Memory and Enthusiasm

Memory

W. S. DI PIERO

and Enthusiasm

ESSAYS, 1975-1985

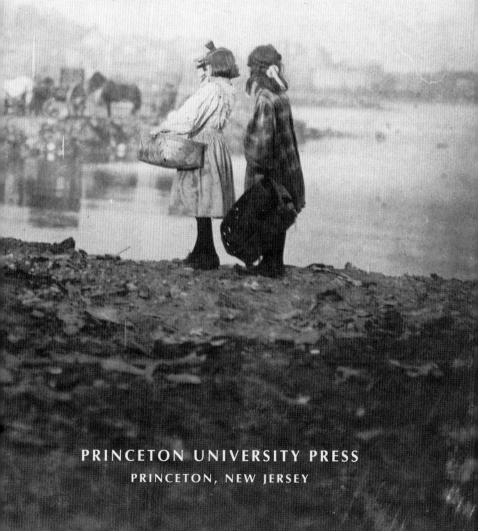

PRINCETON UNIVERSITY PRESS

PRINCETON, NEW JERSEY

Library of Congress Cataloging-in-Publication Data
Di Piero, W. S.
Memory and enthusiasm.
I. Title.
PS3554.165M4 1988   809   88-17939
ISBN 0-691-06756-2   ISBN 0-691-01463-9 (pbk.)

This book has been composed in Linotron Baskerville
and Optima type

Clothbound editions of Princeton University Press books are
printed on acid-free paper, and binding materials are chosen for
strength and durability. Paperbacks, although satisfactory
for personal collections, are not usually suitable
for library rebinding

Printed in the United States of America by Princeton
University Press, Princeton, New Jersey

Title page illustration: "Children at the Dump, Boston, c. 1909."
Photo by Lewis Hine.

The author gratefully acknowledges permission to reprint the following
materials:
   Excerpt from "Waking Early Sunday Morning" from *Near the Ocean* by
Robert Lowell; copyright © 1963, 1965, 1966 by Robert Lowell; reprinted by
permission of Farrar, Straus and Giroux, Inc.
   Excerpts from "Digging," "At a Potato Digging," "Mother," "Anahorish,"
"The Wool Trade," "The Tollund Man," "Bone Dreams," and "The Betrothal
of Cavehill" from *Poems 1965-1975* by Seamus Heaney; copyright © 1966,
1969, 1972, 1975, 1980 by Seamus Heaney; reprinted by permission of
Farrar, Straus and Giroux, Inc.
   "The Bed" from *Selected Poems 1950-1975* by Thom Gunn; copyright ©
1957, 1958, 1961, 1967, 1971, 1973, 1974, 1975, 1976, 1979 by Thom Gunn;
reprinted by permission of Farrar, Straus and Giroux, Inc. "The Bed"
reprinted by permission of Faber and Faber Ltd. from *Jack Straw's Castle* by
Thom Gunn.
   Excerpts from *Death of a Naturalist, Wintering Out, North,* and *Door into the
Dark* by Seamus Heaney; reprinted by permission of Faber and Faber Ltd.
   "Ego Dominus Tuus" from *The Poems of W. B. Yeats: A New Edition,* edited
by Richard J. Finneran; copyright 1918 by Macmillan Publishing Company,

(permissions continued at back of book)

To the four clans:

Di Piero
Epp
Girone
Johnson

CONTENTS

PREFACE

In selecting these pieces from the greater clutter of things I wrote during a ten-year period, I wanted to represent the action I thought I was performing. My intention was to articulate positions, to work out rough formulations of what it felt like to be an American poet at that point in time. I thought I was also devising pieces of an autobiography which might be the matrix for a poetics. What mattered to me was not personality or personhood but experience, specifically the felt intellectual experience of being an American two generations removed from Europe whose saturated Americanism yet retained a dim but certain afterimage of another place. I remember reading for the first time—I must have been eighteen or nineteen—Whitman's announcement in "Song of Myself": "Born here of parents born here from parents the same, and their parents the same." Because my grandparents on both sides were immigrants (among the "launched populations," as Henry James called them), and because the parents of my generation raised us to think of ourselves as Italians but to *be* Americans (we were either discouraged or forbidden, for example, to learn the old language), when I read that line in Whitman I felt in the shadow of an exile, and also completely, forcefully at home. Much of what is here is in answer to Whitman's declaration.

For a while I reviewed new books of poetry, but I've included only a couple such reviews. The others seem now either too callow or too intimate to be exposed again. I include the essays on Antonioni and Altman because they help to shape my themes of work and of American desire. Although I've placed the Sartre essay first, it's the one I'm least comfortable with. If I were to recast it now in light of the biographical and political commentary on Sartre that has appeared over the last several years, it would not be quite so enthusiastic. But I also have to say that I wrote it in 1975, in the stunned pause following several years of extraordinary political events—the smashing of an emergent socialist democracy in Prague by the Soviet Union and the subversion of another in Santiago by the United States; the Cambodian incursions and the troop withdrawal from Vietnam; Watergate and Richard Nixon's resignation—and the passionate clarity Sartre was trying to bring to political and literary discourse seemed exemplary. "Out of Notebooks" is the only piece that does not bear the pinchmarks of public occasion. These are entries from my notebooks, which I've lightly edited to make them presentable and which I selected with a view toward their conversation with the formal essays constellated around them.

The date following each essay indicates the year of composition, not of publication.   1988

ACKNOWLEDGMENTS

The essays in this book first appeared, sometimes in different form, in the following magazines: *The American Poetry Review, Chicago Review, Canto, The Southern Review, The American Scholar,* and *Northwest Review.* "Work," "William James and Henry James," and "The Poetry of William Bronk" first appeared in *TriQuarterly,* a publication of Northwestern University. "A Something of Self: Byron's Letters," "On James Wright and Thom Gunn," and "The Cinque-Spotted Shadow: Coleridge's *Biographia Literaria*" first appeared in *The Sewanee Review,* a publication of The University of the South. "Giacomo Leopardi and the *Pensieri*" was the introduction to my translation of the *Pensieri* (Louisiana State University Press, 1981; Oxford University Press, 1984).

I am grateful to the John Simon Guggenheim Memorial Foundation for a fellowship which supported me while I prepared this collection and wrote three of the essays included here. And I owe special thanks to three editors who have helped and encouraged me along the way: Reginald Gibbons, George Core, and Lewis P. Simpson.

Memory and Enthusiasm

AFTER INNOCENCE

In earlier days I published books in complete innocence;
but I have lost that now.
—Jean-Paul Sartre, "The Purposes of Writing"

Giacometti used to complain to Sartre about space. We stand precariously on our platform earth; all that is not earth is a crushing vacancy, and the freedom of the air is finally an attenuation of ourselves. City dwellers especially, squeezed between steel and glass towers, wear a halo of nothingness. Giacometti shaped his often gaunt figures to contest that aura of the surrounding void. Sometimes space became so oppressive that the clay figures got smaller and smaller, lesser and lesser, until they finally collapsed into powder and dust—art unmade in its making. Sartre meanwhile was spilling out words, compulsively it seemed, trying to fill the nothingness the words themselves described. They were an apt modern pair: the artist whose work came more and more to resemble his own pinched physiognomy, doodling on his lunch napkin in a café while across the table sat the heavy-faced, urbane philosopher-novelist. It is no coincidence that the most astute early monograph on Giacometti was written by his friend, and it is no surprise that the philosopher's obsession with vacancies should underpin so many of his essays, some of which have been recently collected in *Between Existentialism and Marxism* (1975).

Sartre's intelligence has always been abrasively self-corrective, and he has tried in his expansive, garrulous way to redefine the limits of his many activities, as philosopher, novelist, short-story writer, playwright, social historian and commentator, literary and art critic, biographer, journalist, and political activist. If nothing else, *Between Existentialism and Marxism* (a translation of *Situations VIII* and *IX*) reminds us of his extraordinary range of learning and his pursuit of rational

3

illumination. The pieces contained here span thirteen years, from his early essay on Tintoretto (first roughed out around 1957) to his 1970 lecture-essay on Czechoslovakia. In between there are interviews on the art of writing, reflections on Kierkegaard and Mallarmé, a Laingian polemic against traditional doctor-patient relationships in psychoanalysis, stern essays on the political situation in France and on America's recent war in Southeast Asia, and two closing pieces which treat the crisis among contemporary intellectuals.

Sartre's comments on writing have become eminently practical over the years. The heroic ambitions of the aspiring eight-year-old described in *Les Mots* have by necessity been blended into workaday common sense; the pain of writing never really diminishes, but it becomes at least more bearable through familiarity with its daily crises. And for Sartre, serious writing—*heavy* writing—has been a daily occupation for over forty years. It is a little surprising, then, to hear him say that a writer's power depends on a sense of emptiness: "A feeling of emptiness is important . . . and a writer is fortunate if he can attain such a state." Such nothingness, it turns out, is pure potential, "for when one has nothing to say, one can say *everything*." All the more so when, as in Sartre's case, emptiness is the writer's subject. When he says that emptiness confers substance on literature, he rather playfully betrays the kind of dialectical thinking that has characterized his work these past two decades. His mind restlessly explores its own inchoate possibilities, its negative imagery, so that the exploration becomes in itself a positive value and takes on a dramatic—at times heroic—substance. Such dialectical thinking thrives on absolute reversals which are as witty as they are severe. It allows Sartre the freedom to declare in the interview titled "The Purposes of Writing": "If literature is not everything, then it's worth nothing." In a political context it freed him to demonstrate how America's Vietnam policy—on paper, in the abstract—was genocidal. For even if no guns had been fired by American soldiers, America's *intention* to destroy the will of the Vietnamese suffused all her actions there. The idea, what Henry Kissinger deftly calls "policy," is both agent and actor. Sartre sees this same process of suffusion in art: "If a written sentence does not reverberate at every level of man and society, then it makes no sense. What is the literature of an epoch but the epoch appropriated by its literature?"

Artists not only re-create themselves out of the emptiness of failure, but failure is itself a kind of success. And conversely, "success is necessarily failure." To Sartre, the only way artists can go on is by failing to achieve the impossible goals they set for themselves; Leopardi anticipated Sartre when he wrote that such failure makes for a kind of fierce humility. Or, as Giacometti once told him, serious artists are bound to reach a point where they can either throw their work in the trash or display it in a museum. Precisely because the artist "never quite grasps what he sets out to achieve," his failure inspires future efforts. The nothingness or failure of the past underwrites the bigger and better failures of the future. Having defiled one blank page, a poet is more disturbed than ever by the blankness to come, even while feeling all the more compelled to act upon that nagging, defiant vacancy. To push on and obey such compulsion is perhaps the closest thing to secular redemption we can know. But the struggle is not limited to artists, for when Sartre says in "The Purposes of Writing" that "every person is always faced in his own lifetime with the task of wresting his life from the various forms of night," he is speaking also of the Renault assembly-line worker. How does a man like *this* sing back the silence? During the 1960s and early 1970s Sartre has committed himself to just this goal, to reach out to the working class and offer his (rather specialized, mandarin) guidance to help lead them out of their collective night.

A better title for this volume might have been "Existentialism *into* Marxism," for Sartre has not so much disclaimed and abandoned existentialism as he has assumed some of its basic principles into the larger, more public, and more systematic context of Marxism. Or rather, neo-Marxism, which is the designation Sartre prefers, to distinguish himself from his more compromising (and compromised) French and Italian contemporaries, whom he has severely criticized. And he has criticized them largely for what we can only call the lack of existential content in their ideology. Sartre's chief criticism of European Marxism is that it has become totally extrapolated from the context of human self-definition, or *consciousness-in-action*. Sartre's ideology is grounded in the notion of radical freedom, more specifically the freedom of what he calls the "fused group." In this respect he has indeed removed himself from his earlier preoccupation with the isolated individual, the individual-as-other. It is almost as if Sartre's movement toward neo-Marxism were an attempt to redeem Roquentin, to draw that distant and bitter creature back within a directed and self-determining human family, to transform nausea into cunning rage.

In order to keep the human project always in view, Sartre has tried to refrain from using ideology as interference. His comments on the Vietnamese war in "Vietnam: Imperialism and Genocide," cut through the muck of pseudo-ethics that has characterized much journalistic commentary on the war. He is convinced of the fundamental wickedness—a calculated wickedness—of America's international intentions: "Imperialist genocide can only become more radical because the group aimed at, to be terrorized, *through the Vietnamese nation*, is the human group in its entirety." America's intrusion in Vietnam was not an attempt to contain Communism, it was an attempt to contain—or, to use one of Sartre's familiar terms, to *nihilate*—the possibilities of radical freedom as they might exist anywhere. So although his political argument is neo-Marxian, his ethical argument is existentialist, still essentially concerned with human freedom defined in action. Though he has not written any fiction in years, Sartre still turns a novelist's eye on the political events he examines. His analyses are often driven by physical imagery—of bloodshed, burning huts, defoliated jungles—and his outrage is at once sensuous and theoretical.

In criticizing Russia's attempt to impose its own bureaucratic and economic apparatus on a Czechoslovak situation, Sartre finds it monstrous (he calls Russian Socialism "The Thing") because it is devoid of human content. In his essay "Czechoslovakia: The Socialism That Came in from the Cold," Sartre's analysis of the revolution that failed in Czechoslovakia turns into an elegy for the failed dream of an indigenous socialism derived from and based on local nationalistic circumstances. Since his *Critique of Dialectical Reason* (1960), he has insisted on a radical Marxism according to which the socialist state must be an organic reformulation of an indigenous situation. Hence his outrage over Russia's stupid and imperialist insistence, from 1948 through 1956, on forcing the bureaucratic machinery of Russian Socialism upon a Czech situation: "False relations of productions were established under a rigged economy and a reified apparatus of power." The Romantic Socialism of 1848 had been transformed by circumstances—*Russian* circumstances—into the secular Socialism of 1917. But this eventually failed when it became totally depersonalized, when the State became one with the Party. By then imposing its own socialist formula on its satellites, the Soviet Union ignored Marx's fundamental regard for the adaptability of the dialectic to historical circumstances. Russian Marxism became as ossified and impersonal as American policy. As it was both emotionally unsuited and economically counterproductive to the Czech situation, Russian Socialism became in effect anti-Marxist. "Man," Sartre reminds us often, "is a task." Indeed, but more importantly man must *work at himself* rather than be worked on by an inflexible predetermined ideology, whether socialist or capitalist.

Sartre characterizes his postwar shift from the position he took in *Being and Nothingness* as "a movement of rationality which in the end became an irrationalism." In attempting to account for subconscious experience, he has rejected the amorphous applicability of Freudian dream interpretation as too general and nondialectical. In place of "consciousness" Sartre substitutes the totality of *le vécu,* "lived experience." *Le vécu* is that active process which connects one moment of experience to the next, a process whereby one projects oneself out of a circumstantial past into a future of one's own choice; crucially, however, such experience is lived in a world already acted upon and shaped by others. We choose, then actualize, a minicontext for our lives within the larger context of historical otherness. Although the individual functions in a fused group (the neo-Marxist social unit), the group itself must never assume so much predominance that it represses the individual. The great failure of most versions of Marxism is that they forgo radical humanism (which values first and foremost the independence of the individual) in order to achieve an apparently humanistic goal, namely the so-called liberation of the masses. But the masses, in Russia and most of its satellite countries, have at best been liberated into an oppressive bureaucracy which has itself controlled the means of production. The masses, then, are free to be oppressed by their liberator-custodians. It is precisely this grotesque distortion of Marxist-humanist values that Sartre so vigorously attacks. He denounces any system that celebrates the abstraction of State or Party (or Republic or Policy) over the radical freedom of the individual. Marxism, which in its original formulation was a just and economically promising political philosophy, has become a justification for terror and oppression. Sartre's hope is that Marxist guidelines might lead us to a condition where Marxism—indeed, all political formulas—will no longer be necessary, where ideology will be absorbed and dissolved in the larger body of radical humanism. Sartre's neo-Marxian Utopia is a familiar one insofar as it is one where human beings will no longer have reasons to devise newer and more efficient methods of harming each other.

Sartre's Marxist humanism is everywhere evident in his late

essays. Writing of great personalities, of Tintoretto, Kierkegaard, and Mallarmé, he locates each of these remarkable individuals within a historical context; he sees them as having *knowingly* interacted with their period environment. In every respect they, like Sartre himself, inhabited their age rather than merely coexisted with it, citizens of their surroundings, not tourists. In his "Plea for Intellectuals," Sartre would have contemporary intellectuals ("technicians of practical knowledge") follow these three artistic examples, by acting in context, inhabiting the present absolutely. This is not to say that all intellectuals must engage in polemics or be as committed to radical activism as Sartre. I take it to mean that intellectuals must actualize the present—every moment, every thought— as a project of the future. Sartre includes novelists and poets among them, and his emphasis on the writer-as-history is particularly relevant to poets, perhaps to American poets most of all:

> No matter how precious it may be, knowledge of myself and others in our pure objectivity does not constitute the fundamental object of literature, since such knowledge represents universality *without* the singular. Nor, conversely, is the literary object created by a total complicity with fantasies. What constitutes the object of literature is being-in-the-world—not in so far as it is treated externally, but in so far as it is *lived* by the writer.

Not, then, the stupefied sacrificial "I" that has become one fashion in much of our poetry, nor the studiously objective and anonymous "you." Not the whipping post of imaginative rationalism, nor the snazzy indulgence of fanciful improvisation. Sartre is calling for something more ample and generous, more exploratory, less cloistered, certainly less hysterical. *The Divine Comedy* and *Leaves of Grass* seem to me two outstanding examples of the kind of literature Sartre deems necessary. Both are lyric narratives, both huge journeys of the

Self into Otherness, tales of risk and revelation, histories of what Sartre calls the "singular universal."

Mallarmé's maxim is now more relevant than ever before: "Make and in making make yourself." A poet's language projects the poet into the future; that language, which is the poet's action, outlasts him. Every chance is a last chance, even if it is the opening line of a *Poesies complètes*—"*Rien, cette écume, vierge vers . . .*" (Nothing, this sea foam, a virgin line . . .). This series of last chances constitutes the illusion of continuity which a poet needs in order to go on working—"Me going in for my chances, spending on vast returns." In major cases such as Whitman and Dante, the poet's absolute participation in his age, combined with extraordinary personal ambition, makes him an exile. Both these poets insist upon their position at the center of things, Whitman singing himself at the center of the universe, Dante "*nel mezzo del cammin di nostra vita*," halfway along the journey that is our life: being perhaps too much a part of their age, they were bound to be set apart from it. Their public ambition ensured a sometimes wretched privacy. In his essay on Tintoretto, Sartre says that "we are all born in exile," and the works we create are at once an affirmation of exile (our lived experience) and an attempt to escape it. Artists differ from others in that their escape constitutes but another form of exile, another impossible situation, another gambling circumstance to be transformed into lyric narrative.

Sartre's concern with intellectuals has a political motive as well, for he sees them as conspicuous products of a class society. An intellectual is in every way "a product of history," ideally both of his or her personal history and that of the race. Since intellectuals are so much a product of their environment, it is a foolish irony for society to complain of them. A society "has the intellectuals it makes," gets the intellectuals it deserves; in accusing them, society accuses itself. Although Sartre insists that the true intellectual participates in the life of the times as a "guardian of the functional truth of freedom," such participation, as I see it, is really a life-trope. The very desire to preserve radical freedom more often than not alienates the intellectual from most other classes, at least here in America. Strictly speaking intellectuals are neither workers nor petty-bourgeois nor business aristocrats, though they work hard to make their wraithlike presence felt among those others. Americans generally are not much preoccupied with radical freedom, and they usually resent the intellectual who tells them that this is a higher value than common affluence. Sartre's own allegiance to the working class is, I feel, a life-trope for his allegiance to radical freedom. In practice, it is a mighty task to draw the attention of workers away from shop windows to the abstract principle of radical freedom. But then Sartre's objective is finally to educate the workers in the relationship between the two, between the goods they produce and their radical freedom *to* produce. Sartre's lived experience—his polemics, journalism, and tribunalism—constitutes his future project, which I think shall prove to be mankind's future project as well.

Since his conversion to neo-Marxism, Sartre has seldom written in bad faith. He has continued to try to forge his subjective context from the objective world-context around him. It is not so much that he has remained true to his dialectic, as that his dialectic has remained true to him. For many of us born just after World War II, his literary and philosophic influence has been formative, sometimes in indirect ways. For writers his example is difficult to ignore, if only because he struggled so tenaciously, if not always or even often successfully, to honor his maxim that "the need to write is fundamentally a quest for purification."   [1975]

THE PASSENGER

The first time Michelangelo Antonioni looked through a viewfinder, it was to set a frame around a group of madmen. He was filming a documentary in an asylum, hoping to record the daily habits and ambience of the insane. All during the preshooting period the inmates had been very cooperative, indeed deferential, anxious not to make mistakes. But when Antonioni called for lights, he witnessed what must have been a primal experience, which he described in an article written for *Cinema Nuovo* in 1959:

> For a moment, the patients remained motionless, as if petrified. Never have I seen, even on an actor's face, such a look of terror. This lasted only a moment, and then an indescribable scene took place. The madmen desperately sought shelter from the light, as if it were some sort of prehistoric monster attacking them. And their faces, which moments ago had seemed calm, became convulsed, tortured. Then came *our* turn to be petrified. My cameraman didn't even have the strength to stop shooting, and I was incapable of giving any orders whatever. It was the director of the asylum who finally cried out: "Stop! Lights out!" And in that half-darkened room, we could see a swarm of bodies writhing as if in the final throes of a death agony.

Since that first terrible experience with intrusive light, Antonioni has been making films about how the light of recognition, the clarity of knowing, disturbs human complacency. His characters, drawn usually from the middle and upper classes, lead normalized lives numbed by habit until some accidental or unexpected event shocks them into a new honesty about themselves.

When Aldo, the working-class hero of *Il Grido* (1957), learns that his common-law wife plans to leave him for another man, all that was once familiar and comforting suddenly turns strange and menacing; his failure to cope with his own desperation leads him to suicide. In *L'Avventura* (1959) the bizarre disappearance of his mistress causes Sandro, an architect turned contract-estimator, to question the motives for his existence, to confront and admit to his barrenness of spirit. In *La Notte* (1960), the death of a close friend destroys the shaky marriage between Giovanni, a popular "intellectual" novelist, and his wife; they must face the failure of love. Once Thomas, the photographer in *Blow-Up* (1966), realizes he has accidentally photographed a real murder scene, he can no longer trust his perception of reality; his camera accidentally compels him to enter the uncomfortable zone of moral responsibility. In *Zabriskie Point* (1969), a sullen student gets caught up in a "normal" student rebellion, but unexpected circumstances then force him to flee to an unlikely pastoral love affair in Death Valley; his final decision to follow his destiny leads him into a death trap.

In each of these films the underlit world of habit is abruptly flooded with the punishing glare of accident and contingency. When Antonioni's heroes and heroines look to the light, they feel compelled, usually out of desperation with their own boredom, to investigate its source. They decide to follow their destiny, or to *be* their destiny. Thenceforth everything they see takes on new meanings; their perceptions—and hence their feelings—are qualitatively altered by the light. Such knowledge is not always a blessing. It endangers, it taunts, it scourges. Their exploration into the light is an exploration into themselves, testing the truths and untruths of their existence. Sandro no longer designs buildings, he estimates costs for other builders; he is rich, but he hates himself for having sold out his talent. Giovanni has become so "literary" that his novels no longer have much relation to identifiable human experience; he is a stranger to his own feelings. Like Antonioni's primal madmen, these characters, once savaged by the light, have nothing more to cling to than the writhing form of their own unknowing. Most of these films are "thrillers" insofar as they dramatize people who are seeking clues to their being. But Antonioni is always more concerned with the investigative process than he is with any neat solution to the case. Antonioni's most recent hero—and like all the others he is, at best, a reluctant hero—is a media man. He, too, sees the light of change and decides to explore its possibilities, to investigate the operations of Chance and Necessity. He never quite finds out what he has gotten himself into.

David Locke (played by Jack Nicholson), a noted reporter and photojournalist specializing in Third World politics, is on assignment in North Africa to track down and interview a band of guerrillas camped somewhere in the desert. Though he is well equipped with the sophisticated tools of his trade, Locke cannot speak the local language. Nor can he speak decent French, the colonial language. (*"Vous parlons francaise?"* he asks a native.) One wonders how he will communicate with the guerrillas once he finds them. No matter. We learn later, in flashback, that his questions are merely ritual gestures; they are not meant to extract truth from his subjects. (He had once been told by a witch doctor: "Mr. Locke, your questions are more revealing about yourself than my answers to your questions could possibly be about me.") The two guides Locke hopes will lead him to the outlaws both desert him. He is again on his own, as he was before, tracking through the desert in his landrover, when the vehicle buries its wheels in the sand. Tired to his soul of chasing phantoms, scorched by the sun and sand, he smashes the landrover with a shovel, drops to his knees, and wails: "Alright! I don't care!"

Locke eventually finds his way back to his hotel in a small village. In the room next to his, he finds a man named Robertson sprawled on the bed, dead of a heart attack. Locke— He Who Doesn't Care—stares blandly, practically nose to nose, into the dead man's eyes and notices a resemblance. A physical resemblance, yes, but surely Locke also sees his own death, an exhaustion of spirit and will, in the eyes of Robertson. The camera idly tilts upward and focuses on the over-

head fan; when the camera tilts back down, Locke is wearing
the dead man's blue shirt. He has decided, in that brief and
casual moment, to change—or rather to exchange—his identity for Robertson's. It's the first of Locke's two suicides. As he
is switching passports, we hear a conversation between him
and Robertson. An aural flashback? It seems so, until we see
that Locke is playing the conversation on a tape recorder. But
just as we perceive that it's a playback rather than flashback,
we pan left through space-time and see Locke and Robertson
talking on the balcony. Robertson is evasive about his occupation and his reasons for being in Africa. He remarks upon
the cruel beauty of the desertscape. Locke replies that he prefers men to landscapes. Robertson, seeing farther than Locke
can see, says: "There are men who live in the desert." The
camera then pans slowly right, back to the present, where
Locke is still fooling with the passports. In that stretched moment, we see the present as continuous with the past, a continuity so immediate that past and present seem almost coin-
stantaneous.

When Locke next makes a brief stopover in London, he
catches the eye of a girl sitting on a bench in the Bloomsbury
Centre. Nothing is made of this incident; it's a peripheral detail which, like so many peripheral details in this film, will
drift back into Locke's life and give shape to his destiny. In
keeping with his new identity, he decides to follow the itiner-
ary in the dead man's diary. First to Munich, where he finds
in Robertson's luggage-locker an illustrated invoice for hand-
guns and automatic weapons. He then goes wandering
through the city, first following an archaic white funeral car-
riage, then on to a church where a wedding is being celebrated. Despite the major change in Locke's life, the rest of
the world goes about its normalized rituals of change—funer-
als and weddings. He is then met by two men who are buying
weapons from Robertson to arm a guerrilla movement in Africa. So Robertson was—and Locke now is—a gunrunner. Not
a mercenary, however, for the African Achebe (leader of the

rebels) praises Robertson's ideological and moral commitment to the rebel cause. ("Mr. Robertson, you take so many risks for our sake.") Locke the apolitical reporter has become Robertson the engaged revolutionary.

Off-balance, puzzled, Locke is still curious enough to want to explore the possibilities of his new identity. So he goes to Barcelona for another rendezvous. There he makes the acquaintance of a young student of architecture, referred to throughout as The Girl, whom Locke has glimpsed earlier in London. She too is a wanderer, but unlike him she is a more unified, coherent personality. Locke hints at what has happened: "I used to be someone else, but I traded him in." As they travel through Spain—she a passenger in Locke's car, he a passenger riding Robertson's passport—they become friends, then lovers. After a series of failed meetings with Robertson's supposed contacts, Locke begins to grow tired and fearful of the responsibilities he must bear as Robertson. The Girl persuades him to continue pursuing his destiny as Locke/Robertson.

All this while Locke's widow, Rachel, a brassy, neurotic sort of character, has been trying to track down Robertson for some clues to her husband's reported death. In Barcelona, again by accident, she sees him and begins her pursuit. At the same time, Locke is being chased by assassins working for the African government which Achebe's guerrillas are fighting; if they can eliminate Robertson, they can cut off Achebe's source of weapons.

Locke knows now that he's being hunted but decides to play his string out to the end. Sensing danger, he tells The Girl to take a boat and meet him later in Tangiers. He then goes to his next rendezvous point, in a small town in the south of Spain. When he registers at the hotel, he's told that his wife is waiting for him. His wife is The Girl. Locke again tells her to leave: "What the hell are you doing here with me? You better go." The Girl leaves. Locke is stretched out on the bed. People begin converging on the hotel—the Hotel de la Gloria. Locke is murdered, though we do not see it happen. His widow arrives with the police. They and The Girl enter the room and find him dead on the hotel bed, as Locke had found Robertson dead on a hotel bed.

THE ORIGINAL working title of this film was *Profession: Reporter*. During shooting it was changed to *Il Passeggero* (*The Passenger*), then later changed back to its original title for European release. The original title is significant in that it points up the motives behind Locke's decision to change his life. As a professional reporter, he is able to manipulate circumstance. Chance events can be photographed, then edited into coherent but arbitrary thematic patterns. Locke used the viewfinder and voice-over as control devices for ordering reality. He reshapes events into vendible commodities. He tells Robertson that a reporter deals in expectations, his own and those of other people. Locke the reporter can fashion events on film to conform to his noncommittal vision of human events. Antonioni is not interested in the morality of all this; he makes no value judgments in this film. He was recently quoted as saying that "the cinema is not in essence moral; it is emotional." He is interested above all in how the Self behaves in its context.

Work is a medium of knowledge. We work in order to know ourselves and our context. Many of us live by Heracles' axiom: "My labours are my life." Through work the Self extends its identity into the larger context of human society, through work it participates in Otherness and mixes in the communal stir of human destiny. When one's labors (as a reporter, a bricklayer, a soldier, a writer) are made into a shield to protect the Self from participation in the larger body of human responsibility, the Self must shrivel in its own self-containment. Work then becomes an expression of spiritual cowardice, which can lead to suicidal despair. Locke encounters his despair in the desert, where he can read his own spiritual barrenness in the inert, parched self-containment of the desertscape. For Locke had used his professional tools—the camera, the interview question—as a screening device to keep himself at a safe distance from his troubling subjects. His work screens the self from reality. He is said by one of his colleagues to be "an excellent observer . . . and he had a kind of *detachment.*"

Locke is obviously more concerned with the pseudo-events created by his camera than he is with real events. Though his coverage of political turmoil in Third World countries should acquaint him with the moral structures that support such suffering, he feels no desire to *know* these invisible structures. His profession has become an exercise in falsehood and he, a voyeur of sensational apparencies, has come to hate himself for being so good at his work. "David Locke has very concrete problems," Antonioni has said in a recent interview in *Film Comment.* "He is frustrated with his life. His marriage is a failure. He is not completely satisfied with his job even if done successfully." He has, in Pound's words, "withered into noncuriosity." His wild cry in the desert—"I don't care"—is his mad song against everything that has become habitual in his life. He is no longer curious about human destiny, or about human suffering. His profession has become a death in life, and so he chooses, however casually, to reinvent himself. His recognition of the truth about himself occurs, significantly, as a solitary event in the desert. In the world at large, the spiritual abandonment felt by this figure in a landscape is quite unremarkable. It's merely something that happens. Likewise when Locke later decides to assume Robertson's identity, the change takes place in a fleabag hotel in some nameless village. The only soundtrack noises announcing the decision to change his life are the distant whistle of a native flute and the whisking of an overhead fan. But the implications of Locke's decision are profound. For once he is exercising his will to choose. He puts aside the rules of the game, puts aside a life of scripted questions and canned responses; in taking on Robertson's identity he hopes to shed all his old habits, to renew

himself. He had said to Robertson earlier: "Wouldn't it be better if we could just forget all the places, forget everything that
happens, just throw it all away, day by day?"

What Locke does not realize, at least not at first, is that in
committing himself to Robertson's passport and diary he is
also committing himself to a whole set of moral and emotional
habits. One's identity is never neutral, the Self is never a *tabula
rasa*; we are defined—physically, emotionally, intellectually—
by our habits. They are adulthood's scars, our identification
marks. Not only must Locke assume Robertson's habits, but
he must also bear the burden of the remnants of his own. His
first delusion is to think of his new role as a freewheeling adventure. He seems to feel that by cutting himself loose from
his old life he can enter a free-fall zone. When he leans out
the cable car that is lowering him into Barcelona, and spreads
his arms, he does indeed seem a creature of the air. But even
air, Locke learns, is creased by wind; and the sheer weight of
human stuff dooms it to the heave and drag of circumstance.
Locke's past is *not* dead. His widow knows that he's alive. The
future is not a liberated zone, for it is an extension of Robertson's past. As a reporter Locke had been able to stand apart
from events. Now, however, he has unwittingly cast himself in
the role of agent and participant. He *is* an event, but one
which occurs along the continuum of habit. "However hard
you try," he tells Robertson, "it stays so difficult to get away
from your own habits." Then later to The Girl: "I've left behind everything except a few bad habits I couldn't get rid of."
His past is literally unforgettable.

Locke passes from his familiar journalistic world of isolated
supercharged events into an oceanic field in which all events
are somehow interrelated, and where all events in some way
shape one's destiny. Antonioni in the *Film Comment* interview
reminds us that "this is a film about someone who is following
his destiny, a man watching reality as reported." Locke is now
on the receiving end of the world's *reportage*, he is finally
learning how to see. But what he sees is a world of random

events, casual violence, idle details that may at any moment become menacing. He has begun to see this continuum of reality in which any one event may be finally as crucial as any other, where any one circumstance may be insignificant, and any one may just as well prove fatal. It's this tension field which Antonioni reports to us, and its importance is nothing new to him. In 1963, he wrote in the introduction to *Four Screenplays*: "When we say that . . . everyday events often take on symbolic meanings, we must add that it's the *relationship* of all those things among each other in time and space which makes sense to us. It's the tension that forms among them."

Antonioni's pictorial style, aloof, desultory, and always underkeyed, perfectly expresses this tension among objects, and the equability of events. Camera movement, frame composition, mixing, and editing, all conform to the choreography of chance and destiny which the film as a whole dramatizes. Not only does Antonioni avoid melodramatic and analytic closeups (remarkable in itself, since Jack Nicholson's special strength as an actor is his ability to rip a tight frame with the energy of delirium), but he purposefully allows his camera to wander from conventional focal points of screen action. The shots in *The Passenger* are almost always eloquently beside the point. In one of the film's opening sequences, Locke's landrover pokes its nose halfway into the frame, then stops. Locke then walks into the frame, entering a field of action—or forcefield of events—rather than being "discovered" there; then as soon as he enters the frame, the camera dollies sideways so that as Locke passes through his local landscape, the landscape itself is passing away. A few shots later, after Locke has used sign language and cigarettes to bargain with some natives, the camera eye casually drifts away, leaving him behind in the lost frame. Locke then reenters the frame, the human reengaging its physical context. The world, as perceived by Antonioni's camera, has no actual "center of action"; it permits, at best, an occasional convergence of circumstances upon one thing or another. Locke is made to seem just one more datum of the reality we are witnessing, a reality which Antonioni is restoring to us. After Locke's cry of surrender, the camera again leaves him behind as it pans slowly right to gaze upon the peach-colored curves of the desert.

Some viewers mislead themselves by thinking that since Antonioni has the reputation of being a "serious" director (an accusation? a warning?) they must therefore look for symbolic structures in his images. This kind of symbol-snooping is especially wayward with regard to *The Passenger*, where Antonioni is concerned above all with expressing *what is there*. He wants us to see, to bear witness. He is not out to score sentimental or moral points. He in fact runs considerable risks in refusing to overdetermine his images with prescriptive moral or thematic values. The images here are not categories of meaning, they bear none of the hard freight of analogue. Rather, they constitute an organization of perceptions, cold, unembarrassed, and ruthless in their objectivity. Even this organization, however, is yet another form of irresolution. Though Antonioni has clearly selected his materials in advance and refined them to perfection, he has not interpreted them for us. This becomes more evident when we compare Antonioni to other directors known for their aloof, noncommittal pictorial style. Robert Bresson, for example, has fashioned a cinema of objective detail, a kind of pictorial piety. But Bresson's best films—*Mouchette, Diary of a Country Priest, Une Femme Douce*, and the extraordinary *Lancelot du Lac*—all demonstrate, from the beginning, definable thematic biases. The narrative in each case has been interpreted for us in advance; our initial acceptance of these thematic biases frees us at once to respond to the emotions involved. Then too, Miklos Jancsó, in a film like *The Red and the White*, tracks across the Hungarian plains in long discursive takes meant to create an illusion of nonengagement; but here too Jancsó's noncommittal camera reinforces a thematic point, which is man's cool-minded savagery toward other men. I don't mean to disparage any of these directors (as a matter of personal taste, I prefer

Bresson's films to Antonioni's); but of the three, it is Antonioni who refuses to superimpose any moral authority on his narrative, or to prejudice it with foregone thematic conclusions. *The Passenger* is, in effect, pure narrative, cinema of pure event.

It's this evenness and implacability of events that make *The Passenger* so disquieting. Locke's decision to change his life, his meeting with The Girl, his contact with Achebe, and finally his death, are simply events which happen. Even the close-up violence of a public execution is tempered by the cool screen of the moviola, where the event is observed by one of Locke's colleagues. The very transient nature of events deepens the world's melancholy. Despite what the evening news tells us, ours is not a world of titans, nor can horrific events be torn from the world's ongoingness.

What counts is one's keenness in perceiving events-in-their-continuance. Life is thus a journey into our own seeing. To most observers, as to Locke, the scene of children playing in a public garden may not seem terribly significant. But to the hobbled old man whom Locke meets there, these children reenact the tragic eventfulness of all human experience: "Some people see in them a new life, a renewal. All I see is the same old tragedy starting over again." Locke too, since his change, has become more curious about quotidian perceptions. As he enters his room in the Hotel de la Gloria and sees The Girl standing by the window, looking out to the plaza, he asks: "What do you see?" "A little boy and an older woman, arguing about which way to go." Pause. Then Locke again: "What do you see now?" The Girl: "An old man. Dust." Locke then tells her a story, clearly a parable of himself. A man blind from birth gains his sight at the age of forty (Locke's approximate age). At first he is thrilled by the sudden rush of perceptions, but soon he begins to see all the violence and ugliness in the world. When he was blind he hadn't hesitated to cross the street with his stick, but now that he can see, he's afraid even to leave his room. Aware and fearful of chance, menaced by the swarming unpredictability of all he sees, conscious of the melancholy eventfulness of the world, he cannot endure his own seeing, so he kills himself. After telling The Girl his story, Locke tells her to leave. He decides to make this final rendezvous alone. It's his last decision. His destiny now is to wait. And we recall that at the beginning of the film Robertson had described the melancholy beauty of the desertscape as "a kind of waiting." Locke is no longer his old self entirely, but not yet entirely renewed. Living as two men, Locke/Robertson is a no-man. He Who Sees. And who dies unseen "*nel mezzo del cammin.*"

The final, long seven-minute take in *The Passenger* is one of the greatest sequences in modern moviemaking. Not because of its length (Jancsó's takes average from eight to fifteen minutes each), but because this seamless and wholly eventful sequence embodies the ongoingness of reality which Locke himself has come to discover. In its selective brevity, it gives us Antonioni's vision of human continuity. By fusing screen-time with real-time, it invites us to participate in the process of our own seeing.

Locke has asked The Girl to leave. We see him lying on his bed. The camera then points away from Locke toward the iron-grilled window of his room. Through the bars we see the village plaza. On the far side of the plaza an old man sits with his back to a wall, talking to his dog. There's a door to his left (leading where?). The door opens and a man (who?) exits. A driver-training car enters the plaza and buzzes around aimlessly. The Girl enters this dusty field of events, stops, and looks back toward Locke's room, toward us. We hear a blast of trumpets (from a bullring? a record player somewhere?). A little boy enters the plaza, picks up a stone, throws it at the old man, who grunts and curses. Another car arrives, its passengers are the government assassins. A church bell tolls. The Girl moves toward Locke's room, but one of the assassins takes her by the arm and leads her away. The other disappears into the hotel. The waspish throttle of a motor scooter is punctuated by the abrupt muted *pom* of a pistol. And here, the moment after Locke is shot, we pass through the window bars—a moment of terrible exhilaration and release—and begin an omega-shaped journey around the plaza. We hear sirens, a police car arrives, the assassins are already gone. Then Rachel, Locke's wife, arrives in a second police car. We are on the outside, mingling with the ordinary life of the plaza, gazing back now at the hotel. We see The Girl frantically trying to force open the communicating door to Locke's room. Then we zoom in slowly and discover Locke dead. We see his body through the window grating.

What has happened? Where have we been? From behind the bars we had looked out upon the idle details and events taking place on the plaza. Then we moved outside, and in doing so turned our perceptions back on themselves. We have seen things happen, and continue, before, during, and after Locke's death. Everything has been in some way eventful, every detail *could have been* menacing. What if the boy's stone had struck the old man in the eye and blinded him? What if the man walking out the door had been one of the assassins? What if the driver-training car had accidentally collided with that of the assassins? Given the fanciful operations of chance, any of these events could have happened. The genius of this long sequence lies in its suggestion of possible occurrences'. Locke's death is just one more event; as soon as it happens, it gets caught up in the anonymous continuity of human destiny. After everyone has left, we see, over the closing credits, two local townspeople walking through the sleepy, golden brown evening, going home.   [1975]

THE SILENCE OF ORIGINS

When Cesare Pavese committed suicide at the age of forty-one, he left behind one of the most ambitious and important bodies of work of any Italian writer since Giacomo Leopardi. Like Leopardi, Pavese was both a poet and a writer. His amplitude was astonishing: poems, novels, short stories, critical essays, translations, diaries, letters—all written with great compulsion. He was born in Santo Stefano Belbo, a small rural *paese* in the Langhe hills southeast of Turin. Though he grew up in the big city—his father worked in Turin as a court clerk—Pavese returned each summer to Santo Stefano Belbo, establishing even in childhood the crisscrossed tensions between city and country which were to prove so central to his literary work. At the University of Turin he wrote his senior thesis on Walt Whitman, which marked the beginning of his lifelong fascination and struggle with American literature. In 1935, the Fascist regime exiled him to Brancaleone in Calabria. The Fascists had discovered (or had been shown) some letters which he had written to a woman, letters thought "politically compromising." Here in Brancaleone, a seaside town in the deep south, Pavese found himself cut off from contemporary intellectual life; here he put the finishing touches on poems that were later published in his first book, *Lavorare stanca*, an extraordinary collection which went almost completely ignored in Italy. Most of these early poems are lyric narratives, proletarian poems (in Whitman's sense) written by a man who considered himself a literary aristocrat. Pavese wanted to write a poetry which would be "an expression of essential facts, rather than the usual introspective abstraction." The poems narrate the lives of peasants, provincials, city people, their routine solitude and savage wishes, men and women deeply set in their ordinary habits of work and leisure. The landscapes are often unforgivingly primitive; the hills and vineyards seem so Greek that one expects to see men mating with trees. Although Pavese and his critics have both emphasized the influence of Whitman and Masters on these early poems, *Lavorare stanca* (or *Hard Labor*) really owes more to Hesiod, Dante, and Leopardi. Most importantly, even in this first book Pavese was already exploring the revelatory power of ancient myth.

After the war Pavese worked as an editor for the publisher Einaudi and was instrumental in creating Einaudi's illustrious series on ethnology and anthropology. He wrote novels, essays, and short stories (his fiction, too, became "an expression of essential facts") and translated numerous English and American texts, among them *Moby Dick, Benito Cereno,* and *Moll Flanders.* A second volume of poetry, *La terra e la morte,* a more hieratic book than *Lavorare stanca,* was published in 1947. In 1950 he was awarded the Strega Prize, Italy's most prestigious literary award, for his book *La bella estate.* Later that same year he killed himself with an overdose of sleeping pills in a Turin hotel room.

On the day before his death Pavese sent a special delivery letter to his friend and biographer, David Lajolo:

> Like Cortez, I've burnt my ships behind me. I don't know if I'll find Montezuma's treasure, but I do know that on the plateau of Tenochtitlan they offer human sacrifice. For years I didn't think about these things; I wrote. Now I'm finished writing. With the same stubbornness, with the same stoic will of Le Langhe, I'll make my trip into the country of the dead. If you want to know who I am now, reread "La Belva" ("The Lady of Beasts") in *Dialogues with Leucò.* As always, I had foreseen everything five years ago.

And on the table alongside his deathbed lay a copy of the *Dialogues.* What are presumed to have been his last words were jotted down on the frontispiece: "Forgiveness to everyone, and I ask everyone's forgiveness. Okay? Don't gossip too much."

Pavese composed *Dialogues with Leucò* in 1945–1946, while

also writing *Il compagno*, the first of his great novels. Still ahead were *La casa in collina, Il diavolo sulle colline, Tra donne sole*, and the magnificent *La luna e i falò*. The *Dialogues* was poorly received. Most reviewers begged off. Few readers understood it, and those who did were scandalized. Yet this was the book which Pavese cherished most, along with that other public failure, *Lavorare stanca*. He was upset by the poor reception given the *Dialogues*, and references to it are scattered throughout his letters: "the big scandal," "the heretical book that I'm so fond of," "a book with a curse on its head," "my visiting card for posterity," "a book no one reads, and of course the only one that's worth anything," "it doesn't seem possible that Leucò isn't understood, but that makes me happy, it means it's just like the second *Faust*." Pavese was right, of course. The *Dialogues* is a major attempt to account for human origins, and the origins of poetry, in myth. It is Pavese's book of wondrous tales and of suffering wonder.

The *Dialogues* was published here in 1965 in a translation by William Arrowsmith and D. S. Carne-Ross. Unlike most translations from Italian, this one is carefully stylized, vigorous, clear, really written in English. Most professional translators of Italian are not writers and have no sense of style; hence they deliver up patchwork diction and "faithful renderings." The cotranslators of the *Dialogues*, however, obviously understand Pavese's sensibility and manage to translate it into a fluent American idiom. All the quotes from the *Dialogues* here are from their translation.

IN HIS ESSAY *"Poesia è libertà"* (Poetry Is Freedom) written in 1949, Pavese made a working distinction between the origins and the practice of poetry: "The source of poetry is always some mystery, an inspiration, a sense of unknowing in the presence of the irrational—strange territories. But the act of poetry . . . is an absolute willfulness to see clearly, to reduce to reason, to know. Mythos and Logos." *Dialogues with Leucò* is precisely such a fusion of mythos and logos, of mystery and

clarity. It comprises a series of imaginary dialogues between
characters drawn from Greek history and mythology. Taken
together, they constitute Pavese's own dialogues with Leu-
cothea, the White Goddess, once Ino of the slender ankles,
the sea goddess whose veil rescued Odysseus from the tempest. These dialogues need to be read as poetry, much as we
read Leopardi's *Operette morali* (which Pavese regarded as his
chief competition). For as an act of poetry they seek to articulate, "to reduce to reason, to know," the mysterious mythos
of the human past. Read as a poem, with each of the twenty-
seven dialogues a stanza or strophe, *Dialogues with Leucò*
emerges as an epic history of consciousness, the insinuation of
death and blood-fear into the Western psyche, stretching
from the Age of Cronos to the present. It comprises finally
what Pavese called *"una poetica del destino."* These are not dry
discourses on mythic thought, or fanciful reflections on the
ways of gods to men. The *Dialogues* is rather an identifiably
classical, indeed archaic, expression of history, the roots of
which can be traced as far back as Homer. This is the epic
which Pavese felt he could never write in standard verse, and
which he himself wished to be treated as a "mythological document."

The dialogue Pavese referred to in that painful letter to Lajolo, "The Lady of Beasts," contains many of the formal elements found throughout the *Dialogues*. Endymion, the eternal
dreamer, tells a stranger about his quest for Artemis, Goddess
of the Oaks, the wild virgin (who is also "virgin wilderness").
Pavese never makes the common rationalist error of reducing
Greek gods and goddesses to mere functions, the kind of
mythological calculus which reduces, for example, Artemis to
a role (Goddess *of* Chastity) as if she served merely as patron-
ess for certain forms of human behavior. Pavese instead sees
the gods as the Greeks saw them: figures of pure power which
constituted primal states of being. In the *Dialogues*, Apollo is
not god of light, he is Apollo the Lucid, the Light-bringer, the
very principle of clarity and peaceful understanding. Thus in

"The Lady of Beasts" Artemis is dramatized as the living principle of wilderness, wildwood, virginity, the untouched. To Endymion (and to Pavese, writing directly out of his own experience with women) Artemis is "a whole infinity of things," all of which comprise a complex unity of being which Pavese called "*il selvatico*"—"the wild beast, the savage thing, the untouchable that no man can name." Pavese here is obviously testing and exploring his own fantasies about the feminine ideal, the huntress who is also "a slight awkward girl." Like Endymion, the insomniac Pavese is "someone who cannot sleep [yet] longs to sleep," and both are destined to pass into legend as eternal dreamers. In this ancient story Pavese discovers the nexus where his own modern destiny is tied to an ancient dramatic action, where the mythic past becomes a text for transforming his immediate experience into destiny. The artist does not merely cite the past as authority, to shore up his own dramatic compulsions; rather he sinks himself so deeply, so *passionately*, into the past that his own present becomes revealed to him. As Pavese dilates the myth, it comes clear that all human love is, like Endymion's, a dream of unknowing, a melodrama of refusal and retribution. For Artemis is finally something more than an archetypal female, she is the wilderness of unfulfilled desire common to all mortals.

Pavese goes on to explore the relationship between desire and destiny in the dialogue "Sea-Foam," where the dead Sappho, once the great celebrant of the lyric moment, learns that desire outlives the life of the body. In choosing the sea as her suicide vessel ("the sea swallows, the sea annuls") she had hoped to quell her desire once and for all, to *become* her destiny rather than merely "accept" it, to discover the unconscious oblivion of natural things. But Britomart explains to her the difference between accepting and resisting one's fate: "smiling means living like a wave, like a leaf, accepting your fate." Natural unself-conscious things—leaf, wind, sea-foam—exist untouched by the persuasions of desire; theirs is a state of purely passive being, absolutely subject to the movements of destiny designed by the gods. And they have no memory. Mortals, however, and poets above all, are bound to live a life of resistance. They are conscious of their own Becoming, they know that they do not know. Like Sappho, their impulse is not to accept fate but to *be* fate. In Pavese's work smiling is usually a sign of godliness, a surrender of oneself to the eternity of the moment, the flux of destiny. Mortals who know how to smile (in Pavese they are often women, like Helen) live their lives as an open-ended series of discrete moments, without memory, nonhistorical; they resemble the gods, who are sheer power and will, who need no history, no organization of moments, to actualize their brute power. For the gods, who are pure force, each moment is an eternal moment. Thus mortals who accept each moment as eternal take on an aspect of godliness. Such mortals are rare, however, and not always to be envied.

Mortals generally draw what little power they have from history, from the succession of instants that shape the contours of life. How then can a poet live totally for the eternal moment while still consciously participating in the continuity of time? Is desire the same as song? Sappho, poet of the burning moment, came to realize too late that desire is *not* song. Her habit had been "to look into things, into the tumult, and turn it into speech, into song," only then to discover that desire "destroys, and burns, like a snake, like the wind." Sappho fatally confused two processes: *il mestiere di poeta*, the poet's job/craft (and title of an essay by Pavese), and *il mestiere di vivere*, the job/craft of living (and title of Pavese's diaries).

By embracing the oblivion of sea-foam, Sappho thinks to kill the god of desire burning in her blood, and in killing the god thus overcome the divisive tyranny of time. But this too, she learns, is no longer possible, not since the close of the Golden Age. There was once a time, during the reign of Cronos, when death was simply, in Britomart's language, becoming "foam" or "leaf"—all things, all moments, interfused. But with the fall of the Titans and the rise of the Olympian

age, death became the great individuating shadow hovering
over all mortal existence, defining its limits. In the new, severely organized Olympian universe, the mortal self can at
best only dream of such primordial unity of being as existed
in the Age of Cronos. Death now alienated mortals from the
eternal flux of the moment. Who, then, can smile as the gods
smile? If mortals can*not* smile, they are doomed to live in constant envy of the gods and their divine timelessness. This
envy, as Pavese presents it, may be humankind's deepest
source of anxiety.

Pavese might have subtitled the *Dialogues*, indeed all his
work, "Of Monsters, Gods, and Men." In an extraordinary act
of imaginative memory, the *Dialogues* reaches back into the
chaotic past when, as Ovid describes it, "men of their own ac-
cord, without threat of punishment, without laws, maintained
good faith and did what was right. There were no penalties
to fear, no bronze tablets erected. . . . The earth itself, without
compulsion and untouched by hoe, unfurrowed by any plow,
produced all things spontaneously." In that distant time the
world relaxed into its oneness, men had no memory, no divisive self-consciousness, and mingled freely with beasts. Tiresias, in "The Blind," gives us the most vivid description of that
autochthonic age: "Before time was born, the earth was already filling space. It bled, it felt pleasure; the earth was the
only god. In those days things themselves had power. It was
things that happened. Whereas now the gods turn everything
into words, illusions, threats. But the gods can only make
trouble, join things together or pull them apart." In the dialogue "The Cloud" we encounter the old Titanic consciousness in the figure of Ixion, who tells Nephele that in the old
days death was merely "something that happens, like day, like
night." Then the agrarian, animistic world of the Titans gave
way to citified Olympus, mind, law. With Olympus came individuating intellect, a consciousness dividing humankind
from nature. The universe became architectonic. The monsters left over from the Age of Cronos now *knew* they were

monsters. The new divisive intellect created distinctions between sexes, mortals became *conscious* of their alienation from
nature, conscious of the divisions between rich and poor,
youth and age. Sex was no longer a paradisal communion
with earth, men could no longer mate "with the nymphs of
the springs and mountains, with the daughters of the wind,
the goddesses of the earth."

Nostalgia for the lost Golden Age vibrates throughout the
Dialogues, and at every point it reveals something about our
modern selves. For example, once the old Chaos was gone,
there were no more monsters for men to slay. In "The Chimera" Bellerophon is said to be embittered because there are
no more monsters around that he can challenge. He yearns
for "the pride of Glaucus and Sisyphus," the old clarity of
knowing that the monsters were entirely *other*. When these
monsters are gone, man is bound to turn his sword upon himself, become his own worthiest victim, for the monsters now
abide within himself. If death is destiny, and if human beings
decide to *be* their destiny, then for the first time in the history
of consciousness suicide becomes a possibility. In the looming
shadow of Olympus, death is decisive, man is now called "a
mortal," his name is his destiny. In "The Mountain," Titan
Prometheus tells Heracles: "Death entered the world with the
gods. You mortals fear death because you know that the gods,
by being gods, are immortal." Nostalgia for the Age of Cronos
is bound to be transformed into bitter envy—envy of the immortality of the gods. Cursed with memory of the past, aware
of their own helplessness in the presence of the gods, mortals
must now live their lives on the razor's edge, balancing between destiny as it once was and as it now is. Nostalgia rots,
human life becomes a mere calendar of days, limited by
death, abstracted and *ordered* out of the timeless oneness of
the past. Thus one of man's first aspirations in the new age is
to control destiny in some way, to direct the cold waters of
fate through the channels of will. The most tragic example of

this new man is Oedipus, whose catastrophe is itself an act of tragic recollection.

We meet the old king in "The Road," as he converses with a highway beggar. Oedipus's very name is an emblem of mortal division: the head, source of aspiration, riddle-solver, place where the will to remember originates; the foot, motor activity, slave to the rule of the road. Thought and instinct, intellectual pride and physical humility, cerebral time-travel and the dusty present. His confrontation with the monstrous Sphinx brought him down. What finally destroyed him was not his encounter with the visible beast, the Sphinx, but his encounter with the beast of the blood, monstrous memory. Oedipus the Proud still cannot quite accept the resigned attitude voiced by the Beggar, who tells him that everyone, King and Beggar alike, has the same fate. "Leave the rest to the gods," he counsels the king. But Oedipus, the new Olympian man, feels compelled to exercise some personal control over destiny, to shape, if possible, the will of the gods. To *know*. His uneasy aspiration defines the abrasive boundaries of mortal consciousness. Living in the presence of the gods, man is bound to dream of immortality, to envy the gods their boundless power. The mortal distance between head and foot, between aspiration and actuality, creative mind and determined instinct, will become the source of man's great tragic actions. And of his greatest sorrows. Hot, mortal aspiration is doomed to burn and consume itself in the cool Apollonian light of divine perfection.

Odysseus, too, suffers from aspiration, but of a slightly different kind. He yearns for something beyond the daily comforts of Calypso's island, yearns for home, family, history. Calypso tells the hero that he can be immortal if only he would "accept the horizon": immortality means "accepting the moment, no longer recognizing a tomorrow . . . the immortal is the man who doesn't hope to live." These words are wasted on the man who literally lives by his wits, who thrives on risk. Odysseus knows that his desire to travel, specifically to return to Ithaca, is really his chief means of resisting death: "I can't accept, can't be silent." Yet he realizes, too, that by refusing the illusion of immortality he is hurrying toward his death. Life becomes a dare, all risk and desire. In the dialogue "The Witches," Circe recalls that Odysseus "never understood the smile of the gods, the way [the gods], who know destiny, smile." And she remembers Odysseus as a rather verbal character, a compulsive name-giver; each night as he lay by her side he gave her a new name. He even had a name for the dog awaiting him in Ithaca! Name-giving is essentially an act of memory, an imposition of willful speech upon the silence of time. One of the chief distinctions between mortals and gods is that only the former have memory. Yet it occurs to Circe that this, ironically, may be man's sole immortal aspect: "the memory [man] carries with him, the memory he leaves behind." To Circe and Calypso, mortal destiny is a purely exteriorized process. Odysseus, on the other hand, measures his destiny not by the near visible horizon of Calypso's island, or the edge of Circe's bed; his destiny lies inside himself, his fate is an interior territory. His outward journeying is an expression of the journey within. "The object of my quest is inside me," he tells Calypso; then in a brief and startling act of imaginative authority, he tells the nymph, "And so is yours." In this cool Olympian world of law and order, where the gods abide in their heavenly city, man is already beginning to gaze inside himself. Mortality is evolving into compulsive self-reflection, and this will lead inevitably to the terrors of modern self-containment. As man now perceives destiny as something interior, his next stop is to seek history within himself. All of which, Pavese reminds us time and again, deepens mortal solitude.

As aspiration turned inward under Olympian law, so did the monsters of the Chaotic Age. The monsters that were once out there, totally *other*, now swim in the blood of humankind. Birth and death are both blood-rites, we begin and end in blood. "From the time of Chaos," says Eros in one of the dialogues, "there has been nothing but blood. Men's blood, blood of monsters, of gods . . . In order to be born, a thing must die." The sheath of flesh in which we are born is also death's profile. We emerged from the Chaos of beginnings into the Apollonian clarity of self-consciousness and self-reflection. But even as we live in the presence of Law, we are bound to encounter—as Bellerophon the Chimera, as Oedipus the Sphinx—something monstrous, Titanic, in our existence. The beast in the blood. The beast may take various forms: sex, blood-lust, gluttony—whatever steeps us in the seething antiwisdom of chaos. We meet the beast when we touch the things of earth, the chthonic verities. And these constants, Pavese suggests, repeat endlessly, unchanging, and their repetition shapes our destiny. In "The Blind," wise old blind Tiresias describes how he touched rock in sex, when he was turned into a woman for having poked mating snakes with a stick: "The things of the world are rock. . . . Here rock was the force of sex, its ubiquity and omnipresence under all forms of changes. . . . Above sex there is no god." But even the certainty of rock is no consolation. For it repeats, and repeats, and we begin to suffer under the burden of sexual fatigue, sexual despair, sometimes pure loathing. "For all of us," says Tiresias, "it is a wasted effort. I know." Mortal knowledge, then, is at best a knowledge of repetition and recurrence, and this brings us to the central force of the *Dialogues*, the passionate idea that inspirits and compels this book from beginning to end.

The most resonant phrase in the *Dialogues* is, "*Quel che è stato sarà*"—What has been will be. It is spoken (in various forms) by Prometheus, Orpheus, Patroclus, and a Beggar. A Titan, a demigod, a Homeric hero, and a commoner, a chain of personalities stretching from the Age of Cronos down to the last stages of the Olympian Age. The vast overarching cycle of Western civilization—from moiling Chaos to Olympian order to the decadence of primitivist ecstasy and blood-worship—is imitated, reenacted, in the processes of individual lives. The most darkly beautiful dialogue in the book is "The Burning Brand," in which we hear Meleager expressing the by now familiar nostalgia for the past. But Hermes—thief, messenger, lackey of the gods, descendent of Titan Atlas— reminds the boy that each of the admired heroes of the past had a mother, like Meleager, and that they too saw in their mother's eyes their own beginning and end. Conceived in burning passion, a man's birth is his initiation into the burning blood-rite of mortality. Fire gives only the promise of fire. "Your lives are forever contained in the burning brand," Hermes tells Meleager, "and your mother draws you from the fire, and you live half-blazing." Our legacy is a fire in the blood. The passion, chaotic and blood-bound, that conceived us is the passion that is bound to annul us. The cruelest irony of all is that we are not only born into mortality, but we must then spend our lives growing up into a deeper and sadder knowledge of it. Life is largely an education in dying, and the legacy of generations blazes within us. We grow up watching our elders watch us, the fire in their eyes the progenitor of the fire that is now our own. History does not, in the strict sense, repeat itself. But the blood that empowers the mortals who make history reoccurs from generation to generation. "In every man's flesh and blood," Hermes says, "his mother rages." When the slightly bewildered boy asks why Atalanta and Althea killed him, Hermes (who surely bears some grudge against the gods he serves) replies: "Ask why they made you." Generation is all. And it would seem, therefore, that mortals are absolutely at the mercy of the process of recurrence, and that finally they have no real power of their own. But it is here that Pavese asserts his poetics of destiny, by describing and dramatizing the divinely human power of the poet. And the source of this power is memory.

POETS do not "derive" from philosophers. A poet lives and writes primarily off instincts, or, in the painter Francis Bacon's phrase, "off his nervous system." Although a poet's instincts may be shaped or modulated by what he or she reads, a poet is seldom inspired by abstract systems of thought (though possibly inspired, as were Dante, Milton, and Yeats, by the sensuous drama imaginable in certain abstract systems). A poet will feel particularly drawn to a system when it seems to verify or reinforce what is witnessed in the poet's own immediate experience. Pavese was a wide reader, but more importantly he was an attentive reader. He studied, and adapted, the great philosophic world-views of the past—Vico's, Spengler's, and Nietzsche's above all. But his concentration was that of an artist, not a scholar. His was a passion for revelation, not mere explanation (or explication). Pavese *lived* his reading, transforming much of it into imaginative action. "A true revelation," he writes in the foreword to the *Dialogues*, "can only emerge from stubborn concentration on a single problem. I have nothing in common with experimentalists, adventurers, with those who travel in strange regions. The surest, and the quickest, way for us to arouse the sense of wonder is to stare, unafraid, at a single object. Suddenly—miraculously—it will look like something we have never seen before." Pavese has in mind mythic transformation as a thoroughly modern process. As Actaeon stared at the naked Artemis, a modern poet may in turn stare at Actaeon's history and see revealed there the very essence of sexual punishment.

This "staring" is the method of all of Pavese's poetry, and of the novels after *Paesi tuoi*. It is clearly the method of *Dialogues with Leucò*. Furthermore, according to Pavese's poetics, seeing is always and inevitably an act of memory. Pavese's art was never coy or precious, never cramped by the shadow play of Self-versus-World. Far from being a mere description or "capturing" of the moment, poetry is implacably historical. Every emotion has a history, every event a mythos, every moment a sequence of moments to which it belongs. The purpose of poetry—which is to say, the compulsion that inspirits words—is to liberate the moment, to free it into history. Poetry is a rage for continuity, and the argument that meter makes is an argument with time-bound mortality. In his *Scienza Nuova*, Vico wrote, "Imagination is nothing but extended or compounded memory. . . . This axiom explains the vividness of the poetic images which the world had to form in its first childhood" (Book I, L). Poetry thus seeks to enter, by means of imagination—literally, seeing and creating images—the great memory which is human history. The poet does not, however, merely recollect in tranquility. The poet *is* memory. The poet-as-memory generates the past while living in, and creating, the present, and does so by telling huge stories. Pavese dramatizes the role the poet plays in this scheme of recurrence in two of the closing dialogues.

"The Mystery," one of the more luminous dialogues in the book, features Dionysus (Blood-God, Ecstatic Darkness, Grape) and Demeter (Ear-Of-Wheat, Grieving Mother, Seasonal Recurrence, Bread). Both agree that the chief distinction between mortals and gods is that the latter *know* things, whereas mortals *do* things. Moreover, mortals create time. "Everything they touch," Demeter says, "becomes time. Becomes action. Waiting and hope. Even their death is something." Their special talent is to expend work on whatever they find around them. In work they find themselves, find their death. *Lavorare stanca.* "Wherever they lavish their sweat and their speech, a rhythm, a sense, a repose, is born." Speech, too, is a form of work, and poetry is the highest and most ample expression of work.

In the earliest times mortals told tales of the gods because they were unable, as Vico says, to form intelligible concepts about the classes of things. They worked to give gods names, tales, histories. Why, then, Demeter asks, do the gods refuse to help them, who have given the gods so much? Is there no way the gods might make this brief gasp of human life somehow more pleasant? Dionysus's short reply is that the gods have given humans Bread and Wine (given them, in effect, Demeter and Dionysus) and this ought to suffice. Besides, death is what drives them: "Death is what they're born for.

It's death that drives them to their efforts, to memory and foresight." But Demeter, a more imaginative deity than Dionysus, takes issue with the Wine-God's facile politics of blood. She sees that mortals have already "suffered every story they tell of the gods." They have suffered through the imaginative lives they have applied to the gods, they have endured the history of their own highest imaginings. As they continue to mature into self-consciousness, Demeter suspects they will soon seek some new way of infusing meaning into life. They will invent new stories, new possibilities for transcending the brutal mechanics of the blood. This new tale—Tragedy—will, in its telling, confer upon mortals some essence of immortality. The divine urge is bound to fuse with the narrative, myth-making urge. Demeter can even foresee a new mythos that will tell of one who conquers death, one whose self-sacrifice will bestow immortality upon all humankind. Without naming Christianity, Demeter implies that humans will seek to justify their mortal unhappiness by imagining death as a means of rebirth into holiness, the grave as threshold to godliness. Then, she hopes, they will no longer have to "placate [Death] by shedding other blood." But Dionysus, a realist who knows instincts, insists that even if humankind conjures up a new myth of rebirth and resurrection, it will be no guarantee against bloodshed. Blood-lust is inseparable from aspiration, as aspiration is inseparable from myth-making. In wheat and grape, in bread and wine, mortals will see flesh and blood. "As now, as always, flesh and blood will be spilled, not to placate death but to reach the eternal which awaits them." Dionysus is an authority—of all the gods, he knows best about the eating of the gods. "*Sarà sempre un racconto,*" he says. "It will always be a story." While humans enact again and again, under different forms, the mysterious story of their origins and ends, using the same props of flesh and blood and memory and desire, it is the poet who must tell this story, the poets who must *tell* their poems.

Appropriately, Pavese's poetics of destiny spiral down to a

dialogue between Hesiod (theogonist-farmer) and Mnemosyne. Hesiod feels oppressed by mortal routine, the repetition
of mortal habits. They wear a man down, he says. And he has
failed to find a way to escape routine and enter poetry. Mnemosyne—memory that inspirits—corrects the poet's thinking:
the daily round, "the staleness or the toil" of mortal habits,
may be the very sources of divinity, of poetry. In a passage of
almost unearthly beauty, she describes to Hesiod the swamp
of Boibeis:

> A dank swamp of slime and reeds, exactly as it was at the
> beginning of time, a seething, bubbling silence. It spawned
> monsters of excrement and blood. . . . Neither time nor the
> seasons change it. No voice reaches there. . . . Don't you un-
> derstand that man, every man, is born in that swamp of
> blood? That the sacred and divine are with you too? In bed,
> in the fields, before the fire? In everything you do, you re-
> new a divine model. [*Ogni gesto che fate ripete un modello di-*
> *vino.*] Day and night, there is not an instant, not even the
> most futile, which has not sprung from the silence of your
> origins.

Hesiod's inclination is to sit back and adore, passively, Melete.
But she offers him a crucial alternative, an inspiration: "*Prova
a dire ai mortali queste cose che sai*"—"Try telling mortals the
things you know." Try writing poems which *are* memory,
rather than telling tales *about* memory. If every moment
springs from the silence of origins, then the poet must reckon
with that divine continuity, found even "in the valley, in the
fields, at home, beside a hearth and in a bed." Pavese's bias is
clear. If poets are not to be incapacitated by *ennui*, or paralyzed by fashionable pieties, or rendered immediately harmless by whispering well-made poems up their sleeves, their alternative is to tell imaginative tales about divinely ordinary
things. A way of pledging loyalty to the silence of origins.

[1976]

WISH AND POWER

I

Public controversy distorts perceptions, and sudden notoriety often smudges the profile of a newly famous thing. In recent years Robert Altman, a latecomer in American filmmaking, has become the most conspicuous victim of public misperception. Although his films have inspired lively polemic, they have also drawn forth more obtuse, muddled opinion than any other films of the period. Critics and audiences have been dazzled, angered, sometimes baffled by his innovative style, above all by his eccentric narrative strategies. Instead of relying on the centripetal forces of conventional narrative, whereby plot details gravitate toward nuclear characters and events, Altman has exercised a kind of centrifugal style: incidents and characters spin away from the narrative axis, the camera brushes past significant events, the sound track overlaps or truncates "meaningful" dialogue, the editing fragments conventional exposition. It's a cunning, peripheral style, and one of the few real advances in storytelling method since the innovations of the French New Wave. In his films since *M*A*S*H* he has dramatized reality at speeds quite different from those we are used to in narrative cinema, and he has liquefied and refashioned traditional, fixed point of view. Altman casually insists that we train ourselves to see his films in a new way, that we adapt ourselves not merely to a new point of view but to a new method of seeing.

Because of his restless, exploratory methods, Altman has naggingly undermined and blasted critical expectations. He has moved from the flashy, jabberwocky profanity of *M*A*S*H* to the dreamy pessimism of *McCabe and Mrs. Miller*, from the looney-tune fable of *Brewster McCloud* to the puzzle theatrics of *Images*, from the bitter dizziness of *The Long Goodbye* to the melancholy of *Thieves Like Us*. Yet he never makes

41

an issue of his own virtuosity. The elliptical cutting, the eight-track sound recording that mimics and revises the babble of reality, the irreal lighting that shapes character, the peripheral events that lunge into the foreground to determine dramatic action: these are Altman's obvious "trademarks," but he is cunning enough not to have allowed them to harden into mannerism. His versatility, however, has in some quarters undermined his authority. Newspaper critics especially are immediately suspicious of abundance—Altman has made eight films in seven years—assuming that anyone who works quickly must be brilliantly facile. In this instance, the scaled-down expectations of reviewers simply are not equal to Altman's enterprise: his amplitude defeats and embarrasses their mincing generosity.

Nashville was responsible for bringing Altman to the attention of the public at large. Unlike his earlier films, it became a full-fledged media event. Disregarding for the most part the spinning lyric noise of the film and its unsettling ambivalence, critics preferred to seize on what seemed to them an accessible public issue—Altman's vision of America. *Nashville* was discussed in the most unlikely places, from the op-ed page of the *New York Times* to the Johnny Carson show. The topic of public discussion was not really the film itself but rather the commentators' misperceptions of it. Although Altman denied in interviews any intention of making *Nashville* a critical portrait of America in the seventies, critics inevitably misread the film as a moral indictment of America. Yet Altman, in an interview, was quite explicit about his intentions: "When I make films like *Nashville* it's not to say we're the worst country in the world, or what awful people these are. I'm just saying we're *at* this point and it's sad." Instead of righteous satire, he was offering a portrait of American melancholy, a study of personalities under stress, rendered in carousel narrative. The overheated competitiveness of the country-music industry was an ideal context; the brinksmanship and power struggles that characterize show business become all the more ambiva-

lent, and poignant, when the music in question sings American Themes. This too was much on Altman's mind: "Another
thing *Nashville* signifies is that we don't listen to words any-
more. The words of a country song are as predictable as the
words of a politician's speech. . . . *Nashville* is merely suggesting that you think about these things, allowing you room to
think. Many people, I guess, want to know exactly what it is
they're supposed to think. They want to know what your message is. Well, my message is that I am not going to do their
work for them." While Altman continues to operate by suggestion and insinuation, many of his critics still hear only
soapbox rhetoric, which presumably is what they *want* to hear.
His responsibility, as he sees it, is to vex his audience into
thought and feeling. He prefers revelation to mere explanation. Instead of handing down Polonian criticism of the
American way, he was in *Nashville* dramatizing—and often
mourning—the vicious operations of chance in a country celebrated as the land of opportunity—political, financial, and
sexual opportunity. *Nashville* is abrasive rather than critical,
seizing as it does on the confusion between opportunity and
opportunism.

Altman is certainly curious about the American character
and the eccentricities we have normalized. He wants to reveal
those things found only in America, the emotional contours
and cultural habits that distinguish us from others, the imaginative history that makes us what we are. His attitude is one
of curiosity, not pontification; of exploration, not proclama-
tion. Like most artists, he is a skeptic, never entirely trusting
the appearances of things; but he is at the same time celebrative, eager to sing in the presence of what moves him. This
tension between skepticism and celebration gives his films
their peculiar disarming ambivalence, their brilliant unease.
One of the most unexpected moments in *Nashville* comes
when the singer Barbara Jean, arriving at the airport to begin
her comeback, is greeted by a high-school band and a crowd
of scrubbed, chunky baton twirlers. Here surely was a chance

for Altman to poke low fun at American hokum, at provincial
middle-class culture. But, unexpectedly, he has a young
peachy twirler, cradling flowers for Barbara Jean, march directly into the admiring and embracing eye of his camera.
There is genuine affection and a startling absence of irony in
this image. And at the end of the film, although we are not
spared the abrupt horror of the shooting of Barbara Jean, the
hysterical lady in white, neither are we spared the cold and
accurate irony of American Opportunity: even as the great
democratic masses so celebrated in nineteenth-century America offer the young assassin his dramatic opportunity, the
tragic event at the same time offers another opportunity, that
of instant stardom, to the aspiring singer Albuquerque. In his
inspiration and the realization of his vision, Altman is kin to
Whitman: his art is ample and inclusive, he wants to see and
say everything, to get it all down. The result, as in Whitman,
may sometimes have the look of indiscriminateness, but this is
really a strategic mask for the symmetries of plenitude, for
generosity straining at the tether of common sense.

   Nashville is about rituals of public and private power. The
singers and hangers-on who frequent Nashville all act upon
the need to be close to power sources. Most of them seize
every opportunity to draw power from the presidential can-
didate Walker, guided not by serious political loyalties but by
careerism. The Nashville patriarch Haven Hamilton, the frail
convalescent Barbara Jean, the haughty inarticulate trio of
Bill and Tom and Mary, all insist they have no interest in politics, yet in the end they all agree to sing at the Walker rally.
The sympathetic magic of song might allow them to borrow
some of the raw political power of the event. Within this large
context of public power, Altman also sets in motion a number
of minidramas about professional and sexual power struggles,
games of brinksmanship that infect personal relationships.
Barbara Jean's position as country-music queen is threatened
by the glamorous hustling of Connie White; Albuquerque's
husband chases after her in order to "save" her from Nash-

ville; the young assassin, of all the characters the most isolated and solitary, suffers from his own high-strung wish to draw attention to himself. Each character, in effect, wants an increased sense of self-importance, and the most direct and dramatic way of achieving this is by stepping over the fallen or faltering bodies of others.

Power struggles, public or private, feed on pragmatism: A person may do whatever works best to serve his or her personal designs. But the most manipulative and ruthless characters turn out to be not Nashville country-and-western singers but the outsiders, the rock group Bill and Tom and Mary. The Nashville people, especially Haven Hamilton, do indeed believe in the values celebrated in their songs, though their belief is by now blunted by the grinding repetition of sentiment. They are not cynical in believing America to be still a land of milk and honey. Although their song lyrics are often anemic and hokey, they express more or less genuine sentiments. The rock group, on the other hand, are hypocrites in every way. Alienated from each other by sexual drifting and self-servingness, they sing songs that have no real basis in belief; the music is mannered and thin, the lyrics hollow slogans left over from the radical sixties. The mellow truths they celebrate, about loneliness and love, are glamorous instruments that earn them a good living. Tom, the most obnoxious and complex of all the characters, is also the most cowardly and self-serving. He is the show business Don Juan, making bedside phone calls to set up his next assignation even while his most recent bed partner listens on. He is full of canned antiwar sentiments, and his songs are sweet, convincing falsifications of his own feelings. But his arrogance is so apparently self-effacing and understated that it seems almost attractive; he is the perfect rendering of the "sensitive man" so fashionable in the sixties, soft and pliant manners masking arrogant weakness.

Altman sets the opportunistic rock trio against the more sympathetic and conventional character of Haven Hamilton.

Hamilton, the gaudy embodiment of Nashville traditions and
in his way a smug, self-righteous man, bears himself with reserve and dignity. He somehow ennobles even the flamboyant
costumes he wears. Like any toughened businessman he values tradition, yet we learn that he supported both Kennedys.
Most importantly, when called upon to act, he makes his choices
simply and bravely. When Barbara Jean is shot, it's Hamilton
who immediately uses his own body as shield to protect her
from further gunfire. Although he himself is wounded, his
instincts are to protect another, to preserve Nashville's angel.
He is morally outraged that a nearly hallowed place should be
profaned by the kind of irrational violence that *should* be foreign to Nashville. His sense of decency, which runs deep, and
of traditional values carried on in public rituals, is outraged
by the brutal disturbance of communal peace. "This isn't Dallas," he assures the crowd. "This is Nashville." This instinctive
defense of his hometown as a locus of value stands out in
sharp contrast to the equivocal values voiced not only by the
Walker campaigners, but also by most of the other Nashville
singers. His courageous gesture transcends pragmatism, cultural sloganism, and careerism; transcends, in effect, the most
obvious *appearances* generally identified with Nashville.

Altman's tone, however, and his attitude toward his characters are often ambivalent. Even though Haven Hamilton
performs more than one admirable act, we are never allowed
to forget that he is also an arrogant businessman. And Tom is
allowed some of the cool, bemused sympathy we reserve for
Don Juans. Altman's tone, then, can be at once abrasive and
affectionate. We have become so accustomed, however, to the
generally explicit, flattened tone of American movies that we
tend to feel not only uneasy but also defensive when con-
fronted with something more ambiguous and expansive. We
do not expect a film so overrun with familiar American images and attitudes to treat them in a new way. Our tendency
as viewers is to protect our own ritualized responses and to
make the darkened theater a place of safety rather than of

menace. By embracing a broad range of personalities in his films and by allowing them to pursue their own destinies without the blunt intervening hand of the filmmaker, Altman is close in sensibility to Renoir. And like Renoir, he resists making political and moral judgments. *Nashville* offers no explanation of America to itself, but it does render a very singular vision of the complexity of American experience. And I think that Altman's intelligent affection for his characters is tied to his ambiguous affection for American diversity. He is much taken by the peculiar blend of the wild and the forlorn which gives the American character its rough edges, the chattering, expansive, speedy smugness that seems built not only into our behavior but into the environments we surround ourselves with. Everywhere we go there is music—in supermarkets, offices, restaurants, houses, automobiles, factories. The music is meant to be ignored: this is its proper nonpurpose. Altman picks this up as an aural cue to one aspect of the American experience, and he uses it as a unifying element in *Nashville*. The people in the film do not really listen to music, they behave in its presence. Finally, the music does begin to seem like organized noise.

Altman's art, like Whitman's, is first of all revelatory, often interpretive, seldom explanatory. His work is too sensuous to be explanatory, too full of the messy, half-realized, inarticulate experience that gives his films an oddly numinous quality. Because of its amplitude, *Nashville* yields its own apparent contradictions, its own nonexplanations. For these reasons, the closing sequence deserves its mixed fame. Rather than a neat, summative, programmatic vision of contemporary America, it yields instead a vision of the heterogeneous elements of American experience and of the tensions that bind and enliven them. The pure unreason of the violence against Barbara Jean remains unexplained: The young killer, who has the clenched, ascetic look of a young anarchist, may be shooting up at the American flag, or at Haven Hamilton. The shooting itself is underplayed, since Altman is more con-

cerned with what happens afterward. We have a moment of
unexplained violence followed immediately by Hamilton's act
of conventional bravery. The disorder allows Albuquerque
her long-awaited opportunity to sing before an audience. Disaster thus creates opportunity, and this sudden realization of
opportunity, insofar as it reaffirms a crucial American value,
brings with it a provisional restoration of order.

More important than the lyrics of the closing song (with its
ambiguous refrain: "You may say that I ain't free / But it don't
worry me") is the self-referential incantatory power of song,
of organized noise, with its primitive power to soothe and manipulate, to turn benign or malevolent: song as democratic
redemption and fascist appeal. While the crowd chants, the
camera pulls back slowly. The colorful throng seems
shrunken against the hulking modern Parthenon ("made of
poured concrete and steel: the Athens of the South"). On
stage, isolated from the crowd, are the cheery blond new-
comer and a black back-up choir. Above looms the covering
presence of the flag, the symbolic organization of all the
mixed elements that stand, slightly dazed, beneath it. In this
bold context, the theme of the stars and stripes—its tricolor
harmonies, its pluralism set against a fixed field—ceases to be
ironic. The flag suddenly seems an appropriate metaphor,
though certainly at best a *working* metaphor, for the mixed
vision the film has offered us. But the film does not end here.
Intercut into this generalist vision are spastic, isolated closeups of the crowd: babies, rednecks, freaks, elders, and two
conspicuous police officers, one of them female, winding
alertly through the crowd. These shots remind us that the
generalization "society" exists only by virtue of its discrete
parts, its anonymous human units; society is before all else an
aggregate of personalities. Once we have absorbed this large,
expanding picture, the camera makes another decision. Tilting upward away from the crowd, it leaves both crowd and
flag behind and fixes its gaze on the blue and innocent sky.
The music finally, mercifully, fades out. Moments later, in si-

lence, the sky too fades. This final progression of images does
not resolve the film according to the melodramatic conventions of American narrative cinema. Instead of a vision of
provisional order and harmony (the standard resolution of
Hollywood films), and instead of the false consolation of political or moral platitude, the camera eye *enacts* transcendence,
lifting itself above the crowd, above human diversity toward
the oneness of sky. It is a powerful enactment of the will to
dream, the decision to transcend the appearances of pluralism and emerge into a transcendent, unified reality, an alter-
nate world. It is Altman's instinctive equivalent, I think, of
Emerson's aspiration toward the oneness of the Oversoul, a
coherent wish for transcendence. He of course thinks his way
toward this possibility through images, through his round-
robin metaphors of plenitude and unity. But the narrative
poetry is embedded in the self-contained metaphoric story.
Altman does not so much tell a story as he *tells* metaphors,
tells a poetry of deeply related images, and his films after
Nashville continue to tell this poetry of guarded aspiration and
promise.

II

Buffalo Bill and the Indians, or Sitting Bull's History Lesson, begins
where *Nashville* left off, with a vision of sky and mountains
and the American flag flying high. The camera eye descends
slowly, once again into show business, but this time the show
is a dusty historical spectacle of Missouri settlers battling Indians. From the pure presence of Nature we slide down into
the staged artifice of entertainment, of Buffalo Bill's Wild
West Show, where a revised version of history is being re-
hearsed so that it may be sold to willing audiences. Altman's
vision descends quickly from silence into noise, into the glib
speech of commerce, the marketplace of American wish and
power. Based as it is on the legends of Buffalo Bill, the Wild
West Show is grounded in falsified history, and it uses the
American Indian, the fixed center of native culture, as its
main ploy; it takes culture and distorts it to serve Bill's ends,

to become "civilized" entertainment. In the interests of progress, culture may be falsified, too. Civilization is more important, since it promises greater profits.

The linguist Edward Sapir, in his essay "Culture, Genuine and Spurious" (1924), distinguishes between culture and the civilization which is its vehicle. It is quite possible, he says, for an advanced intelligent civilization to be a very poor culture-bearer. America certainly possesses high civilization, conspicuous material wealth defined almost exclusively by advanced tools, a society where leisure is the highest ideal. Culture, on the other hand, depends not on tools but on a homogeneous mythic truth that must underpin the psychology and actions of an entire people, truth which results from a passionate desire to refine experience, to understand pious communal origins. Culture depends on an understanding of the sky and of humankind's residence on earth beneath such sky. Civilization places its trust in less permanent things. Sapir argues that genuine culture is not graduated, is neither high nor low: "It is merely inherently harmonious, balanced, self-satisfactory. It is the expression of a richly varied and yet somehow unified and consistent attitude toward life, an attitude which sees the significance of any one element of civilization in its relation to all others." The Wild West Show is certainly a mode of advanced civilization; not only is it *efficient* in its entertainment (it even has an "Inventions Department"), but it is self-conscious about its materials and impious in the presence of inefficiency. Progress is whatever works. Everything is judged according to its appearance—it is, after all, the show business. What it lacks, however, is what Sapir calls "spiritual essence," a belief in something that is not itself, that stands over and against human-made products. Bill's show may be a success, but it lacks spiritual mastery, lacks the historical abundance and unself-conscious permanence that infuse the mountains and sky. It is not numinous. Altman's film, perhaps the only truly contemplative American film of the mid-seventies, explores these distinctions, dramatizes the sadness that emerges from supercivilization when it lacks culture, broods on the suppressed envy that lies just beneath the surfaces of American experience, which so often is grief disguised as plenitude.

Show business is high civilization, a world of well-tooled artifice and illusion, the greatest being the illusion of history, a dream of Buffalo Bill as great Indian fighter. The show is certainly well designed, convincing in its appearances. But it lacks spiritual essence, lacks the one historical truth that might have given it real culture: Bill's identity is not a historical truth but the crude product of Ned Buntline's hack imagination. Far from being a great buffalo hunter and Indian fighter, Bill was above all an illustrious manufacturer of illusions. And the legends that began to cluster around his name were mostly dreamed up by a dime novelist visiting from the East. In order to preserve both his image and the show which markets that image, he must live up to the personality created for him. But in trying to honor his artificial public identity, Bill has become a civilized paranoiac who fears his own legend. He already suspects that his show, his dream, is very dandy waste, but waste nonetheless; it may be civilized entertainment, but it is not culture. It derives not from natural piety or the wisdom of the heart, but from businesslike cynicism and media hype. In Altman's version, Bill is beginning to distrust his own pulp greatness.

Into this hermetic, voluble world comes the threatening stranger, Sitting Bull, silent as a mountain, needing no hype to validate his spiritual power. Bull really does have visions; he sees what others do not, because his soul is great. Everything he says or does has its roots in the creation myths of his tribe, the primal piety of man in the presence of his gods, acting out of radical motives. As a man, he *comprises* culture. Unlike Bill, whose world is wildly contaminated by Nate Salsbury's pseudo-language, Bull needs no words to explain or rationalize his existence. Bill, the civilized creation of literary gossip, feels almost morally obliged to explain himself and to

exercise (as flamboyantly as possible) the power of his position; Bull, son of the silent earth, now dispossessed of the
means and tools of his own civilization, is pure revelation.
From the moment Bull enters, Bill is on his guard, cautious
and envious of this unlikely American. Each claims a history
drawn from the same historical context, but Bill knows that
the Indian is the real thing and hence the only dangerous
thing.

Buffalo Bill's main power source is self-esteem. He has assumed the manufactured image of himself; since it is so useful, so profitable, it must be true. Sitting Bull threatens Bill's
self-esteem, his control over all aspects of the theatrical production which is himself. Bill thinks he has scored a huge success in acquiring Bull as an attraction in the show, but it turns
out that the Indian has come only because of a dream which
told him that he would there meet the Great White Father,
President Grover Cleveland. To Bill's mind, this is a very spurious "reason," since it has no practical grounding. Bill cannot
understand because he does not have such power-dreams.
Certain that he is matching Bull's game of brinksmanship, Bill
agrees to let him stay but reminds his nephew Ed that "the
difference between a white man and an Injun in a situation
like this is that an Injun don't know the difference between a
question and an answer. That's why they ain't ever sure when
they get what they ask for." Duped by a man of power, Bill
can only resort to paleface rhetoric to preserve his self-
esteem. Question-and-answer is the most convenient kind of
business discourse: the language of exchange and bargaining.
Sitting Bull, however, speaks the more direct language of
need; his words are impelled by the destiny his dreams dictate. Bull's culture demands that he interpret fantasy, dream-
stuff, as one of the power sources behind his spirituality. Buffalo Bill and Salsbury, on the other hand, take the facts of
history and rearrange them into palatable illusions; they manufacture historical fantasies as something quite divorced from
their own spiritual essences. They deal in titillation, not inspi-

ration. In staging Custer's Last Stand, Bill has Custer scalped
by Sitting Bull. When someone objects to the historical inac-
curacy, Salsbury justifies it according to show business pragmatism: "We're in the goose-bump business." Halsey, Sitting
Bull's interpreter, also tries to correct Bill's staging: "Sitting
Bull was not present on the battlefield. He was making medicine and dreaming. Sitting Bull will allow you to show his
dream. He saw many horses upside down and blue skeletons
floating to the promised land." Not only does this not coincide
with Bill's idea of show business, but Bull's dream exists in a
cultural context totally alien to Bill's own. Bill must have big
American entertainment, explicit and goose-bumping; Bull's
oracular dream would not make good pulp. Moreover, the
Wild West Show is not, as Salsbury says, "in the yesterday
business"; the past exists not as radical memory but as raw
material for future deals. Salsbury refers to Bull's contract as
"the most futurable act in our history." Historical fact exists to
be packaged as a future commodity—this allows even a cul-
turally impoverished civilization to flourish.

All these materials lend themselves easily to satire, but in
Buffalo Bill Altman again adopts an unexpected tone. Rather
than characterize white men as malicious fools or show-busi-
ness sharks, he allows each character to stand close to the
shadow line of grief, to the collapse of self-deception (and
hence of self-esteem). If *Buffalo Bill* is a satire, it is elegiac satire, steeped in melancholy and uncertainty. Ironically, and
painfully, the only person to whom Bill can confide his fears
is Sitting Bull. The most seductive scene in the film is the one
in which Bill, delirious on whiskey and lack of sleep, halluci-
nates the presence of Sitting Bull. Provoked by the Indian's
astonishing self-containment, he spills out some necessary but
disarming truths and reveals some of his own hysterical wisdom. "God meant for me to be white!" he exclaims. The white
man's birthright is different in kind and degree from Sitting
Bull's; his legacies are different, too, and in their own way
terribly burdensome. Bill is aware of the choice he himself has

made and the responsibility he has taken on as a paleface showman: "It ain't easy. . . . I got people with no lives living *through me*! Proud people! People to worry about." He knows it is too late to make up for that which was missing in the first place, a sense of piety and of historical memory. The white man's dream is, and always has been, essentially different from the Indian's dream, and white America has had such little time to do so much that, as Bill tells it, we should not be held guilty for cutting corners on history. Civilization, in effect, is a different kind of aspiration than culture; its power must be evident in appearances, the clout of artifice and utilitarian rhetoric. And white America made its choice long ago. Bill goes on to confess his own urge to immortality; like an Indian, he wishes to be remembered by his children's children, but the source of his immortality, unlike an Indian's, will not be rooted in great deeds or spiritual power. "I do what I do for *me*. Because when you do that, you're gonna live a little longer. It makes me true! Because truth is whatever gets the loudest applause." Bill draws his power, his truth, from living for others' acclaim. Public acclamation of an artificial identity is the soundest confirmation of meaning in his life, and it promises some kind of immortality.

Show business is perhaps the most commonplace ritual of American civilization, and as Ernest Becker says in *Escape from Evil*, "ritual is a technique for giving life," conferring the power to outlive oneself. The difference—a tragic one—is that Bill sees himself as the source of his own power. Sitting Bull, too, obeys a set of rituals, but his strategies of immortality depend absolutely on a source of power which is *other*. Bill is a paradigm of American civilization in that he recognizes no numinous power, no spiritual authority beyond his own. In his impoverished desire, he is a figure of American grief. Here too, Becker's formulation is appropriate: "Man needs self-esteem more than anything; he wants to be a cosmic hero, contributing with his energies to nothing less than the greatness and pleasure of the gods themselves. . . . *Hubris* means forgetting where the real source of power lies and imagining that it is in oneself." When the power source is oneself, and when one's rituals are those of show business, one must then live not for oneself but for others. This too is a cause of Bill's melancholy. Pointing to a heroic portrait of himself, Bill asks Bull: "Ain't he riding his horse all right? If he ain't, then why did all of you mistake him for a King?" He suffers from the discrepancy between what he knows himself to be and what he knows the crowd expects of him. Whenever he rides into the show ring, mounted heroically on his white charger, Brigham, he barely manages to stay in the saddle. He is, literally and figuratively, slipping, about to lose his image, and he knows it. Obtuse as he may seem, and certainly no visionary like Sitting Bull, Bill still sees enough to suffer. Lacking culture, however, he lacks a spiritual system that might help him organize the disparate perceptions he has of himself and others. Ned Buntline says that Bill "likes to think he's a dreamer, but he's really just a sleeper." Bill's sullen American yearning, cast in the darksome and honky-tonk moods of this film, is directed toward the radical culture he knows he lacks. But his yearning, too, is anxious and uncertain, since he is not sure he even needs or wants such culture. He has already acquired great material power, but somehow this power has still not satisfied a deeper wish that civilization lacks the language to express, let alone realize.

III

The power relations in *Nashville* and *Buffalo Bill* are largely public, practiced by entertainers whose anxieties are acted out before large, attentive audiences. In both films the protagonists are media heroes, fabricators of civilization. In *3 Women*, however, Altman withdrew (once again, unexpectedly) from public to private zones of power. *3 Women* is very much about the anxieties and densities of power, but the drama here is reclusive, and the conflicts are suffered not by the fabricators of civilization but by its anonymous consumers. Altman again

carefully modulates the American context. Instead of the
swarming vitality of American plenitude, he concentrates on
a more controlled vocabulary of metaphors, rigorously designed and *placed*, which makes *3 Women* stylistically a more
poised and fragile film than the earlier two. If the poetry of
Nashville and *Buffalo Bill* is public, abundant, open-aired, and
utilitarian, the poetry of *3 Women* is cloistered, ascetic, self-
referential, aesthetic. In the patterns of emotion dramatized
in its (often oneiric) metaphors, *3 Women* is almost a symbolist
investigation of impingement, emotional sabotage, and viola-
tion of personality. In the earlier films personality was the bat-
tlefront of power, where identities were left battered but in-
tact. In *3 Women*, impingement causes actual changes in
personality, normalized monstrosities.

The worst victim of impingement is the woman who at first
seems most aggressive. Millie works at a geriatric health spa.
We first see her wading in a heated pool, steering along an
old disabled woman. Altman places his metaphors at the very
beginning, for Millie walks half-immersed in water, half-dis-
torted, half-"drowned." If the finale of *Nashville* was Altman's
expression of Emersonian wish, in Millie he gives us a contemporary misversion of Emerson's self-reliant American.
She is a cheery monster of American consumerism, prattling
about microwave ovens and new fast-food recipes. Her fero-
cious sense of self-esteem, aggressive but dull-witted, puts
people off. Her self-assertiveness is so obtrusive and over-
stated that she seems all surface, a tissue of TV and supermar-
ket values. And yet she is protective of these values, since they
do comprise her selfhood. In her rush to be as contemporary
and as independent a woman as possible, she estranges herself from her own context; she authors her own separateness.

Millie's tidy world is invaded by the stranger Pinkie, who
comes to work at the spa. Pinkie is a Texas girl (like Millie)
and her freckled innocence somehow combines both the
cheer and menace of small-town American life. She seems at
first Millie's opposite, homely, withdrawn, uninformed, with

one pair of panties that she rinses out nightly. The seed of
personality-doubling has already been planted, not only because the two women come from Texas, but because Pinkie's
real name is Mildred. These coincidences will soon turn into
compulsions, and Altman already begins to establish meta-
phorical symmetries. Pinkie's quick and strategic attachment
to Millie is mocked visually by the presence of identical twins
who work at the spa and who hold a spooky attraction for
Pinkie. They become a model for Pinkie's own behavior; this
innocent from the country will patch together her own personality from the scraps and remnants taken from others. If
Millie borrows her personality from TV, magazines, and supermarkets, Pinkie takes hers from the personalities that surround her. Millie takes her as a roommate, and soon Pinkie is
reading Millie's diary, wearing her clothes, mimicking her
speech patterns, and generally insinuating herself into Millie's
private world.

The two frequent a desert bar called Dodge City, a tacky
Old West saloon run by Edgar (once a stunt stand-in on the
Wyatt Earp show) and his pregnant wife Willie. Here Altman
again reveals his ability to define a special kind of brash
American vulgarity. Willie is an artist who bears herself with
the silent, closed dignity of Sitting Bull, and as in *Buffalo Bill*
silence here is a sign of self-containment and personal power.
Willie drifts through the desertscape like a wraith, leaving behind power signs, paintings of scale-armored humanoids. She
paints her demons on the walls and floors of swimming pools;
her creatures seem ravaged by their own isolation and by
their cumbersome sexuality. Some have elastic striated male
torsos and flat drooping breasts, others have huge phalli.
Their predatory look and sexual menace call to mind Albany's lines from *King Lear*: "Humanity must perforce prey on
itself / Like monsters of the deep." Pinkie shows the same attraction to Willie's monstrous doubles as to the twin sisters,
and when she later attempts suicide, she does it by leaping

into a pool, going to meet the monsters whose shapes rhyme just as the names of the three women rhyme.

In *3 Women* style itself is the narrator. Altman builds the movie on a suspended, coherent poetic design; the story is narrated in its metaphors. The film's visual coherence depends on two metaphors of place: desert and pool. Each personality is identified with a natural element. Millie is the desert princess, her wardrobe and apartment interior bright with sun colors; the brilliant yellow of her dresses imitates the piercing yellow of the desert cacti and yucca (desert flora is pale and bright, but not quite the garish banana yellow we see in the film; Altman, too self-consciously perhaps, color codes his metaphors). Pinkie, on the other hand, sees reality most often through watery distortions. Very early in the film, prefiguring her attempted suicide, she dunks herself in the spa pool. When she spies out her apartment window, her gaze passes through a fish tank. Willie, the most self-possessed of the three, passes easily from the dry depths of pools to the cactus landscape: when Pinkie attempts suicide, it is Willie who lunges into the water to rescue her. As the women impinge upon one another, they swing through shifting planes of light, from the slippery greens and blues of the spa to the brittle pastels of the apartment complex to the glaring yellows and browns of the desert. The images to which the characters are drawn also enact the interpenetration of identities, of natural functions. Willie's pool monsters are obviously desert creatures, scaly, saurian. Blurry underwater perceptions and duplications of image are played off against the violent, parched clarity of the desert. Altman dramatizes not merely figures in a landscape, but also the landscape itself as an imitative figure of the spiritual contest waged among the three protagonists. As they move through these zones of lucidity and distortion, the zones of self-knowledge and living for others, the three women begin to stake provisional claims on one another's selfhood. Pinkie takes on Millie's effusiveness, whereas Millie begins to learn from Willie's silences.

When Millie, anxious for the self-esteem that sexual conquest brings, returns home one evening with a drunken Edgar, Pinkie is stunned by her roommate's "borrowing of Edgar." Suddenly, borrowing is no longer a harmless game; Pinkie feels great sympathy for Willie, and her pleas to Millie not to sleep with Edgar grow out of her fear of harm done to Willie. Rebuffed, her games now darkened by the subversive reality of sex, Pinkie seeks a way out. In keeping with Altman's poetry of oblivion, she seeks death by water, plummeting into the pool to meet the sexual monsters at the bottom.

When she emerges from the coma induced by her fall, Pinkie is changed. Having surrendered herself to the dark creatures, she now begins her doubling in earnest. While convalescing, she begins to claim more fragments of Millie's personality, even asks to be called by her real name, Mildred. She paints her toenails, appropriates Millie's (yellow) car, picks up Millie's friends, flirts with Willie's husband. Pinkie also suffers from partial amnesia. In *Nashville*, the characters remembered only what they wished to remember, and these were usually memories of power, of the Kennedy campaign and the end of that world in Dallas. Buffalo Bill Cody manages to cope mainly by forgetting his own drab origins, soaking them in whiskey and power dreams. In *3 Women*, Pinkie in her loss of memory is free to wield power; she has no memories to define her own personality (which is always shaped by memories and past experience). To be absolved of identity is to be liberated, purged for the future. In her presence, Millie becomes unusually timid, deferential, obsequious. The waters of the pool have brought on enforced forgetfulness. Pinkie, like William Cody, knows only her wish for power.

The power does not last long, however. One night a dream comes to claim her, a dream filled with images of the past, the hallucinatory reality of doubles, twins, monsters, and Willie, all twisted and warped by the opacity of water, the dream medium. The montage sequence that dramatizes Pinkie's emergence from forgetfulness is, in Altman's rendering, a stun-

ning figuration of the way stored images fuse, collapse, and
percolate in the subconscious, as Pinkie makes her bizarre
journey from unknowing and mystery into clarity. In effect,
she *swims up* into the provisional clarity of self-possessiveness.
This change is immediately challenged by yet another. As the
stunned Pinkie climbs into bed to be warmed and consoled by
Millie, Edgar barges in to announce that Willie has gone into
labor.

Altman uses the childbirth sequence as a dramatic fulcrum
where the balance of power among the three women is finally
tilted and decided. This scene, like Pinkie's suicide attempt, is
glazed by the memory of water, of sexual depth and unknowing. Our view is flexed and smeared by the water line that
floats so unnaturally up and down the frame of vision while
Willie is in labor. Once again Pinkie is being tested by water,
and she fails the test, shrinking back from the primal event.
Unexpectedly, Millie, who spends her days wading in pools
for the aged, is the one who endures the initiation by water
into full selfhood. Pinkie's idle games of doubling collapse under the pressure of real circumstances; her fabricated identity
cannot survive this traumatic experience in which the fanciful
adolescent "freakiness" of doubled images becomes an adult
reality. To the innocent Pinkie, the issue of one human from
the body of another is the most terrifying event of all. It is
finally too real. The scene turns matter-of-factly tragic when
the infant emerges from Willie bearing her own chilling silence. Millie, unaided, is left with the stony child on her
hands, and her personality is tempered, *fired*, by the experience. Here, Altman suggests, is terminal impingement; after
this crib death, this grieving enactment of stillborn selfhood,
the lives of the three women can never be the same.

The underkeyed moral and physical bravery revealed in
this scene reminds one briefly of Haven Hamilton's moment
of instinctive bravery; Millie's courage is also instinctive, but it
is intensely private. When Willie plants her feet on Millie's
shoulders during the birth, the two seem fused into one em-

battled, courageous, pained woman. Their dealings with human predators (Millie with Pinkie, Willie with Edgar) lead finally to this encounter with the general predator. Altman's
tale thus comes full cycle in its poetry; a film about power relations and identity-thievery evolves into a tale about generation. The tale told by the metaphors is finally this: Until it is
tested by mortality, all identity is provisional, makeshift, ex-
pedient. Once mortality has brushed against us, personality
hardens, selfhood becomes fixed, and identity drives down
permanent roots. We recall the opening scenes of the film, the
wrinkled, deteriorating elders wading so carefully in the pool
at the spa—the aged awaiting death, attended by the young
who themselves act as midwives to the yet unborn.

The film's closing moments are stern, serene, imperious.
The gleaming promise of yellow now belongs to a huge Coca-
Cola truck that rears up from the desert to make a delivery to
Dodge City, now operated by the three women. Edgar has
died of a gunshot wound, clearly the victim of one of the
women. Dodge City, in its new version, is a tribal village without men (a bitter inversion of the manly Dodge City of movies). The three women comprise a family. Pinkie, now called
Millie, calls Millie "Mom"; she sits at a cashier's desk popping
gum and reading fan magazines, the eternal adolescent eternally dependent. Willie, still silent, still paints. But Millie, the
poetic center of the film whose "color value" has been the key
to the film's figurative tale, is changed utterly. Once the creation of other people, a conflation of popular tastes and vibrant self-esteem, she is now very much her own woman, self-
contained, domineering, unsmiling. Although the three now
comprise a household, they are ruthlessly *three*, each an individual possessed of selfhood, each distinct. A new power balance has been achieved, and this time it seems awfully permanent. The permanence is nearly inanimate, locked in the
middle of the desert, still brutalized by the insistent yellow
sun. There are no pools in sight now, none of the watery
opacity and sexual menace that have brought about this final

condition. Instead, the most conspicuous element in the landscape, which also is the last vision Altman offers us (so unlike
the final transcendent vision of blue sky at the close of *Nash-*
ville), is a heap of worn-out tires, civilization's junked products
left to bake in the sun.   [1978]

OUT OF NOTEBOOKS

1978–1979

The commentators are celebrating "a return to narrative," by which they mean poems that take notice of things happening in sequence. But if it is to have any necessity, narrative poetry must tell states of becoming. And the poet's sense of the existence of an anonymous listener is more important than it is in lyric poetry. Narrative poetry does not take notice of things, it enacts the process of things.

★

The law laid down (again) in a feature essay in a poetry magazine, codifying more confusion and uncertainty about verse composition. The essay presents and tries to justify some contemporary conventions: "voice" is the new form of poetry; tone is the new prosody; the lyric is essentially a blend of tone and personality; poetry generally is a verbal configuration of personality, a talisman carved in the image of the personality of the poet; the poem therefore is a charm, should charm, be charming. The standardization of method, by which many try to imitate as a formula for "a successful poem" the methods of technological production, here receives confirmation by standardized critical pronouncement. How desperate we all must be for community of some sort, even if it is only the false community of likenesses. Save us from our singleness!

★

Shortly after Minny Temple's death, Henry James wrote: "I asked her about her sleep. 'Sleep,' she said, 'Oh, I don't sleep. *I've given it up.*' And I well remember the laugh with which she made this sad attempt at humor. And so she went on,

sleeping less and less, waking wider and wider, until she
waked absolutely!" In the same letter he says, "It's the *living*
ones that die, the writing ones that survive." An entire life's
work can thus be the testament of regret.

For days you feel turned inside out, as if the nervous system
were lining of the flesh's fabric, now all exposed. Whatever's
out there chafes and grinds. Words, the air, the sound of leaves
blown across the pavement. These become desire's claims.

Robert Lowell spent considerable energy readjusting the rhetoric of self-presentation. He wanted a protagonist whose
household demons intruded upon and screeched at public
history. From the first (and best) of the *Notebook* series, he
wanted poetry to announce the life as it was being lived, burdened with fact. By the time the *Notebook* versions became *History*, the rhetorical exertions seemed more and more mere
public eloquence, a new kind of lyric oratory. In the melancholy of his last years, the years of *Day by Day*, he seemed to
have to force himself to take interest in his imperious personality and its freight of facts. He says in one of these poems
that he asked to be obsessed with writing, and part of that was
the obsession with revised rhetorics. He's one of our best
poets of domestic tumult, of political sorrow, and of writing-
room contentiousness. But how many new dawns, new saving
moments, can any life need? Or tolerate?

James resented critics who attacked books, resented the sheer
number set loose on new works. The critics, he suggested (he
who dutifully turned out hundreds of pages of newspaper
criticism), ought to try their hand at writing fiction, to appre-

ciate its difficulty. Since then the situation has turned around.
Now we have more writers than critics. And many critics
sooner or later write some poetry or fiction. Now there are
too few decent critics set loose on so many books.

I dreamed I was looking at a book (*Portrait of a Lady?*) with
mixed disordered pages in different typefaces, some mysteriously astray from other books, other stories, all bound beautifully as one text. Page 782 followed page 34. The numbers
were important only for their shattered sequence. The chaos
promised mystery, and eventual revelation, so I started to
read it.

Nietzsche, in *Ecce Homo*: "My formula for the greatness of a
human being is *amor fati*: that one wants nothing to be different—not forward, not backward, not in all eternity. Not
merely bear what is necessary, still less conceal it . . . but *love
it*." That love is a tremendous task and requires a complete
limitless residence in the present which lyric poets may be incapable of. In *Zarathustra* he says, "Pain too is a joy. . . . Have
you ever said Yes to a single joy? . . . then you said Yes, too,
to *all* woe. All things entangled, ensnared, enamored." And
yet that is what any poet demands, the restored fullness and
passion of those entanglements.

The skulls Cézanne painted in his last years are *memento mori*,
but they are still apples and pears, transfigured. His subject is
still the formal life of nature made over into paint. The recognition of mortality one feels in these last works is articulated less by the talismanic figure of the skulls than by the
brooding sepulchral coloring and the extreme stillness of the

forms. The power of the reckoning: the passion of the material.

★

The character of the lyric poet is expressed in Lancelot's first question to the unknown damsel he meets in the forest after a long journey: "Fayre damesel, know ye in this contrey ony adventures nere hande?"

★

To borrow a method from Francis Bacon. After finishing a figure in a painting, he takes a rag or sponge, smears a section of the canvas, then leaves it, abandons it as is. Willed arbitrariness, the danger of the act (in destroying form won by toil), the random violence, to *derange* the figure into a new meaning. Violent formlessness becomes naturalized, made part of the form. A strange and wild sort of integration. It is a matter of allowing instinct an even more decisive control over the form of the poem, once the form has already begun to "set." To encourage the strange word-traces of the dream life, the sudden rearrangements of phrase, all invasive oddnesses, and wield them in deciding the poem's final form. The smear of words, the dislocations, need to result in a new formal consonance (otherwise the practice becomes uninteresting play, or frivolous chaos). And this can come about, I think, only if the poetry issues from whole temperament, not from sectarian interest in technique. The smear is or ought to be an instrument of disclosure, finally, and a way of altering the nature of the invitation that poetry visit us.

★

To travel through the landscape of self into the world, the terrain of otherness. ("One must learn to *look away* from oneself in order to see *much*: this hardness is necessary to every climber of mountains.")

★

Lyric narrative: less a way of telling stories than of telling a history of metaphors of becoming. The feeling tone is (too often?) terror.

★

The importance of narration—of the imagination of sequence and consequence—is that it illuminates mystery. In its purest form it illustrates origins and endings, the arc of existence. To narrate that otherness is to narrate ourselves.

★

A friend tells me about a new audio recording technique that results in "absolute fidelity" to the source. The need to reproduce as "faithfully" as possible sounds, events, images, and sequences (and to manipulate the speed with which they are reenacted, "replayed") comes from a need to make the past a sort of physical installation portable into the future. Experience thus is transformed into decorative artifact, something already past, even in the moment of its occurrence. We think it something already past. We sacrifice, therefore, as a culture, the dare to become sovereign knowers of the present, of the hardness and terror and fineness of existing entirely in time, sacrifice it to our craving to devitalize time by delivering it, perfected and preserved, into the future. That cult of preservation matches the technology of obsolescence. Both are flights from the present. The technological imagination is a great thing, but like any exercise of the imaginative faculty it is a form of deliverance. In poetry, the imagination delivers us, in the time and memory of the poem, from the crush of contingency so that it may restore us to a more complete and detailed knowledge of ourselves as contingent beings. The technological imagination, as it is often practiced now, delivers us from the present without any real and necessary restoration. That is why it can so easily turn us against ourselves.

It abstracts us. We become more and more what we have made the mind of the machine make us.

★

Descriptive speech: reconstructs or replicates the piece of reality seen in the mind's eye when that vision conforms to the configuration of the thing seen in the physical world. It acknowledges and imitates that objective reality.

Metaphoric speech: enhances, intensifies, transfigures the piece of reality seen. It insists not on the discrete attributes of the thing seen but on an intuited *relation* among the individual parts that compose an entire object (the skin of an apple, the curve of its pulp), but also the relation between it and some other piece of reality (the apple and the skull). Metaphoric speech also dramatizes the activity of the mind relating itself to the object of its gaze. Metaphor is therefore a code of relations, the animating in language of the tension that joins the reflective life of mind to the world of objects surrounding it. Metaphoric speech, the speech of desire in lyric poetry, is an act of mind intent on the destination of otherness.

★

Coleridge and relation. "Frost at Midnight," "This Lime Tree Bower," and "Dejection: An Ode" enact the presence of consciousness testing the ways of its aspiration. The discoveries he makes along the way mark the moments of Romantic Surprise, the disclosure of the possible clarity of one's regard for the world. It is domestic, inwarding, almost secretive. It is enthralled by its antithetical possibility—by failure, derangement, despair. Unlike Wordsworth, in Coleridge (and Keats) the sense of the poet's ambition vanishes in the telling of mental event.

★

How escape the confines of occasion without giving up its definitions? How *live into* relations? The self into otherness. The one into the blissful, terrifying, absolutely real more-than-one? The enormous "you" of lyric: the imagined destined receiver of the lyric message. Maybe reaching toward—*talking toward*—another is a normal cry for public intimacy. It is the first real moment of publication.

★

Dante not only talks himself through his journey, reflecting and interrogating as he moves, but he also edits himself as he goes along:

> *Non lasciavam l'andar perchè ei dicessi,*
>   *ma passavam la selva tuttavia,*
>   *la selva, dico, di spiriti spessi.*
> Though he still spoke, we kept on walking
>   And making our way through the wood,
>   I mean the wood of the thronging spirits.
>   (*Inferno*, IV)

He catches himself up in his own metaphor, the "selva scura" of the poem's opening lines, and so he hastily explains himself. He offers at once the realistic detail and the self-consciousness of the telling.

★

Since poetry is so much possibility and speculation-in-the-making, each poem, however self-contained or defined by the lineaments of occasion, ought to bear some exponential promise. (The poem as "minimalist gesture" is something I can hardly understand.) I hold no idea of the perfect poem, except in my dream life, where it's always an image of a poem or a music. But I insist (maybe too much) on the rude need for a vision of contested becoming.

★

When I think of poetry as public event, I imagine a lyric taking place in a middle distance somewhere between the incan-

descent interior of the poet and the receiving ground *out there*.
Poetry's language looks both ways at once. Its position out
there is the public space of the poem, its installation in full
view of (and therefore available to) the public mind. But the
poet never writes *toward* that space.

The wish to be all mind, flesh dissolved into thought, all acts
mere gestures of ideas. That is one kind of unity of being, or
a shambling dream of it. It excludes only everything—the first
charge of existence: embodiment.

1980–1981

Dante's invocation at the beginning of *Inferno* xxxii: *"sì che dal
fatto il dir non sia diverso"* (so that the telling will be no different
from the fact). He insists on the importance of rendering the
data of vision, the facts of the imagination. To assume the obligation of rendering the clarity of the details the poet himself
fabricates in memory—this is still the moral obligation of poetry. The telling does not just relay a fact or observation (or
infernal datum); the telling itself constitutes imaginative fact.
The form-making impulse and the truth-telling obligation
fuse.

Two of Darwin's facts, reported in *Voyage of the Beagle*:

> Certainly no fact in the long history of the world is so star-
> tling as the wide and repeated extermination of its inhabit-
> ants.

> There is no reason to believe that the Fuegians decrease in
> number; therefore we must suppose that they enjoy a suffi-
> cient share of happiness, of whatever kind it may be, that
> renders life worth having. Nature by making habit omnipo-
> tent, and its effects hereditary, has fitted the Fuegian to the
> climate and the production of his miserable country.

★

One doesn't lose one's faith; one falls from, *out of*, belief, as if it were a terrace in the mind. The falling is a negative condition, zero minus something. You never strike bottom, you just keep falling and get accustomed to that direction.

★

Schiller's advice in *On the Aesthetic Education of Man*: "Live with your century, but do not be its creature; render to your contemporaries what they need, not what they praise." He must have had Goethe in mind. These days, the desire to please, and therefore be praised, is blent into the sentimental wish to "tell your audience what they need to hear in order to live their lives."

★

I said to myself that hearing Mass after nearly fifteen years would be merely a sort of social call. But what moved me about the ceremony—did I expect not to be moved? did I expect to stop falling?—was so different from what used to pulse inside me all those years ago. The Mass seemed no longer a ritual loaded with grace, but a volatility, a faith burnt up and renewed with each gesture, each word, resolving moment to moment into divine power incarnated then dissipated, the awful glory of the dying man-god. Maybe one has to fall first, and keep falling, to feel that quickened glee of divine immanence, and to know cooly—to feel along the heart—the terror of the story of the God who, having visited among mortals, returns to the sky after being locked away inside the earth. Calling himself, in the flesh, back from death, he explodes the vessel of earth, melts the stone, leaving in his wake a message, some stories, the precipice of belief. (The woman's first thought when she finds the tomb empty, the roughneck angel, a Caravaggio angel, standing angry at the tomb, assuming no one will understand what he has to say, and not much caring, is that someone *has stolen* the human god who will redeem us all.) Nietzsche was the purest, and in his way most pious, anti-Christian in insisting that one must live wholly and entirely—*comprehensively*—in this webwork of earthly existence. There can be no imagined obliging transcendent Other *which offers promise of another life*. I can't begin to understand the happiness of those who have come to rest content in one view or the other. One's relation to the imagination of the divine is always a struggle, an act of self-definition in progress.

★

At a small gallery in Virginia, a local artist had a one-man show that ran for several weeks, during which time not one of his thirty paintings was sold. On one of his increasingly rare check-up visits, in a fit of enraged disappointment he began to scream in the presence of a handful of visitors, then he took a can of spray paint and, in a gesture I imagine like Baptiste's in *Children of Paradise* when he crosses out with greasepaint his image in a mirror, he began to spray an enormous X on each canvas. Every picture got the same treatment. Then he threw down the can and left.

Two or three bystanders immediately approached the gallery owner and inquired about the prices of the newly x-ed out canvases. Word spread. Within a week of the artist's outburst of self-cancellation, more than half of his paintings were sold, earning him about $20,000. The paintings were of familiar southern subjects—plantation homes, magnolia groves, benevolent darkies—rendered in the most conventional ways. Once x-ed out, they became, of a sudden, modernist and therefore acquired value. The buyers were not really buying the painting, they were appropriating anecdote, something that would remind them of an actual occurrence of human anguish. The anecdote (or story-structure) was the "life art" of the otherwise dead-duck painting. This had nothing to do with the way the public enjoys the story of others' suffering, but rather their desperation to acquire some embodiment of actual grief, actual passion. In a gruesome way, the buyers wanted their story—their lives—to flow briefly in and through that of the artist, as if to say there really is some connection, something binding one to another. Save us, again and again, from our singleness!

★

Living in what Simone Weil calls an Age of Psychology, where all states of mind, all perceptions, are to be equally valued. (Everything is important, therefore nothing is important? The new equivalence? What freedom issues from this?) Poetry in an age of psychology: the equivalent importance of all impressions. Poems as interchangeable parts in the "descriptive insight" machine. The result, however, is the diminution or thinning out of mental qualities.

★

There are those mysterious lines that seem delivered, dictated by something greater and entirely other than the poet. Sometimes I think of those language traces as a sort of neurogram, a way of writing a condition of nerves governed or guided by a force, or power, now unremembered but still active. But at the moment of writing, of the dictation, it's as if the nerves were exposed, the body pulled inside out: the external world registers instantaneously, and in an incredibly painful charge, on all those impulses, relays, sortings, resolutions, and rearrangements—all the manic electricity of consciousness. What matters most is that encounter, registered in the delivered language, between the external world and the restless, discontent, groping, apprehending interior.

★

Keats's remark about Negative Capability seems to be becoming a literary cult object. The commentators are full of it these days. Some, though, use it as a justification of ignorance. Embrace doubt and uncertainty, the current wisdom has it, for it will do you good. Indeed, it will ennoble you. I suppose it's easy to heroize one's fearlessness in the presence of uncertainty. We travesty Keats's inquiring, sensuous intelligence, however, if we cite him as an endorsement of the unwillingness to pass judgment, to evaluate, to assert or deny. Negative Capability is no counsel for failed nerve. Keats was advising himself to be patient in the quest for definitiveness. It is the counsel of patience of the imagination.

The peculiarity of Herbert's intelligence is his ability to engage two powers at once, and articulate both, nearly line for line in poems like "The Collar," "The Windows," and "The Flower": the first is disposed to quarrel, question, be skeptical, scrupulous, even intellectually prideful, belligerent, inquiring; the other is an almost priapic alertness and preparedness, at once receptive and aggressive (and a little nervous), in the presence of imminent bestowals of grace, of deliverance.

★

From the Taoist text Kuan Tzu (330 B.C.): "The earth is the origin of all things, the nest and the garden of all life. . . . Water is the blood and breath of the Earth, flowing and communicating (within its body) as if in sinews and veins." Therefore poison the blood, foul the nest, scatter filth in the garden, as a promise to our children. Therefore profit. Progress, human industry, in the name of "technological imagination."

★

We most fully live in the present when we are in pain. The past becomes a block of useless stuff, rubble, recognizable only because it is monument to a time when pain was not. It is a lost, ruined Eden. The future is imaginable only as oblivion—of pain, of ourselves. There is no reach or stretch of time called "future," there is only "the end of pain," a deliverance. Then, afterward, the future might begin again.

Oh that I once past changing were,
Fast in thy Paradise, where no flower can wither!

1982–1983

R. P. says that the activity of poetry is an attempt "to transcribe the greatness of our existence." To receive this greatness and intensify our knowledge of it in the symbolic forms of poetry is perhaps the only way in which the writing of poetry may be said to be a natural activity.

The interview has become the most proliferating literary form of our time and is not to be confused with table talk, with Eckermann's Goethe or Traubel's Whitman, three of whom were at least worth listening to. Poets seem to write less critical prose. This isn't in itself a bad thing. But instead of writing they talk, and the talk is recorded, published, then cited as deep authority in creative writing classrooms. Talk is cheaper than ever. And the interview inadvertently serves and perpetuates the organizations of power in our playback culture.

The most devastating and impious assumption: the world in all its hard bright particulars exists so that we can write poems about it. (Or that it exists by virtue of language's capacity to make statements about it.)

Public culture is obliged to ennoble what's trivial. That is part of its function in an industrial democracy. It happens at all levels, not only in television and popular music but also in the sphere of book and magazine publishing. Democracy assumes that even what is undistinguished can, or must, be elevated by virtue of the sovereignty of individual genius.

The most disturbing quality of certain poets associated with Yvor Winters is that their poems are simulacra of thought, self-contained and definitive in their formulations which, in their steely completeness, boast normative good sense. A poetry that makes all experience answerable finally to good sense is intellectually *vanitosa*.

Since human beings have probably written or spoken or sung poetry (or chants or songs) longer than they have practiced other kinds of expression, its beauty presumably had use and could not be distinguished from its religious or ritualized practice. Cave painting probably followed on some formal vocalization of the magic power registered in those paintings. The songs were repetitive, and religious in that they meant to summon and control relations between humans, the animals they hunted, and the powers that guided and destined the hunt. Song bore the full integralness of what was felt to be important in the culture, at a time when such discriminations were easy to make because the press of necessity was more constantly felt, less mediated by the apparatus of civilization. Poetry preserved and continued communal consciousness. This impulse hasn't died out entirely. Edwin Muir was a self-conscious transmitter of what he felt were the core myths of our society. But since 1945, the tribal uses and shared values of poetry have thinned out. Poetry now is primarily a conductor of discriminations and deliberations of selfhood and its qualities. It has become more psychological (in S. Weil's sense), more obliged to an overly nuanced studiousness of personality and less concerned with relations. Cultural memory now functions often not as a *quality* out of which poetry issues, but rather as interesting subject matter.

Poetry, symbolization in language, symbolization of thought, not thought itself. (Can poetry think?) The symbolization is characteristic activity in that it bears forth the character of the poet. Its expressive impulse cannot be distinguished from its form-making impulse. It is its symbolical nature that accounts for the feeling, a familiar one, that it is greater than we are.

The "thoughtful" pattern of symbolization cannot be separated from language, words, but it should not be mistaken for "raw" thought. The way painters speak of "form language" is apt. A poet's words are, in a sense, not important. Rather the arrangements of words as constantly altering and self-revising figurations of the poet's intellectual and emotional landscape. The revelatory patterns, the form-language.

★

Sometimes you have a dream that wakes you, and in those first opaque streams of consciousness you still see, or aftersee, some piece of the dream (a boot, a bobby pin, the peeled caulking around the door) but the entire structure of the dream remains amorphous, fluid, any moment about to shimmer away, though you know it's *this* integral picture that you need and want to see. The feeling-tone of the dream is all too urgent (you're still crying, or giggling, or trembling) but you still can't see in your mind's eye the whole clear structure that induced the tone. That is what thinking about poetry is like. The dream is the actual writing of the poem.

★

Against Baudelaire: Sensation as an aesthetic program.
Against Berryman: The poem as sacramental in the
          worship of one's own suffering.
(Against me: the feeling of poetic form as definitive
          inconclusiveness.)

★

Sometimes every object becomes magnified, distorted. Buildings seem taller, plumper, literally stuffed with things and
people. Everyday things, a pen or spoon, a cigarette, a button,
suddenly elastic, swell or bloat. Faces of strangers and friends
bulge and shine with some grave inner light. Then comes the
pulsing at the core of that expansiveness, a quickened over-
ripening of things. Surfaces throb. All objects of attention
loom larger. Ordinary fever dreams. (Yesterday, in a meadow,
under the hot midsummer sun, it was a gigantic bumblebee
working the crocus.)

★

Conversation with someone about religion, and again I went
round and round the question of mediation. Give up Roman
Catholicism and you withdraw or expel yourself from the civilized apparatus of mediation that the Church constitutes and
which is formulated in so many symbolizations—in scripture,
in the exegesis of the Church Fathers, in images in paint, mar-
ble, wood, in the designs for containment and exaltation of
church architecture. Give up that two-thousand-year-old
structure of civilized "zoning" and you are in a wilderness,
with few of the instincts you need to survive there. The conventions of prayer, its norms and habits, are gone. If you
manage to pray, what you now do is something savage and
improvised and formless.

I'm walking with my wife to look at a small river that has some inexplicable nostalgic value. When we arrive, the river is nearly in flood, not only running high but also twisting wildly back against its current, like Stubbs's horse twisting toward the lion on its back. My wife leaves, urging me to follow, but I lag behind, still watching the torrent when suddenly I realize I'm looking into the form of the river. The general churning and heaving disintegrates into thousands of perfectly enunciated—for the seen forms have the force of speech— loops, curlicues, waves, and spirals. I know at that same instant that I'm looking into Van Gogh's late paintings, into *Crows over a Wheat Field* and *Cypresses*. Seeing into the vitality of the pattern (every brushstroke, every little action of the water, pulses like an artery), I feel the dream knowledge that natural force finds its fullest imitation in art, but the knowledge wakens me into tremendous sadness.

★

"But consciousness," Jung says, "continually in danger of being led astray by its own light and of becoming a rootless will o' the wisp, longs for the healing power of nature, for the deep wells of being and for unconscious communion with life in all its countless forms."

★

Keats had the most intensely self-corrective, self-adjustive mind among the great poets of his time. The reflectiveness became a style in the odes, and it speaks for the remarkable wholeness of his life, the continuity between mental quality and the plastic formalizing of it in poetry. Coleridge possessed similar quality, but not the wholeness and continuity. In him reflectiveness and self-correctiveness became a paralyzing scrupulosity, perhaps because he was *turned* toward specula-

tive philosophy as a means of expression whereas Keats was
turned entirely toward expression in the forms of poetry.

In the culture where I was raised, every family had a horseshoe hanging somewhere in the house as a good luck charm.
The usual place was on the lintel overhanging the cellar stairs,
so that halfway down you passed under the horseshoe's ben-
ediction. Some families painted them gold. If one was
knocked loose or fell, it was a bad omen, for the talisman had
thus lost some of its protective power. A new one would have
to take its (identical) place. If done quickly, the power of the
object might be restored. No one of my parents' generation
had ever been on a horse, or ploughed a field with draught
horses, or sold wares from a horse-drawn wagon. They were
the typical children of immigrant shopkeepers and manual laborers. I think horses were at once magical and dangerous
creatures to them, though the vegetable monger, the tinker,
and for a while even the milkman, in those days still sold their
goods from horse-drawn wagons. (The hollow knock of hoofs
was one of the familiar early morning sounds of my childhood.) The first time I was allowed to hold a horseshoe—before it was installed in the cellarway—I must have been about
seven years old, and the thing was shockingly heavy and cold.
Its authority was at once weighted *and* volatile, unpredictable,
uncontrollable. The power of belief in its meaning was mysteriously but palpably *there*, actualized, but also obviously
without the authority of the Church and unaccounted for by
the Baltimore Catechism I was then memorizing at school. I
assumed belief in the horseshoe's powers just as my parents
did, for it was tribal necessity, and a clear material manifesta-
tion of a communal terror—of bad fortune, in an economy
which could ill afford it. Jung says that in many peasant cultures the horseshoe is an equivalent for the horse's foot, that
its meaning is apotropaic. ("The analogous effect of the phallus is well known; hence the phalli on gates.") If the horse-

shoe, or the horse's hoof (and the phallus), share the same
magical purpose, it must have to do with fertility, regenera-
tion, continuity. Planting and sowing and harvesting, against
which rhythms press the shadowy monsters of bad luck
(drought, pestilence, natural disasters of all sorts)—a culture
stands alone and helpless, even if it is doing its productive
work within an industrial economy. And I suppose the place,
the tunneled descent into the cellar, was also a fertility setting.
The power of the object was, at any rate, proportionate to the
helplessness my people felt in the presence of fate. For me, I
could not articulate but felt very strongly the conflict—a kind
of grinding or chafing—between the God of love and the
scheme of Redemption through grace as I learned it at school,
and the rough paganism of living in a universe of random
force precariously controlled at times by mortals' efforts to
appease the gods, requiring talismans as aids to living in a
world of contingency. Without knowing it, I was stretching a
membrane of religious orthodoxy over a cavern of pagan
mystery. I was not then aware of the difference, the double-
ness, but I know that I have continued to live it out.

★

William Carlos Williams, looking middle-aged as he does in
most photographs. But I am watching his hands, which are
the most beautifully formed hands I've ever seen, slender but
powerfully muscled, and they shine with some inner light.
Out of nowhere he takes a small, brightly furred creature in
his hands and begins to tell me about its vitality, its life principle. As he speaks, quietly, confidently, his fingers press
gently into the animal's fur and begin to dig into the skin,
slowly prying the animal apart like a peach or fig until its in-
ners are visible. Holding the torn creature (it still squirms,
though held firmly) the poet exposes, then strokes and prods,
the feathery white muscle tissue, explaining all the while that
the animal's strength and agility—its *power*—is due to these
unseen structures.

★

Public literary culture in America: a buffalo carcass, around which buzz hundreds of fat flies. Then come the larger carrion-feeders. From a distance it looks like a great festive occasion. All that activity. All that excited, titillating buzzing. All that ripe rich color.

★

I knew a middle-aged woman who had been suffering for two years from arthritis in her shoulder. She was a factory worker, accustomed to dozens of minor ailments, but this new pain made the simplest and most unaware activity of waking each morning the most painfully complex. Medical advice helped very little. The doctor gave her injections of some sort and told her about "the cost of growing old." (Nature, in other words, was punishing her for living long and working hard.) Not long afterward she was talking to a man who worked with her and whom she respectfully referred to as "the nice nigger." Hearing her complaint, he suggested he try to help her by a laying on of hands. Desperate to be rid of the pain and angry with the dismissive solace of doctors, the woman, a devout Roman Catholic, consented and promised to contribute to the man's small Baptist congregation if the treatment worked. He laid hands on her shoulder, said, "Lord, drive Satan out of Lena. Drive Lucifer out. Drive him out." The pain ceased and has not returned. Lena was enormously grateful, and astonished, but she refuses to tell people about it. Had her healing been in answer to a novena, or candles, or a Mass said in her name, or if it had been effected by one of the spiritualists she has always visited, she would have spread the news fast and loudly. But that healing had a strange and therefore fearful source. Its mystery can't be normalized by any of the familiar forms of mediation she has lived her religious life by. Having been touched, finally, once, by what she must call divine power, she is embarrassed.

★

In our poetics we still have a sort of ragged, try-it-on, frontier manner, pragmatic, undogmatic, exploitative, acquisitive. (With that goes a sometimes shambling affection for ignorance, or know-nothingness.) In the poetics of Western European countries there are cultural and political formations that have been developing and undergoing revision for so many centuries that the generative and corrective powers have fused into one ambition, one gesture. Ours may have been, may still be, a mockingbird culture, but the mockingbird has a jubilant, cunningly various song, has in fact a song of its own and is a fierce squawking protector of its nest. William James is representative of the American poet, barging and sweet-talking and singing mad songs through an American here-and-now, with the wisdom of Western Europe right there at his back. This is from a manuscript page of *Varieties of Religious Experience*: "It *comes home* to one only at particular times. ... The more original religious life is always lyric—'the monk owns nothing but his lyre'—and its essence is to dip into another kingdom, to feel an invisible order." To tell the feeling of that invisible order, to tell the felt sense of its presence or evanescence, is a proper ambition for an American poet.

1984–1985

What Yeats called "personality" was important to him in the poetry he was writing in the twenties, but for him personality was ritualized, and fully externalized, as Mask. It wasn't what we normally mean by it, that is, personhood, the "natural" quality or character of the person in the poem, which usually amounts to a likable, presentable sort of benign self-absorption. In our talk about poetry we usually mean quite the opposite of Yeats's self-conscious ceremonialism. Our assumptions are perhaps closer to what the Victorians felt was the

identity of the moral quality of the poem with the moral quality of the person detectable in the poem.

★

If the way we talk about poetry isn't a testing of old assumptions and received ideas, our conversation becomes debased,
devalued. The language we use to talk about poetry can influence the language of poetry. It's inevitable that the sound of
some of our poetry chimes dully with the sound of interviews
and politic reviews. Truisms and classroom maxims thus become enshrined and called expertise.

★

The poetic imagination needs at least the illusion of perceiving a road ahead, a possibility of continuity, without which
each newly composed poem would be intolerably burdened
with its own enforced deliberate momentariness. The next
stage is momentous fixity, where poetry gets grooved into the
stony surface of its own ever refined sense of self-importance.
Poetry then becomes a beautiful, petulant child (and thereafter a merely neurotic adult?). That is why the Romantics,
Keats and Coleridge especially, stressed possibility, process,
re-volution, the fiery activity of redefinition. They were con-
noisseurs of idealizations precisely because they so distrusted
idealizations of any sort. Blake and Shelley were the harshest
critics of the tyrannies the mind exacts to induce consolations
and rescue us from nervous seekings. Writing and revision
were, in effect, the same activity.

★

From the shadows falling between the eucalyptus trees where
I like to walk, wavering on the same wind that carries that
healing odor, comes the hurt dignified cry of bagpipe music.
A woman on a small path, by her car, alone, treading almost
motionless between the long scarred shadows in slow time to
that cry, her step measured by no cadence I can hear. It's as

if she stopped of a sudden, stepped from the car, and began
to play. The call.

In his essay on Goethe, Ortega says: "Every life is, more or
less, a ruin among whose debris we have to discover what the
person ought to have been." What, then, if that person in life
designs quite consciously that ruin, almost as a mock ruin or
diorama? What of the person who arranges torment, predis-
poses tumult, contrives dissolution? That ruin is already, in
life, a "set piece." What interpretive record can there be of
such a life?

Not so. I've now heard that music on other days, in other
moods, but always in the same place, under the eucalyptus
trees, and she walks the same path, keeps close to her car. The
call becomes habit.

What's really useful? Perry Miller's description of Jonathan
Edwards: "He was passionately interested in experience, his
own, his wife's, his people's—or the universe's—because in experience was to be detected the subtle working of the pattern;
but he was supremely uninterested in personality, his own or
anybody else's. Especially, we may add, his own." I want a poetry of that kind of experience, not one that lives entirely by
the quality of the idiosyncratic person made present in the
poem. I want to be caught up by the inwardings of experience, by what James calls that strungalong sort of flowing
reality of consciousness—and the forms of poetry complete
the feeling of that experience.

We say something is "the worst" to persuade ourselves of the
devastating power and force of the happening, that it is the

new extremest measure, and also to dignify the suffering that the event brings us. When really we can only speak of present ills as something "worse" than what once was. "Worst" is a future idea, a future passion. We say "worst" because we need to believe there is a limit to the pain and that we have, luckily, already achieved it, touched it. It is a promise to ourselves that nothing worse can happen now.

A Sioux who fought at Little Bighorn said that the soldiers carried lots of money, which he and other braves stripped from the bodies. They knew what the silver was but not the greenbacks. The children played with these, made teepees out of them, gathered dozens of bills which they stuck together to make toy shawls, though much of the money was stained with blood.

And the urge toward form is a greeting of the world of facts and things. It is imagination's answer—more than greeting or salutation it is *answer*—to the mindful solidity of existence.

GIACOMO LEOPARDI AND
THE *PENSIERI*

To most American readers, the work of Giacomo Leopardi remains, more by oversight than by design, a still vague but glorious rumor. Many are familiar with the great lyrics— "A Silvia," "L'infinito," "La ginestra," and "A se stesso"—and with the brilliant imaginary dialogues of the *Operette morali*. But it must also be said that Leopardi impressed himself so deeply on European intellectual history of the past 150 years that Nietzsche, for example, could speak of him as "the greatest stylist of the century," ranking him alongside Goethe as one of the great poet-scholars. And that Leopardi's great obsessions still inspirit a good deal of modern Italian literature, whose major figures—Montale, Ungaretti, Svevo, Vittorini, Pavese—have in turn influenced recent American writing. It is only a slight exaggeration to say that Leopardi is everywhere present in the tradition of classical modernism.

Leopardi's place in early nineteenth-century letters is a rather peculiar one, and not simply because he was one of the great solitaries of the age. The early nineteenth century in Italy was a time of intellectual fervor, much of it due to the polemics emerging from the Romantic movement that had descended from France. Italian Romanticism did not lack strong and interesting voices. Tommaso Grossi, Melchiorre Cesarotti, Giovanni Berchet, and Silvio Pellico were all influential in shaping the intellectual tone of the age. For the most part, however, they remained yoked to the intellectual contingencies of the period. Like Robert Southey and Thomas Love Peacock, they were so claimed by contemporary cultural values that they remained neatly contained within the definitions of their time; to later generations, their voices lack urgency and seem harmlessly archaic. Leopardi, on the other hand, was not contained by the conventional polemics of his time, such as the heated debate between Classics and Romantics. His ambitions were certainly grander than those of any of his contemporaries. Like Blake, he seems one of those artists who spill out of their own time and flood intellectual frontiers; and like Blake, he risked extremism of the most provocative sort, probing and testing the boundaries of consciousness rather than merely delineating them. Although the work of some of his contemporaries still urges itself upon us—most notably Manzoni's *I promessi sposi*, Foscolo's poetry and his prose book *The Last Letters of Jacopo Ortis*, and Pellico's *Le mie prigioni*— they are no match for the huge speculative intelligence and lyric strength of Leopardi's work. And it is precisely this speculative intelligence that has remained inaccessible to American readers.

Leopardi's sensibility, his way of feeling and of thinking about feeling, dramatized the tragedy of values that was to become the central story of Western culture after 1848, that neurotic embrace of public self-esteem and private self-loathing rooted in the politics of social power. The influence of this sensibility crosshatches intellectual history. If Nietzsche was the most immediate and prominent heir to Leopardi's critical temperament, Leopardi's influence in our own time has been most evident in the writings of Cesare Pavese. The coincidences are eloquent. In 1938, Pavese confided to his diary: "Leopardi's 'illusions' are with us again." One of these illusions, many of which are anatomized in the *Pensieri*, regards the token altruism and generosity of others. In our dealings with the world, Leopardi says, we are always inclined to think that people will take pity on our misfortunes, perhaps even volunteer a helping hand. Charity is, after all, the first precept of Christian behavior. But Christian values have become for the most part a gross, though elegant, imposture: nothing in this world is freely given without something sooner or later being taken in exchange. At best, Leopardi suggests, charity is an instrument of self-esteem. "No one," Pavese writes in his diary, "absolutely no one, ever makes sacrifices without expecting something in return. It's all a matter of buying and selling."

In 1950, at the peak of fame and worldly success, Pavese committed suicide in a hotel room in Turin. In 1824, Leopardi analyzed what seemed to him our peculiarly modern style of suicide:

> What do all these voluntary deaths mean if not that men are tired and fiercely despairing of this existence? In ancient times men killed themselves as a heroic gesture, or for grand illusions, or from violent passions etc. etc. and their deaths were illustrious etc. But now that heroism and grand visions have disappeared, and passions are so sapped of energy, why is it that the number of suicides is so much greater? And not just among great men who have failed in the grand manner, nourished on grand dreams, but men of all classes, so that even grand suicides are no longer "illustrious." . . . It means that our knowledge of things brings about this desire for death etc. Men now take their lives coldly. (*Fragment on Suicide*)

These reflections on suicide also describe the dissolution of the conventional heroic personality that had long been another of Europe's most precious illusions. Here as elsewhere Leopardi called falsehood by its real name. If conventional heroism was no longer a medium for defining one's meaning, something else had to be taking its place. What Leopardi saw in the early years of his century was a civilization more and more preoccupied with its own unknowing, a world in which emptiness and forced inaction were so present as to seem a new, all-pervading substance. In this revised moral landscape, heroism for Leopardi became an interiorized condition that required, as Walter Benjamin noted in a 1928 review of a German translation of the *Pensieri*, "perseverance and insight, cunning and curiosity." And one of the great forces against which the new hero had to test himself was *ennui*, or *noia*. Here, too, in his awareness of and struggle with *ennui*, Leopardi announced and investigated what would soon become, in Baudelaire's work, one of the most compelling subjects (and problems) for poets.

The more we know, Leopardi says, the more we want to die; all learning is an education in mortality, all knowledge leads finally to a knowledge of annihilation. He could speak of this with real authority. He was one of the most learned men of his day, his intellect and imagination as ample as Coleridge's, his honesty as spacious and as devastating as Blake's. And we know from his poems, letters, and daybooks that he entertained the possibility of suicide—as his entire life was an exploration into Possibility—so we can be sure he was familiar with its barbarous invitation.

Throughout his brief and difficult life, however, Leopardi opted time and again for energy and survival, often improvising his existence out of the contest between knowledge and illusions:

> Illusions, however weakened and unmasked by reason, always stay with us and form the major part of our lives. Even if we know everything, this still isn't enough to dispel them, even if we know the illusions are vain. Nor, once lost, are they lost in such a way that their vital roots are also destroyed: if we go on living they are bound to flower again despite all our experience and certitude. . . . I've had the same thing happen to me hundreds of times, to despair completely because I was unable to die, then resume my old plans, building castles in the air regarding my future and even feeling a little passing cheerfulness. (*Zibaldone*, August 18–20, 1820)

Leopardi's life, as we shall see, was a constant dispute between knowledge and illusion, and from this he fashioned his writings, the best of which are quarrels, dialogues with darkness, teasing and inciting the possibilities of the human project.

Anyone who makes himself a student (and therefore a critic) of illusions and of human possibilities must be willing

to follow wherever his explorations lead and to call things by
their real names. Illusions must be made to yield to the power
of one's will-to-speculate. In Leopardi, as later in Nietzsche
(who wrote in his preface to *The Antichrist*, "One must be honest in intellectual matters to the point of hardness ... one
must never ask whether the truth will be useful or whether it
may become one's fatality"), this will was absolute, and it was
necessarily joined to great courage of mind and sentiment.
The results, as we might expect, are not at all genteel:

> Everything is evil. I mean, everything that is, is wicked; every
> existing thing is an evil; everything exists for a wicked end.
> Existence is a wickedness and is ordained for wickedness.
> Evil is the end, the final purpose, of the universe. Order, the
> state, laws, the natural process of the universe are all quite
> simply evil and are directed exclusively toward evil. The only
> good is nonbeing; the only really good thing is the thing that
> is *not*, things that are *not* things; all things are bad. All that
> exists, the totality of the many worlds that exist, the universe,
> are nothing but a minor blemish, a mote in metaphysics. Ex-
> istence, in its general nature and essence, is an imperfection,
> an irregularity, a monstrosity. But this imperfection is a very
> small thing, truly just a blemish, because all existing worlds,
> however numerous or grand they may be, though not for
> certain infinite in number or size, are consequently infinitely
> small compared to what the universe *could* be, if it were infi-
> nite. And all that exists is infinitely small compared as it were
> to the true infinity of nonexistence, of nothingness. (*Zibal-
> done*, April 19, 1826)

Such writing, such thinking, is likely to make even the most
tenacious reader cringe. Leopardi's absolutism is staggering,
undistracted by wit. But we learn immediately thereafter that
he poses all this as one more risky, unfashionable, unlikable
possibility: "This system, though it offends our ideas, which
hold that the end of all things can only be goodness, may perhaps be more tenable than Leibnitz's formulation, or Pope's,

that 'everything is good.' I'm not anxious, however, to extend my system so far as to say that the existing universe is the worst of all possible universes, thus replacing optimism with pessimism. Who can ever know the limits of possibility?" It is in all events wrong, then, to dismiss Leopardi as merely an eloquent pessimist. He, like Gramsci after him, would have thought pessimism at best a "vulgar mood." What drove him on was his desire for clarity and his need to explore possible truths.

Another thing that distinguishes Leopardi from his contemporaries is his clear and unrelenting perception of the self-reflective and self-revisionary nature of consciousness. He was able to describe, analyze, and transform into poetry the painful maneuvers of mind turning back upon itself. He possessed that special ability to observe himself observing and to feel himself feeling. Leopardi and Foscolo shared a classical passion for lamentation and complaint, and their tone (rather than content) identifies them as near contemporaries. But Leopardi plunged more deeply into the complex mysteries of yearning, and his song is at times a psychology of morbid self-consciousness—it animates for us the condition of being conscious of consciousness. A morbidity, it must be remembered, that he always contested and hoped to defeat. With such a high theme—the dynamics of yearning frustrated so regularly by the barrenness or failure or paltriness of human possibility—Leopardi's work, the bulk of it, is tragic in mood and intent. The necessary sorrow of existence lies in the disjunction between the infinity of our desires and the frustrations imposed by human limits. We can see what we can never be.

Leopardi looked for a fixed center of the universe and found none. Unlike Manzoni, that other colossus of nineteenth-century Italy, Leopardi refused the consolations of Christian belief, refused to believe that nature is governed by Divine and ultimately benign Law. Nor did he swear allegiance to classical norms. Though he had a great but often mixed admiration for Greek culture, he did not enslave him-

self to the worship of things ancient; he was too familiar with
the Greeks to be pious toward them. Leopardi's universe is
recognizably modern, a blasted place, and nature is *il brutto
poter*—brute force, mindless, governed by natural selection,
empowered by its own necessities, oblivious to humankind's
needs. In the *Zibaldone* he writes: "Nature, compelled by its
law of destruction and reproduction, and in order to preserve
the present state of the universe, is essentially, regularly, and
perpetually the persecutor and mortal enemy of all individuals of every sort and species that Nature itself brings to birth.
Nature begins to persecute them the very moment it gives
birth to them" (April 11, 1829). And in one of the *Operette
morali*, "Dialogue between Nature and an Icelander," the
lonely mortal makes his case: "I have to conclude, then, that
you are the manifest enemy of mankind, of all other animals,
and even of your own works. I realize now that we are
doomed to suffer just as we are fated to be unhappy, and that
it's as impossible to lead a peaceful life as it is to lead an active
one without misery. You trap us, you threaten us, you sting
us, you spite us, you tear us apart—always nothing but injury
and persecution." In such an inimical universe, life will tend
more and more to become a struggle of brutalized resistance.
That resistance is one of the central subjects of the *Pensieri*.

IN HIS autobiographical fragment, *Storia di un'anima*, Leopardi wrote with chilling brevity about his beginnings: "All I'll
say about my origins is that I was born of a noble family in an
ignoble town." Giacomo's father, Conte Monaldo Leopardi,
was a kind and noble gentleman given to shaky business en-
terprises and very conservative politics. The Leopardi family
at that time was one of the most important families of Recanati, a small city that sits on a low hill in the Marches some
fifteen miles from the Adriatic coast. Monaldo was a self-
styled man of quality, a strong personality with an abiding
sense of self-importance. Social custom, which plays such an
important part in the *Pensieri*, was the fixed standard against

which Monaldo measured and judged all human behavior. In his later years he boasted of being the last man in Italy still to wear a sword, and in his memoirs he says that he always sought to dress "in a noble and decorous manner." Esteem—of himself, and that of others for him—was the center of Monaldo's life, and most of his activity converged on that still point where esteem is inflated by will. Again in his memoirs: "All that I have ever come in contact with, has been done according to my will, and all that has not accorded with it seemed to me poorly done." In the *Pensieri*, Leopardi hardens this even more and says that the strong live in accordance with their own will, the weak in accordance with the will of others.

The strong-willed Monaldo married the Marchesa Adelaide Antici, the daughter of a Recanati nobleman. The marchesa, too, was a strong-willed individual, even more so than her husband; soon her authority in *casa Leopardi* eclipsed his, and she became the real governor of their household. She ran a frugal household, as a way of reconsolidating what was left of the Leopardi fortune after it had been drained by Monaldo's failed financial schemes. The marchesa's thrift was more than matched by her stern religiosity. She was in many ways a passionately self-sacrificial woman, fully devoted to the bizarre forms of Christian self-scourging then encouraged by the Church. In *Storia di un'anima* Giacomo describes her as a woman who "was not in the least superstitious, but most orthodox and scrupulous in her Christian faith and practice." Pain, to Leopardi's mother, was a benison, and suffering a passport to salvation. Giacomo was convinced that his mother envied other mothers whose children died at birth, "for these children, escaping all perils, had flown directly to heaven." She thought beauty a great misfortune—the suffering that attends physical deformity was a gift from God. "Seeing her children ugly or deformed," wrote her son, the hunchback, "she gave thanks to God."

Giacomo, born June 29, 1798, was their first child. We are told that he was a healthy and spirited boy. In his childhood games with his younger brother Carlo, Giacomo would always insist on playing the most heroic roles. He had a great love of fairy tales and ghost stories; like so many children, he was thrilled by his own terror. The lively child grew up into a studious boy. By the age of twelve, having studied for years under private tutors, he already had more than a working knowledge of Latin and had mastered the fundamentals of theology, physics, and rhetoric. The first great movement in Leopardi's life came when Monaldo opened the doors of his library to the boy. Giacomo was then fourteen and ready to pursue his education on his own. His father's library, accumulated over many years, offered generous if at times eccentric resources for a young classical scholar. There were all the tools for learning languages—grammars, dictionaries, glossaries, textual commentaries—and the young student began to accumulate languages enthusiastically. There were texts in Hebrew, Greek, Latin, English, Spanish—the library became Giacomo's refuge where he hoped to teach himself the history of his race. He was fondest of philology and the classical authors, and his passion for learning seemed inexhaustible. These were the years of rigor in which he acquired what he called his "peregrine and recondite erudition." Between the ages of thirteen and seventeen, he began to write in earnest, producing a number of learned works—a history of astronomy, an essay entitled "On the Popular Errors of the Ancients," translations of Moschus, plays, verse, philosophical "dissertations," and other ambitious works. The adolescent would enter the library in the morning and study till late at night. When the evening sea-chill swept through *palazzo Leopardi*, he had to wrap himself in rugs to keep the cold out of his bones. Even as the flame guttered on the candle, Leopardi remained hunched over his small reading desk in the library, hounded by the need to learn, a compulsion he himself did not fully understand. It was, in his own words, a period of "*studio matto e disperatissimo*," of mad and incredibly desperate study.

One day in his eighteenth year, Giacomo looked in a mirror and saw himself *senza illusioni*. Though he always referred to himself as *un gobbo*, a hunchback, he wasn't quite. He suffered from scoliosis, a curvature of the spine that often occurs during childhood or adolescence. The years of intense study had twisted his body permanently, the scoliosis had raised a small double hump on his back and chest. His desire to know and to learn had created what he thought to be a physical monstrosity (*una mostruosità*, one of the key words in his vocabulary). Among men, he says in the *Pensieri*, appearances count for everything. At the age of twenty, he wrote to his friend and mentor Pietro Giordani: "I have miserably and irremediably ruined myself by rendering my external appearances hateful and contemptible . . . [and] this is the only part of a man that most people take into account. Not just ordinary people, but even those who want virtue to have some physical adornment, when they find me utterly lacking such adornment they certainly will never love me—they won't dare love a man who possesses only beauty of soul" (March 2, 1818). Love and illusion. Most of Leopardi's life was suspended between these two terrible needs. Life nurtures itself on one or the other, or both combined. And both consume: "I consider love the most beautiful thing on earth, and find nourishment in illusion. . . . I don't think that illusions are totally vain, but rather that they are, to a certain degree, substantial and innate in all of us—and they form the whole of our life."

In his early manhood Leopardi began to languish in Recanati. Like any provincial place, it had little to offer an ambitious man of letters craving recognition. And to one as sensitive as Leopardi, the insular meanness of provincial gossip must have proved especially painful. At twenty-one, Leopardi had never yet been away from Recanati; indeed, he had spent precious little time outside the walls of the family *palazzo*. He was still completely dependent on his father for financial support. The Leopardi household, once his monastic sanctuary, now began to seem a prison to the aspiring philologist-poet, and Giacomo's days there descended steadily into melancholy and self-pity. Moreover, although Monaldo was proud of his son's scholarship, he was not at all keen on the poetry that Leopardi was writing: at a time when the Austrians occupied large parts of northern Italy and had spies everywhere, the patriotic odes that Giacomo had been composing made his practice of poetry a pastime rather dangerous for the entire Leopardi household. But there was a deeper and more compelling reason for Leopardi's desire to break away from his family, a reason he describes in *pensiero* II: so long as he was dependent on his father, he could never be psychologically whole, he would remain forever an extension of his father's purse, a mere function of his father's will. Leaving *casa Leopardi* was not simply a question of pride, it was one of survival. Finally, in his twenty-fourth year, Giacomo was able to break—or at least stretch—the familial bonds and accompany one of his uncles to Rome.

Big-city life shocked the provincial youth. Rome turned out to be more than Leopardi had bargained for. Soon after his arrival there, he began to feel crushed and exasperated by the indifference of the city, a *noncuranza* felt all the more keenly by a young soul seeking fame and fortune. (Leopardi was to remain very sensitive to the problems and dilemmas experienced by young men entering society; much of what he says about this in the *Pensieri* is based on his personal experience.) Rome seemed outsized, monstrous, too monumental. He wrote to his brother Carlo:

> Small-town life may be boring, but men there at least feel some connection to one another and to the things around them, because the range and ambience of these relationships are modest, limited, made on a human scale. But in a big city a man lives without any relation whatsoever to the things around him; the context is so vast that no individual can possibly fill it or even be fully *aware* of it, and hence there's no point of contact among them. You can imagine, then, how

much greater—and how much more terrible—the tedium of
a great city must be than that of a small town. Human indifference, which is a horrible feeling, or rather an *absence* of
feeling, must inevitably be concentrated in big cities. (Dec. 6,
1822)

Rome was a city where the social elite of the age gathered.
Physical deformity of any kind was bound to elicit disdain,
embattled indifference, or snobbish pity. Having finally managed to escape the loneliness of Recanati, Leopardi now felt
even lonelier and more wretched than before, and he began
to yearn (almost despite himself) for those familiar affections
he had felt at Recanati.

He had gone to Rome hoping to dispel the solitude he endured in Recanati. He was eager to experience a larger, more
comprehensive social environment. The *figlio di famiglia*
yearned for real human community, for the company of intelligent men and women (intelligent enough, he hoped, to
appreciate *his* intelligence). But he felt that the architectural
scale of Rome conspired against human communication. It's
worth noting in some detail Leopardi's response, because it
gives us an early view of what would later become his own
peculiar radical humanism. To the young poet, Rome's heroic
spaces were, in the end, antihuman. To his sister Paolina he
wrote: "Rome's colossal size serves no other purpose than to
multiply distances, multiply the number of steps you must
climb to find whomever you're looking for. These huge buildings and interminable streets are just so many spaces thrown
between men, instead of being spaces that *contain* men." Later
in his career, he broadened his argument on behalf of human
proportions and the importance of the individual, insisting
that one must not allow oneself to be totally absorbed (and
hence disintegrated) by any larger abstract unit, by society,
political party, state, or intellectual coterie. Like all radical hu-
manists, Leopardi distrusted anything that hinted of mass
identity and decimation of the individual self. In his time, he

was perhaps closer in his radicalism to the aged Sartre than to his contemporary Mazzini. After a couple of failed attempts to gain employment in Rome, Leopardi returned to Recanati, this time hoping to find "nothing but friendship and love"— the two vital signs he had so profoundly missed in the capital.

Predictably, however, soon after his return home he felt again oppressed by his dependence on his father. Thus, when in 1825 he was offered a job by a Milanese publisher to work on an edition of Cicero, he immediately resolved to leave Recanati again. But he found Milan, then a center of political activism and Liberal opinion, quite as impersonal a place as Rome. Leopardi craved notice and esteem. He received very little of either. After a few months there, he traveled south to Bologna, which he had passed through on his journey to Milan. Here in *La Dotta*, a city of intellect that was also city-as-village, Leopardi felt very much at home. He was at ease on Bologna's gently curved streets, where the porticoes defined a self-contained, man-sized space and where the sidewalks seemed so perfectly adapted to personalized communication. Here was a place where an individual could partake of a larger community and feel himself a functional member of a city without being swamped by it. Leopardi was soon accepted into literary society and became rather famous for his poetry and scholarship. People sought out his conversation. He found himself a success and was, for a time, happy. In the *Zibaldone*, he offered a provisional definition of happiness: "Happiness is nothing more than contentment with one's own being and one's mode of being, satisfaction, perfect love of one's own condition, no matter what that condition may be, even if it's most despicable" (August 30, 1826, Bologna).

After spending brief periods in Florence and Pisa in 1826 and 1827, Leopardi returned to Recanati, having failed to obtain regular employment with which to support himself. Carlo, who had been the poet's chief source of solace and friendship, had by this time left *casa Leopardi*, so Giacomo now felt more alone than ever. His solitude was made more bitter by the petty meanness he encountered whenever he left the *palazzo*. Walking the streets, he was heckled and tormented by boys, his deformity an easy target for ridicule. He felt pressed on all sides—by the pesty boys, by his father's subsidy, by his mother's possessiveness, and by his own grand aspirations. Even the challenge and consolation of his books were no longer readily available to him. For years he had suffered from ophthalmia, and now the disease made it extremely difficult for him to read for any length of time. Now even his books conspired to cause him pain. He continued to write poems whenever he could and to plan long prose works, one of them a "system" of his philosophy. If he had any hope for salvation, it was the totally secular salvation of the clarity of his own mind. His urge to live became one with his need to clarify and explore the processes of his wretched consciousness.

In 1830, Leopardi was invited to Florence, where a wealthy patron offered to support him in his work. Again he left Recanati, now for the last time. In Florence he met for the second time Antonio Ranieri, whom he had known briefly during his first stay in Florence and who became Leopardi's closest friend and protector during the remaining seven years of the poet's life. After three difficult years in Florence, where his already fragile health continued to deteriorate, Leopardi took his doctor's advice and moved with Ranieri to the balmier climate of Naples. In 1832, he closed his daybooks, the *Zibaldone*, which he had begun many years before. In his last years he composed three of the finest poems of the century, "A se stesso," "La ginestra," and "Il tramonto della luna." In 1836, he left Naples to escape the cholera epidemic that threatened the city. He could, and did, escape the cholera, but not the deterioration of his body. He died on June 21, 1837.

SOMETIME in 1832 Leopardi began to prepare for publication a booklet of aphorisms and reflections that he did not live to see printed. In 1845, Ranieri published them under the title

CXI Pensieri. Many of the *Pensieri* were excavated by Leopardi from his *Zibaldone*, the series of daybooks he kept from 1817 to 1832, though he had not added much to it after 1829. To appreciate the rather special (and specialized) shape and function of the *Pensieri*, one must have some idea of what the *Zibaldone* contains. Leopardi's first *Zibaldone* entry speaks of the beginnings of Italian literature and of the function of the Good and the True in art. For the next fifteen years, through 4,525 manuscript pages, he kept an almost daily record of his thoughts, observations, and feelings. The range of knowledge displayed in the *Zibaldone* (or *Miscellany*) is astonishing and at times wonderfully unpredictable: philological notes; etymologies; attempts to formulate a poetics; reflections on society, authors (classical and modern), metaphysics, and morality; aphorisms on women, tobacco, liquor, clothing, politics, public relations, biology, genetics, psychology, and a variety of other topics, as well as autobiographical anecdotes.

Leopardi's purpose in writing the *Pensieri* was to compose "a book of reflections on the characteristics of men and on their conduct in society." He wanted the *Pensieri* to be quite a different text from the *Zibaldone*, both in style and purpose. To realize this ambition, he chose to draw freely from materials he had already touched upon in the *Zibaldone*, but he did not limit himself to these raw materials. I emphasize that these were raw materials, for in order to make his text cogent—and the *Pensieri* is nothing if not compact, tight, coherent—he had to rework, compress or enlarge, formalize and redistribute those materials he selected from the *Zibaldone* and which appear there in a more amorphous, leisurely, and expansive form. The *Zibaldone* is an epic account of Leopardi's sensibility, but the *Pensieri* is considerably more than just a chapbook of conclusions siphoned off from these vast explorations. One of Leopardi's recent popular biographers, Italo de Feo, insists that we must first of all take into consideration the importance the poet placed on "clarity and propriety of expression, which in the *Pensieri* reached the highest level

Leopardi ever touched upon in prose." Most importantly, these 111 "thoughts" all converge on one central subject: the individual's activity in groups. The *Pensieri* constitutes a manual for self-preservation in modern Western society. It tells us how society in general functions and what an individual must do to survive the inevitable collision between one's own willful individuality and society's anonymous collective demands.

Leopardi begins his case with a practical generalization. It's important that we assume what he assumes, "that the world is a league of scoundrels against men of generosity, of base men against men of good will," for all of his subsequent observations are corollaries of this axiom. We may question the veracity of this premise and Leopardi's authority to make such a mighty generalization (he was, after all, a very solitary man), but once it is accepted, everything that follows takes on a most persuasive cogency. The *Pensieri*, then, must be read not as a random assortment of aphorisms hacked and carved from the rough quarry of the *Zibaldone*, but rather as a coherent narrative of ideas, a carefully organized, self-contained text in which each part is related to some other.

If the world stands opposed to all that is good, then all of the individual's activity in society becomes a game of combative one-upmanship whereby scoundrels conspire to dominate men of *virtù*—a modern vulgarized form of classical *arete*. The scoundrels, Leopardi says, are by far the majority; while the meek and the honest struggle to survive, the wicked strive to prevail. Since the latter are so obviously at the advantage, most people will side with wickedness in any encounter with the good; everyone wants to be on the winning side in a dispute, even if it's the side of meanness and deceit. Scoundrels moreover are excellent public-relations men; they know how to manipulate their public image—and that of others—in such a way as to win supporters for their cause, their chief instrument being deceit. They pretend to be strong and courageous—a mask for cowardice and vain arrogance—because they know that this instills fear in others. Through fear they acquire power, knowing that common people mistake power for strength, a Napoleonic conceit that still functions in Western politics. This is not, however, Leopardi's understanding of genuine strength. A truly strong man is one who does not concern himself with the machinery of fear and intimidation, for he feels no need of them. His strength is not founded on deceit and imposture. But, Leopardi says, it is almost impossible to win over the hearts and minds of people except through deceit. The strong man, in effect, is bound to suffer from bad public relations. Though he may be strong in substance, he lacks a strong public *image*; in a world where appearances count for everything, such a man is more likely to be thought a weakling. People will sooner be won over by the glibness of bullies—for in glibness lies public power—than by the silent self-containment of the strong.

There are, however, certain social values that function ambivalently in this apparently absolutist structure. Artifice, for example, has both a positive and negative value, depending on its application. Scoundrels depend on artifice to gain advantage. But artists use it as a means of serving the true and the good; metaphor, an instrument of truth, is artifice. Moreover, a measure of artifice is essential for getting along in human company. If a man wishes to make himself likable, he must pretend interest in the conversation of others; since such conversation is usually dull or boring, one can *only* pretend interest. When a man compromises in this way, does he falsify himself? Does he join the league of base and petty men? Not necessarily, for such a man still possesses self-esteem; he is making a necessary compromise so as not to be excluded from the human group. Likewise, if a man chooses to participate in groups—it is always a conscious choice, or at least should be—he must learn to accept the meritocracy (often spurious) upon which all social action is based. Leopardi does insist, however, that if one wishes to remain true to oneself, one's distinction in society must be grounded in truth. He further distinguishes between two kinds of superiority: *hauteur*, which is always forced and artificial, and an instrument for power; and natural (or "classical") superiority, whereby one achieves one's aspirations in an honest way. The two types are easily recognized. The haughty man is arrogant and imposing, his will a kind of blunt instrument. The naturally superior man, however, tends to be withdrawn, simple in manner, humble, self-contained. Unfortunately, most often the bullies prevail, while the simple superior men become victims of envy and *ressentiment*. In several instances in the *Pensieri*, Leopardi reminds us that ordinary people frequently resent natural superiority, and they loathe genius. Their hold on self-esteem is so insecure, so embattled, that they feel threatened by the mere presence of a man of true strength, all the more when he seems indifferent to social power-rituals.

Another axiom of human behavior is that "the world speaks absolutely consistently in one way and acts absolutely consistently in another." To ignore hypocrisy is hypocritical; furthermore, such innocence invites disaster and eventual exclusion from the community. Can hypocrisy ever be eliminated? Possibly, Leopardi says, if we were to tell the truth, if we were to "call things by their real names," if we were to give more credence to substance than to artifice, then the gap between words and deeds would be closed. Then there would be no need for gamesmanship, and human communication would no longer be forced to rely on euphemism and circumlocution. This is certainly a noble (and still unrealized) project. Leopardi, always alert to dangers and as a philologist concerned with the actualization or falsification of language-in-action, admits that anyone who tells the truth is likely to be hated and will probably be thought a simpleton. Society sooner tolerates evildoers, sooner admires confidence men, than it tolerates someone who names them. Even people who privately oppose a politician's policies, for example, will rush to shake his hand in public; such power seems almost a sacred charm. This, Leopardi says, demonstrates our weakness; it does not, however, excuse our wickedness. Leopardi's ex-

traordinary tolerance of normal human shortcomings and the
compassion he feels for human foibles derive from his own
recognition of the importance of illusion. One of the most
gentle (yet firm—Leopardi is always firm) passages in the *Pensieri* occurs in XXIX: "In everything he does man needs some
illusion and glamour, since truth is always too flawed and impoverished. . . . He lives for the promise of something more,
and better, than what the world can actually give. Even Nature is deceitful toward man: it makes life congenial and tol-
erable only through imagination and artifice." A little later, he
notes that "men are miserable by necessity yet determined to
think themselves miserable by accident."

Leopardi traces the hatred mortals feel toward one another
back to the hatred of animals for their fellow creatures. Ultimately, Nature is the mother, the author, of all conflict—even
the harmonies found in nature are sustained only at the cost
of death and normalized dissolution. He further suggests that
the law of natural selection applies also to human beings,
where survival belongs to the wiliest and best adapted. Life in
society, then, requires adaptation. Though a man be honest
and forthright in all things, for example, he must still keep
his affairs (especially his financial affairs) to himself, for his
secrets will not be honored by others. When in public, a man
must guard his natural weak spots, for these are the first to be
noticed by others, and the first attacked. Above all, a man
must preserve self-esteem, though watchful that it does not
become so bloated as to suffocate him. This self-esteem, along
with the internal strength described earlier, usually goes hand
in hand with simplicity of manners: if you are strong, be prepared to find your simplicity (like that of Stendhal's Fabrizio)
interpreted as arrogance, with unpleasant consequences. At
all events, strength is essential to self-preservation, since "the
world never faults a man who refuses to yield."

In the *Zibaldone*, Leopardi makes his case for radical skepticism: "Human reason, if it is to make any progress whatso-
ever, can never divest itself of skepticism. It embodies truth.

Reason cannot discover truth except by doubting and departs from truth whenever it judges with certainty. Doubt not only allows us to discover truth (in keeping with the Cartesian principle), but truth itself consists essentially of doubt. He who doubts, knows—knows as much as can be known" (September 8, 1821). In the *Pensieri*, he instructs his readers in the practical application of skepticism. In the world, we must assume that duplicity and double-talk are inescapable. People seldom really mean what they say. Apparently sincere offers of assistance and support are usually "nothing more than sheer syllabic noise." The only fixed point on the constantly sliding scale of social values is one's own moral quality: "Man is unable here on earth to trust in anything but his own strength." All social behavior derives from, and serves, self-interest. Moreover, what one *seems to be* is always more crucial (and more profitable and more readily justifiable) than what one truly *is*. Before all else, a man of substance must realize that "the world does not care much about substance, and often absolutely refuses to tolerate it."

If society is a jungle or perilous savannah, then deference and obsequiousness can only undermine one's will to self-preservation. Given the slightest opening, people will crush their weaker fellows: "Esteem cannot be bought with deference." Better to hold one's ground at whatever cost than seek the esteem of others by degrading oneself. Too much deference is a sign of low self-esteem, and men generally are quickest to attack those who lack self-respect.

Although the advice Leopardi offers in the *Pensieri* is stern, it never descends into mere grumbling or into intellectual bullying. Its purpose is analytical. This tactical manual of social customs—Benjamin called it a "working oracle" that teaches "the art of discretion for rebels"—constitutes finally a profoundly critical document of modern social behavior and a sketch in miniature of the reversal in human values that has taken place between ancient and modern times. The ancients, Leopardi reminds us again and again, insisted that a man *be* good, whereas moderns demand that a man only seem good. The concept of the world-as-enemy-of-the-good dates back only as far as the beginning of the Christian era, he notes in *pensiero* LXXXIV. It marks the beginning of an epoch in which false appearances have become a social norm and lying an axiom of human behavior, something to help us make it through the day. Throughout his career, Leopardi was concerned with the steady decay of human community. The *Pensieri* is a brief investigation into the origins and effects of that disease. If it lacks the sardonic grace of the *Operette morali* and the fragmentary exuberance of the *Zibaldone*, it is nonetheless an intense, insinuating book and remains Leopardi's most practical prose work.   [1979]

DIGS: ON SEAMUS HEANEY

From the exemplary careers of Yeats, Pound, and Eliot, the contemporary poet inherits a definition of poetic office that requires him to be a bearer and interpreter of cultural history and to demand of himself a vigilant internal ordering of learning, belief, theme, and method. There is also, however, a sort of auxiliary office to which poets are appointed, a public frame clapped together from current taste, public relations, critical opinion, and the goodwill of influential publishers. Under these circumstances, rumor, partisanship, and all the other devices that contribute to the manufacture of fame collaborate to install a poet in a position of eminence. The Irish poet Seamus Heaney, now in his early forties, is the latest to receive such privileged regard.

Since 1965, Heaney has published five major volumes of verse; the most recent, *Field Work* (1979), was brought out in America by Farrar, Straus and Giroux. That same publisher has now collected in *Poems: 1965–1975* Heaney's first four books and has issued as a companion volume *Preoccupations*, a gathering of prose pieces written between 1968 and 1978. Such attention is so rare among major publishers that one hopes, almost as a reflex, that this recently assigned public office will not disrupt or distract Heaney from the more traditional task of the poet, which is in the end the only one that counts.

Heaney has a clear picture of the internal career—that arc of need, design, and execution—which urges and steers a poet through his themes. Like his modern predecessors, he takes his duties seriously. His work, poetry and prose alike, is rooted in the need to claim and express the rough exigencies of history. He seeks coherence and continuity. "Digging," the opening poem in *Death of a Naturalist* (Heaney's first major book) and the initial poem in this new collection, announces the work that will follow. Writing by a window, the poet hears the "clean rasping sound" of his father digging turf, and in that sound hears his grandfather's work before him. Digging becomes at once a signal of origins and legacies and a sounding of Heaney's own poetic ambitions. He has "no spade to follow men like them," so he will dig instead with his pen: "Between my finger and my thumb / The squat pen rests. / I'll dig with it." The metaphor is meant to articulate the method by which the poet will carry on, while at the same time departing from, the family tradition. Although the fancy may be somewhat strained and self-important, Heaney's intention is clear enough: he wants connections, continuities, and historical justification for his art.

In one essential particular the truth of the metaphor is redeemed, for in many of his poems Heaney does dig with his pen, unearthing histories of families, country, and self. But in the poem's opening lines, he also describes the feel of the pen in his hand as "snug as a gun." The figure is at first glance impressive, and its apparent authority is boosted by the clicking backward rhyme; but what has this terrorist image to do with agriculture, archaeology, or intellectual exertion of any sort? I question the integrity of this core metaphor because it prefigures a larger problem in Heaney's work, one I will come back to later. But it must be said that his ambition, which is in most ways admirable and pure, on occasion leads him to will connections by virtue of overwrought metaphor. The result is good writing which is not always good poetry.

The danger for someone of Heaney's talent is that his aspiration will spiral his work away from integral metaphoric truth. But when aspiration and metaphoric truth fuse, the poetry is exact, deliberate, and natural, as in "At a Potato Digging": "Heads bow, trunks bend, hands fumble toward the black / Mother. Processional stooping through the turf / Recurs mindlessly as autumn." This poem is an extraordinary meditation on natural dependencies, Irish sorrow, the body as bearer of history, the legacies of deprivation and blight.

The language has a gritty sonority blent of the sonorities we
hear in Keats and in Dante's Hell cantos:

> Stinking potatoes fouled the land,
> pits turned pus into filthy mounds:
> and where potato diggers are
> you still smell the running sore.

The dark that figures in Heaney's *Door into the Dark* is near
and actual: it is the dark of stables, turf stacks, forges. And
the landscapes bounding the darkness are sharply drawn, as
are the characters who live and work among them; implicated
in their surroundings at every turn, their lives become dramatic inflections of land and light. Here, as in *Death of a Naturalist*, there are lyrical portraits of ordinary people serving
functions usually conferred upon them by history. Peat gath-
erers, diggers, dockers, thatchers, diviners, farmwives—all
take on an unexpected radiance in these poems. Heaney
catches the density of their lives with the same passionate dis-
interest and attention that he gives to the densities of the mineral world, to the slippery entrapments of boglands ("Melting
and opening underfoot, / Missing its last definition / By millions of years"). He works the language hard, just as one of
his favorite subjects is a world hard worked, caught in its plenitude of actions, turnings, recognitions. Here, for example, in
"Mother":

> I am tired of the feeding of stock.
> Each evening I labor this handle
> Half an hour at a time, the cows
> Guzzling at bowls in the byre.
> Before I have topped up the level
> They lower it down.

The poems in Heaney's *Wintering Out* grow almost predictably from his desire to explore primal resources and primal
connections between landscape, language, and people. Presences are defined by the sounds and structures of words: "*An-*

ahorish, soft gradient / of consonant, vowel-meadow"; "To shear, to bale and bleach and card / Unwound from the spools / Of his vowels"; "Our gutteral muse / was bulled long ago / by the alliterative tradition." It's in *Wintering Out* that Heaney argues for the world as a language to be heard and entered, a language bounded, inflected, and impelled by regional history. The most remarkable poem, however, is "The Tollund Man," a profound wish for the company of the dead, for the violent knowledge they withhold. He would dig into the layers of preserved time, into the stratified anguish of Irish history, and become a resident in "the old man-killing parishes," locked in the earth, "lost, / Unhappy and at home."

A poet often writes prose to articulate an investigative technique or explanatory procedure, by which his intended discovery, probably initially intuited, may be claimed and justified. An exhibition of need and will, it is also an act of self-declaration. The essays in *Preoccupations* demonstrate Heaney's aspirations, his awareness of his own position in the poetic tradition, and an account of those patterns of exploration which comprise the nervous system of his verse. Heaney is almost obsessively concerned with what we might call the natural history of language, its origins, morphologies, homologies. Whatever the occasion—childhood, farm life, politics and culture in Northern Ireland, other poets past and present—he strikes time and again at the taproot of language, examining its genetic structures, trying to discover how it has served, in all its changes, as a culture bearer, a world to contain imaginations, at once a rhetorical weapon and spiritual nutriment. He writes of these matters with rare discrimination and resourcefulness, and a winning impatience with the received wisdom. In his essay on Hopkins, for example, he describes one kind of poetics which regards the emergence of poetry as a feminine action, "almost parthenogenetic," a seeping forth of language that "tends to brood and creep, crop and cluster, with a texture of echo and implication, trawling the pool of the ear with a net of associations." In another es-

say, Wordsworth's "hiding places of my power" provide an occasion for Heaney to announce his own view of poetry: "poetry as divination, poetry as revelation of the self to the self,
as restoration of the culture to itself; poems as elements of
continuity, with the aura and authenticity of archaeological
finds . . . poetry as a dig."

Heaney's essays are studded with reiterated phrases and
notions, but such repetition is less a sign of indolence than of
a coherent, strong-willed intelligence testing and revising its
themes. We hear more than once of Eliot's "auditory imagination" and "dark embryo," of Yeats's "bundle of accident
and incoherence," of Shakespeare's "Our Poesy is as a gum
which oozes / From whence tis nourished." And to these Heaney contributes his own passionate, conspiratorial language:
of poems "earthed" in provincial recognitions, of words "as
bearers of history and mystery." The very selectivity of quo-
tation, its rather narrow range, indicates Heaney's predilec-
tions. Poets reveal the vision they have of their careers in part
by revealing those predecessors they choose to ignore as
much as by those they claim as occasions for statements about
their work. Without faulting Heaney's choices, one would at
the same time very much like to hear him on Browning (Heaney's own dramatic monologues are very fine), and on the rural Hardy of the "feel of old terrestrial stress" and "Earth's
old glooms and pains," and on W. S. Graham.

At every point, Heaney shows himself a discriminating
diagnostician of the poetic tradition. He explains the way in
which poetry issues from the roughly shaped, vaguely stirring
beginnings in intuition and compulsion. He draws firm distinctions between his predecessors, clarifying that diversity
(and divisiveness) which gives such quarrelsome vitality to poetic tradition. Here he is, for example, on Keats and Hopkins:
"Keats has the life of a swarm, fluent and merged; Hopkins
has the design of the honeycomb, definite and loaded. In
Keats the rhythm is narcotic, in Hopkins it is a stimulant to

the mind. Keats woos us to receive, Hopkins alerts us to perceive."

The most crucial distinction Heaney makes regarding the writing of poetry is that between craft, which is "the skill of making," and technique, which "involves not only a poet's way with words, his management of metre, rhythm and verbal texture; it involves also a definition of his stance toward life, a definition of his own reality. It involves the discovery of ways to go out of his normal cognitive bounds and raid the inarticulate: a dynamic alertness that mediates between the origins of feeling in memory and experience and the formal ploys that express these in a work of art."

North, the last volume collected in *Poems: 1965–1975*, suffers from the dominion of craft over technique. The territory, as in all of Heaney's books, is clearly demarcated. *North* is in large part an anthology of death chants, songs of bones and boglands, anatomizations of the body of language and history, another dig into the geological strata of culture, its residues, seepages, signs. A number of the poems, however, like the early "Digging," demonstrate the triumph of rhetoric over theme, of mere good writing over investigative vision. By "mere good writing" I mean exclusive attention to the sheen and noise of language, such that flamboyance and invention, however sincere and in service to however serious a theme, come to displace clarity and integrity of feeling. Poems like "Bog Queen," "The Grauballe Man," and "Kinship," which at first shine forth with the sort of writing that one might praise for its ingenuity and intensity, are finally so clenched, or so overwrought in metaphor, that the poetry becomes too much a theatrical event or mere "performance." When style comes unstuck from feeling, subject matter dissociated from thematic explorations, the result is the kind of poem that bullies the reader into admiration. There were traces of this in Heaney's earlier work. I've already noted the pen/gun/spade figure in "Digging." But there are other instances: blackberries that "burned / Like a plate of eyes"; "stepping stones like black molars"; a cow's eyes as "shallow bowls."

I want this judgment to stand in the light of the passionate intelligence and sensitivity to natural technique which distinguish much of Heaney's work. Given the quality of some of the poetry in *North* ("Gunfire barks in question off Cavehill / And the profiled basalt maintains its stare / South: proud, protestant and northern, and male. / Adam untouched, before the shock of gender"), the following lines, from "Bone Dreams," seem by contrast a great rattling of words, manner detached from feeling:

> Come back past
> philology and kennings,
> re-enter memory
> where the bone's lair
>
> is a love-nest
> in the grass.
> I hold my lady's head
> like a crystal
>
> and ossify myself
> by gazing: I am screes
> on her escarpments,
> a chalk giant
>
> carved upon her downs.
> Soon my hands, on the sunken
> fosse of her spine
> move towards the passes.

I'm not suggesting that Seamus Heaney is going stale, or that his inspiration is failing, or that he is writing too much. But I want to say that at this point in his work, now that the public office has imposed itself upon the private, and now that *Field Work* has shown that he still has not resolved what seem to me major questions of craft and vision (questions appropriately asked only of a poet of major talent), he may now need to be more vigilant than ever. A poet's career is always in the making—or remaking—and one must be careful not to mistake fine craft for true feeling, deft mechanics for the intricate felt life of forms.   [1981]

NOTES ON MEMORY AND ENTHUSIASM

For Thamyris boasted that he would surpass, if the very Muses,
Daughters of Zeus who holds the aegis, were singing against him,
And these in their anger struck him maimed, and the voice of wonder
They took away, and made him a singer without memory.
—*Iliad*, Book II

Early in his career, before he changed his mind about the importance of modeling from nature, before the instructive experience of painting *The Potato-Eaters* and before his crucial friendship with Gauguin, Van Gogh placed absolute faith in the instantaneous recording of natural forms. He was so exhilarated by the possibility of catching the inflections of light and color while they were occurring—of fixing the moment as the paint itself began to set—that he was quick to disdain memory and those painters who relied too much on its vagrant influence. In 1882 he wrote to his brother Theo: "But when I see young painters compose and draw *from memory*— and then haphazardly smear on whatever they like, *also from memory*—then look at it from a distance and pull a very mysterious, gloomy face while trying to find out what in heaven's name it looks like, and finally make something of it, always *from memory*—it sometimes disgusts me, and makes me think it all very tedious and dull." For Van Gogh, an instinctive literalist of sensation, memory was bound to cheat. What mattered most was replication, not recollection, of the figures and densities of the actual. Imitation of nature was thus *enacted* in paint, whose color, texture, and movement share the accidents of the world it seeks to imitate. Painting borrows from its subjects the properties which are then manipulated to imprison or frame some portion of the world. When he spoke of the physical stuff of paint, Van Gogh became almost ecstatic; his requests to Theo for colors he himself could not

116

afford ring like incantations—carmine, emerald, cadmium, indigo, cobalt.

The bountiful irony is that while in practice he relied so dogmatically on the replication of the real, he poured out almost daily, in an extraordinary flourish of mnemonic powers, those long, detailed, closely argued letters to his brother in which he cast his recollections of the painterliness of the real world. The furious hurried look of his brushwork becomes in the letters a poetic technique, though more measured, less vertiginous:

> Through the window of a very elegant English bar, one will look on the dirtiest mud, and on a ship from which, for instance, attractive merchandise like hides and buffalo horns is being unloaded by hideous dock hands or exotic sailors, a very dainty, very fair young English girl is standing at the window looking at it, or at something else. . . . There will be Flemish sailors, with almost exaggeratedly healthy faces, with broad shoulders, strong and plump, and thoroughly Antwerp folk, eating mussels, or drinking beer. . . . A tiny figure in black with her little hands pressed noiselessly along the gray walls. Framed by raven-black hair—a small oval face, brown? orange-yellow? I don't know. (end of November, 1885)

He doesn't know? Had he been on the spot, getting the scene down in paint, he surely would have known. With his rage for exactitude of form-language, Van Gogh trusted only in the registering, on location, of natural forms. Memory—a disrupter, revisionist, antic colorist—could only contaminate the purity of literalism. And yet those hundreds of letters—efforts to catch the mix of sentiment, idea, and perception, to recover from storming memory disciplined and directed *arrangements* of told experience—are every bit as compulsive in their gathering up of actual details as are his pictures. Even after he had submitted to Gauguin's urgings that he rely more on the transfiguring imagination, Van Gogh continued to distrust memory.

According to literalist dogma and practice, memory can never be a sure form of knowledge and therefore cannot serve as a model for artistic expression. A literalist aesthetic may result in great painting and drawing, but in poetry its results are bound to be minimal, or barren. The importance of memory in poetry is rooted in ancient tradition. In the *De Oratore*, Cicero tells how the poet Simonides of Ceos was called away from a banquet where he had been hired to recite. In his absence the roof of the hall collapsed; all the guests, and the host (who had welshed on Simonides' commission), were crushed beyond recognition. The poet was later able to identify the corpses, however, according to the seats they had been occupying at the disastrous moment. He had a memory set, or model. The incident persuaded him that the arrangement of mental images according to an architectural pattern was the key to perfect recollection and, by extension, to refined and persuasive discourse. Cicero comments: "Admonished by this occurrence, he is reported to have discovered that it is chiefly order that gives distinctness to memory."

A more extreme statement of the importance of memory, and one which has become a vexing legacy of the Romantic movement, appears in Book 3 of Rousseau's *Confessions*: "I have studied men, and I think I am a fairly good observer. But all the same I do not know how to see what is before my eyes; I can only see clearly in retrospect, it is only in my memories that my mind can work." Memory, then, is a required clarifier of experience, a cognitive necessity. Not only is it a housing for knowledge, but the mind can work only by engaging its past experience, its history. It is the engagement, in all its instability and uncertainty, that matters for Rousseau. He goes beyond Simonides in that he does not insist on an a priori memory model but suggests instead that the mind improvises a model during the course of recollection. Most astonishing, however, is his remark that exactitude of perception comes only "in retrospect," in memories. Assume this (it's a self-serving assumption, of course, but more to the point a useful one) and one must then admit that the artist, in order to tell the truth, is also free to burnish, recolor, flex, and rearrange the materials of history. Rousseau's statement, which would become part of the groundwork of the theory and practice of poetic composition in Wordsworth, Shelley, and Coleridge, offers a perfect negative of Van Gogh's literalist aesthetic: a poetics of imperial memory.

MEMORY is the oceanic flux of images, spectral feelings, lore, all the history-bound matter of intellection and sensation stirring in the present. It promises futurity, extension. In Book x of the *Confessions*, St. Augustine describes it as a hoard, "a storehouse for countless images," "a vast immeasurable sanctuary," and "vast cloisters." Memory is that condition of mind as it is inhabited by its own manufactures and gleanings, where the voices of the past tangle with those of the present. Augustine admits that we rely entirely on its powers even though we do not understand them. "Yet I do not understand the power of memory that is in myself, although without it I could not even speak about myself." It bestows most of what we know about ourselves and our histories even while of its sources we always know too little. Employing memory, we are possessed by it. Its powers are familiar enough. It terrorizes and heals. Bursting upon us unexpectedly, it knocks loose the underpinnings of self-knowledge so that the plenitude it brings seems at once a paralyzing ignorance. It contains what the race has been, and its imperial presence charges us to try, earnestly and futilely, to contain *it*.

Recollection is the movement of mind to hold and frame a selection from the unshaped mass of memory, to suspend momentarily its endless stirring so that an image (dusk, earring, razor, plum) or patterning of events (Alexander's army stomping snow, the day's weaving undone each night, the new house keys cut this morning) may be situated in the present as an object of contemplation. Recollection may be voluntary, elective, a searching out of some piece of the past in order to determine its relation to yet other pieces; it is a summons served on memory. Its purpose is to set in order, however provisionally, details picked from memory's unsorted debris.

Voluntary recollection is supported or cut across by involuntary recollection, whereby the mind's products, in Augustine's words, "come spilling from the memory, thrusting themselves upon us when what we want is something quite different." Involuntary recollection is frequently triggered by association, the haphazard breeding and coincidence of sensation and idea, undirected by the will, which may at first seem nothing more than Coleridge's "phantasmal chaos." The odor of honeysuckle generates a picture of two children tilting watering cans on each other's head; an anonymous whistle outside a window at dawn recalls the thick hands of an uncle planing timbers; the shape of the word *tilt* calls up a weatherworn picket fence once built by that uncle.

If voluntary recollection is intentional activity, an active drawing forth from the enormous mind of memory in order to constitute meaning, involuntary recollection is fortuitous, familial, a rebounding of what at first seem unrelated bits of history but which may, with visionary unexpectedness, randomly dispose themselves into significant patterns. Both kinds shed light on the human project. And for the poet who regards himself as a collector and recoverer of cultural energies, of what Eliot called "the changing mind of Europe," and who turns his attention to the various ways in which the past infuses the present, Mnemosyne, Mother Memory, rules as a stern, constant, and exalting figure.

COMMENTING on Giordano Bruno's theory of image-forming in the arts of memory, Frances Yates writes in *The Art of Memory*: "Nothing comes out but what has first been formed within, and it is therefore within that the significant work is done." The need and aspiration to give a structure to the mat-

ter of remembered life—to *re-collect*—taken together compel
the traditional invocation to the Muse. Though no longer announced, such invocation still stands back of most lyric poetry. The poet asks: *Let me see the pattern so that I may speak what
is true and necessary.* Dante's outcry in the second canto of the
Inferno, where he speaks of the journey and the pity which
memory, sure and unfailing, must retrace ("*che ritrarrà la
mente che non erra*"), is a precept for any poet who believes that
recovery and discovery are the same movement of mind.
Dante's words are appropriately willful and demanding:

> *O Muse, o alto ingegno, or m'aiutate;*
> *o mente che scrivesti ciò ch'io vidi,*
> *qui si parrà la tua nobilitate.*

> O Muses, O high imagination, help me now.
> O Memory that wrote down what I saw,
> Show your bright virtue, here, now.
> (7–9)

In the *Convivio* Dante defines *nobilitate* as "the perfection in
each thing of its proper nature." Memory's *nobilitate* therefore
lies not only in its fidelity to past experience but also in its just
integration and organization of the details of lost time. At the
threshold of Dante's poem, memory is called upon to sustain
a journey through the manifestations of universal darkness
and light, of ignorance and knowledge, from the mineral in-
candescence of Hell to the beatific unfoldings of light in Paradise.

Since the *Comedy* is a remembered journey, the perfection
of its telling—its *nobilitate*—depends largely on the poet's fidelity to his memory model, that pattern which, like Simonides' seating arrangement, governs the process of recollection.
The poem's subject is the acquisition of knowledge. Dante's
memory model, which is processional, sequential, tracked, is
thus also a model for knowing—recollection as a Way. The
poem is acted out upon the topography of remembrance.
Dante designs his urban, pastoral, and celestial locales as con-

centric rings so that isolated incidents, bits which singularize
the universal, may fix in memory the larger recurrent modes
of suffering, purgation, and bliss which exist in eternal circu-
larity. As the Pilgrim descends into Hell we are told that there
are thousands of other souls at each level which Dante cannot
see, as if each infernal tier were a model in miniature of memory's overpopulated pool from which the poet will select only
the most emblematic (and the most personalized) to be set
forth as objects of contemplation. Dante in effect dramatizes
both the origin and act, source and result, of individuated recollection.

Dante's final vision of Paradisal light is authorized by the
intricately designed progress of the first two canticles. Authorized, that is, by virtuous recollection, which is a task. His vision of the Triune Circle marks the perfection of memory:
the divine geometry of light witnessed by the wayfarer breaks
forth from the perfected act of recollection. There is an extraordinary moment in the last canto of the poem when the
poet speaks in the present tense, while composing, rather
than in the narrative past tense that sustains most of the
poem:

> La forma universal di questo nodo
>   credo ch'i'vidi, perché più di largo,
>   dicendo questo, mi sento ch'i' godo.
> Un punto solo mi'è maggior letargo
>   che venticinque secoli a la 'mpresa
>   che fé Nettuno ammirar l'ombra d'Argo.

> I believe I saw the universal principle
>   of this Unity; I believe because now,
>   telling it, I feel my joy grow and grow.
> This one instant brings me greater oblivion
>   than twenty-five centuries brought to the enterprise
>   that made Neptune marvel at the Argo's shadow.
>   (XXXIII, 91–96)

Dante persuades himself, and his reader, that he actually experienced the vision he has already recounted; he knows this because in recollecting the vision he feels a flooding joy. Yet in this moment of recollection perfected, as he concludes the tale of his journey, he at once realizes that even as he recalls the vision, he must reckon with its pastness; with this reckoning comes a sudden obliteration of memory. The instant, the told recovery of that celestial fusion of Mind and Love, induces oblivion, a forgetfulness comparable in magnitude to the many centuries of lost time since the voyage of the Argo. The recollection perfected in the telling of the poem, in the combustion of composition, volatilizes memory.

Something similar happens, though on a smaller scale, in certain kinds of lyric poetry where memory, put under the most intense concentration of recollection, is lost, burnt up in the telling, as in Hart Crane's "Praise for an Urn":

> Scatter these well-meant idioms
> Into the smoky spring that fills
> The suburbs, where they will be lost.
> They are no trophies of the sun.

Gregory Bateson has coined the phrase "patterns which connect" to elucidate the hierarchies, homologies, and interdependencies that link all elements in the biosphere. In *Mind and Nature*, he asks: "What pattern connects the crab to the lobster and the orchid to the primrose and all four of them to me? And me to you? And all six of us to the amoeba in one direction and to the back-ward schizophrenic in another?" We might take over Bateson's phrase as a means for understanding the radical connections and disjunctions in literary history. When poets take a predecessor as a working model or paradigm, what must they in their own practice keep? What exclude? What fragmented hierarchies of the predecessor's achievement can be shored against the younger poet's own career? And to what purpose? Poems are frequently essential conservations and dismissals of earlier poems, ancestral ways of telling. In recasting the Orpheus story a poet may keep, almost as an act of good faith, the immanence of Orphic power caught by Rilke in the *Sonnets to Orpheus* while at the same time revising the Eurydice episode as a memorialization of domestic dissonance or marital terror. He or she may find in the Homeric poems patterns of force and cunning that can be transfigured into contemporary expressions of will and necessity, while at the same time discarding entirely the incantatory power of familial legacies that figure so crucially in those poems. To engage any pattern, even if the engagement is destructive, is to recollect the written past.

POUND'S *Cantos* constitute an epistemology, a method for apprehending knowledge by means of elective and associative recollection. The poem announces itself with the strictest sort of literary recovery, a translation, a re-citing of the Homeric *nekuia* from *Odyssey* XI, which is clearly Pound's invocation to Memory. Having grounded the poem in this act of self-conscious reclamation, he then launches into a vast gathering up of what he regards to be the most consequential details of the past. The memorialization takes the form of a sustained act of ventriloquism. To enact the changing forms of culture, the ways in which the mind engages the past in the present, Pound throws his voice far and wide: the charged heroic diction of Homeric speech; the dandified elegance of drawing-room conversation; the chopped aphorisms of oriental philosophy; the idiom of curt professionalism ("I said: You buy your damn coal from our mine. / And a year later they hadn't; so I had up the directors, / And they said: . . . well anyhow, they couldn't / buy the damn coal"); the supple American vernacular which Pound travestied, or misremembered ("an' doan you think he chop an' change all the time / stubborn az a mule, sah, stubborn as a MULE"). The dazzling mix of voices demonstrates a mind entirely caught up in, at times swamped by, the languages in which memories are embedded.

Although both the *Comedy* and the *Odyssey* were working models for Pound, they were engaged only sporadically to serve his own improvisatory design. In 1927 he outlined the early conceptual structure of the *Cantos* in a letter to his father:

1. Rather like, or unlike subject and response and counter subject in fugue.
A. A. Live man goes down into world of Dead
C. B. The "repeat in history"
B. C. The "magic moment" or moment of metamorphosis, bust thru from quotidien into "divine or permanent world." Gods, etc.

With this third movement we are in the world of Dantean light, but Pound knew from the first that he would not, could not, seek the same hierarchical orders of light, the sequence of luminous thresholds, that conducted the Pilgrim to his destination. Nor was he concerned with the Homeric *nostos* and the restitution of household, although variations on the Homeric pattern recur in the *Cantos* in the form of national and domestic economies. Conceptually, the *Cantos* do not allow for a Penelope or Ithaka, nor could Pound's method allow for arrival of any sort, since his strategy for recollection precluded this. There can be no arrival when there is no journey. And the mind that entertains all the mnemonic materials in the *Cantos* cannot be said to travel in any classical mimetic sense. It is instead fixed, sedentary, ruminative; it welcomes and absorbs presences, it does not strike out toward them. The mind of the poem—the "I" in all its transformations, all its voices—is a host more than guest; a keeper, not a traveler. All of which demonstrates what Pound did *not* derive from Dante, although they remain connected by the pattern of epic remembrance.

Pound's technique of recollection derives largely from his interest in the sculptor Henri Gaudier-Brzeska, who in his essay "Vortex" laid down the history and precepts of vorticist practice:

> Sculptural energy is the mountain.
> Sculptural feeling is the appreciation of masses in relation.
> Sculptural ability is the defining of these masses by planes.

Transposing Gaudier's theory to poetry, Pound came to regard the individual poet as the axis around which turned all the influences of tradition, the centuries of race consciousness, the particulars and generalizations of the past as they whirled around the present. Words were energy units which contained all the convergent matter, elective and associative, of the past. Vorticist method could not be converted into a memory model, since it depended so much on random improvised fetching. Vorticist technique was movement, not pattern; a way of receiving history, not a way of organizing it. Its aesthetic does not quite allow for any migratory pattern or mnemonic template, such as governs the movement in the *Odyssey* and the *Comedy*. What vorticist theory did provide was an *environment* for restless meditation. It was not an internal model for structuring poetic materials but rather a model by which the artist could dispose himself toward receiving them.

Pound treated the written and spoken matter of history—books, conversations, documents, lore, letters—as slabs of undressed stone ("sculptural energy") to be viewed in their relations one to another ("sculptural feeling") then selected, hewn, reshaped, and set self-consciously in associative arrangements ("sculptural ability") registered by the organic recollecting mind of the poet:

> So very difficult, Yeats, beauty so difficult.

> "I am the torch" wrote Arthur "she saith"
> In the moon barge βϱοδοδάκτυλος Ἠώς

> with the veil of faint cloud before her
> Κύθηϱα δεινὰ as a leaf borne in the current
> pale eyes as if without fire

all that Sandro knew, and Jacopo
and that Velásquez never suspected
lost in the brown meat of Rembrandt
and the raw meat of Rubens and Jordaens
(LXXX)

Pound recalls a conversation: Yeats asks the dying Beards-
ley "why he drew horrors," and the painter replies that beauty
is a task, a remark that later informs yet another conversation
in Yeats's own "Adam's Curse." Beauty as dangerous toil trig-
gers another remembrance, of Arthur Symons's "Modern
Beauty"; "I am the torch, she saith, and what to me / If the
moth die of me?" From the associative material a design idea
begins to generate: beauty, love, light, peril—the perfection
of that which fades while it's watched. The dawn, Sappho's
brododaktulos eos, goddess borne on the sickle moon, is a signal
of promise, of immanence. Many of the stories about Eos have
to do with her kidnapping of young men, so that with her
appearance comes also, to Pound's mind, the apparition of
the morning star, an avatar of Aphrodite, here and elsewhere
regarded as *kuthera deina*, dread Aphrodite, whose powers
may be a blessèd poisoning and who appears elsewhere in the
Cantos under the aspect of Circe, whose promise is the power
to transform men into beasts and pollute all good reason. The
cloud veiling the ancient morning presence is figured forth in
the clouds of Pisa, where Pound is composing the poem. To
this cluster of associations Pound adds the revisions of the
feminine figure that took place in the history of painting: the
ethereal expressions of Botticelli and Jacopo del Sellaio (who
knew "the secret ways of love") were darkened and weighted
by the "brown meat of Rembrandt," love corporealized and,
in its loss of light, vulgarized.

The lines dramatize the way in which the revealing mind of
the artist goes about its work of frantic recovery. Each epi-
phanic, fragmentary bit is invited into the vortex of composition, where it is momentarily deployed (or enjambed) in

cordance with the pliant, improvised, noncontiguous norms
of thematic association. These lines, like many others in the
poem, are an enactment of recollection as delirium.

POUND acknowledged Dante's poem as an exemplary narrative of exploration, but more to his own purpose were the in-
fusions of light authored by *il ben dell'intelletto*, the Good
Mind. In *The Spirit of Romance* (1910) he wrote: "[The *Comedy*]
is the journey of Dante's intelligence through the states of
mind wherein dwell all sorts and conditions of men before
death; beyond this, Dante or Dante's intelligence may come to
mean 'Everyman' or 'Mankind,' whereat his journey becomes
a symbol of mankind's struggle upward out of ignorance into
the clear light of philosophy." Pound, too, wanted that sustained examination of "states of mind," modes of preparedness that would enable him to read all the signs of those affections that have "carved the trace in the mind / dove sta
memoria." Dante's balanced concentric design, however, is replaced by Pound's busy thematic enjambment of artifacts. Me-
dieval cosmology and Catholic dogma provided Dante with an
accessible memory model; Pound of course had no such cultural apparatus at hand, and he chose not to appropriate or
fabricate one for the purpose of his poem. Pound must therefore function as the central mind of the poem, which not only
receives and selects from memory's hoard but which also designs orderly arrangements, frequently episodic, by which
recollection will be charged with meaning. Pound's later comment that the poem does not cohere may have been his own
recognition that the *Cantos* lacked a memory model, a seamless binding internal pattern.

Both poets drew on their erudition, but in very different
ways. Dante literally makes learning his guide. Virgil, the
shade of that text which as a young man Dante got by heart,
leads and protects the investigator down the scales of suffering, then up the terraces of forgiveness. Pound engages his
learning in a less dramatic, more compulsive way; rather than

allowing it to guide or draw him through his themes, *he* entertains *it*. The recovery of erudition in itself provides worthy occasion for epic meditation. For all its boisterous modernist technique—its cult of energy, its cubist juxtaposition of disjunctive cultural information, its whirlwind of data invited into the poem—Pound's epic is just as remarkable for its monumental pauses, its *longueurs*, where the central mind of the poem mulls over and shifts around its amassed recollections.

Dante kept his teachers with him as dramatic presences who promised knowledge. Pound, assuming the role not only of culture-bearer but also that of culture-publicist, himself assumes the role of teacher. (His own didactic enthusiasm apart, Pound also intended his poem to be a selective history of teachers and teachings.) The voices we hear—of Malatesta, Adams, Jefferson, Confucius, Whistler, Pound—are often *aimed* at the reader and are clearly meant to dispense learning, to profess. Dante, whose intelligence and enthusiasm were surely no less obsessive than Pound's, renders instead, in terrifying detail, the process of learning with all its dangers of inquisitiveness and curiosity.

Consider one detail early in the *Inferno*. Dante learns that the winding tail of Minos signifies the circle of pain to which a newly arrived shade will be condemned. What the Pilgrim will learn later is that Minos's action sketches the initial figure of the spiraling topography which he, Dante, will explore. Moreover, the self-flagellation of Minos also designs in advance (and gives Dante early notice of) the modes of suffering—the contortions, lashings, constrictions, all results of corrupt will—which will serve as landmarks in the descent. And Dante will remain, after that encounter with the instructive monster, a student of Divine justice. The *Comedy* is concerned more with the acquisition of knowledge than with its dispensation.

Pound begins his poem without any recollection of arrival. It is therefore inevitable that recollection as a prosody of

memory, a system of measures, will be violated and over-
whelmed by the sheer mass of mnemonic information that he
allows into the poem. His premonitions of an earthly paradise
of intellect are bound to be haphazard and contentious:

> spiriti questi? personae?
> > tangibility by no means *atasal*
> > but the crystal can be weighed in the hand
> formal and passing within the sphere: Thetis,
> Maya, ᾽Αφροδίτη,
> (LXXVI)

At such moments the *Cantos* memorialize fitful glimpses of
possibility. Dante's journey is triggered by a remembered arrival, and his poem is written to recover the entire process
leading to it. The *Comedy* is conceptually so coherent that the
grand pattern of all three canticles can frequently be inferred
from the most incidental details. The rain of filth in *Inferno* VI
is not simply a prefiguration of the downward journey facing
the Pilgrim and of the law of gravity that governs the place, it
is more importantly the negative presentation of matter and
motion that shall be purged and reversed when Dante climbs
the Mount of Purgatory. And during the descent, the sulphu-
rous exhalations and uplifted sparks that mark the way will
eventually be transfigured from their negative aspect to the
positive radiance that awaits the Pilgrim in Paradise, the destination and home of Good Mind. Dante thus begins to arrive
in Paradise the moment he sets foot in the underworld.

No artist was more self-conscious than Dante, but for all the
minute calibrations of light and dark throughout the *Comedy*
one still feels that the poem is being improvised in the telling,
that it is generating itself, its own peregrine recollections,
rather than being *composed* and artfully arranged. This is due
not only to the processional interlocking of verses allowed for
by terza rima and the frequently noted dramatic device of the
"two Dantes," actor and narrator, but also to the poet's ex-
ploitation of his memory model. The *Comedy* dramatizes not

only flux and movement but also waiting and preparedness; the farther the Pilgrim walks, the more intensely prepared he becomes. His activity gives evidence of pure waiting. While it is one of the most detailed analyses of spiritual self-consciousness in our literature, the *Comedy* is also autotelic in a cunning, insidious way: the actualization of metaphoric patterns is at every point commensurate with the "surface drama." That is, the mind that makes the journey discovers, by traversing the landscape of its ignorance, the symmetry of its own operations. The pattern of mentality is *revealed* in the patterning of the journey. And Dante's learning is engaged—the past engaged in and by the present—in the very process of the telling. The narrative is at once an unveiling and a recovery.

"ENTHUSIASM" derives from the Greek "*enthousiasmos*," that state of inspiration, of being filled or possessed by the god, for which poets might be praised or chastised. In a more secular application we can still speak of enthusiasm as the condition which combines a poet's concentration, preoccupation, attentiveness, and excitability. In social life it is usually called intensity, a vaguely accusatory description of a poet's extreme and discomforting alertness. What others perceive as neurotic inwardness or physical hyperactivity is merely a necessary expression of internal enthusiasm—the poet's obsessive concentration on a chosen subject as he or she works it over in the imagination, registering and decomposing, then reconstituting and articulating, the stuff of the real world. Before the world is spoken for, before a poem takes its provisional final shape, the poet focuses on that interior complex of relations that bind the matter of memory, while remaining equally vigilant toward the world outside, the kingdom of otherness. Both forms of attention are a constant testing of the possibilities of revelation.

Enthusiasm is also a condition of preparedness, of being ready for an unveiling. The gaze, or stare, inside and outside, is the medium for the unveiling. I believe this is what Pavese had in mind when in the preface to *Dialogues with Leucò* he described the conditions for revelation: "A true revelation, I am convinced, can only emerge from stubborn concentration on a single problem. . . . The surest, and the quickest, way for us to arouse the sense of wonder is to stare, unafraid, at a single object. Suddenly—miraculously—it will look like something we have never seen before." The "problem" may be any recollected bit: one's lover brushing her hair; a nightingale's song; a young man transformed into a stag; a yellow scarf snagged on a bush. Concentration, which is work, involves waiting, a disciplined expectancy that may at times seem wrapped in an aura of idleness, as a child will seem idle when first pausing to study the efficient moves of a squirrel in autumn. No wonder, then, that when poets are not thought too intense they are just as likely to be affectionately dismissed as indolent. When they are working hardest, they may seem to others not to be working at all.

The lyric is a formalized articulation or enactment of enthusiasm. In Yeats's "Among School Children," enthusiasm takes the form of historical scanning, an argumentative review of the "problem" of matter versus spirit. Hart Crane's "Garden Abstract" is another pure expression of enthusiasm: the poet witnesses, and *turns* in the language, that moment of transformation when the girl "comes to dream herself the tree, / The wind possessing her, weaving her young veins." In both poems the lyric voice is pitched high, exalting recollections claimed in exalted speech; and in both poems (and generally in Crane's and Yeats's poetry) enthusiasm serves a theme. In "Garden Abstract" the drama of erotic possession, of the natural order sexually interfused with the human, culminates in a falling away of memory and the annihilation of those feelings dependent on it: "She has no memory, nor fear, nor hope / Beyond the grass and shadows at her feet."

William Carlos Williams is a different case. He wanted enthusiasm—the celebrative stare, the pause for revelation, the waiting—to suffice entirely as both ground and finished act of the poem. That is, for Williams a poem need be nothing more than an act of enthusiastic noticing, a spelling out of the lyric imperative "O look!" It is this aesthetic that stands back of such early poems as "Proletarian Portrait," "To a Poor Old Woman," "The Young Housewife," and "Metric Figure." To *register* in language what he sees is itself an intensification or heightening of consciousness which serves to clarify the design of the visible world. A poem, therefore, need not be an investigation into a theme or quarrel with oneself. This mode of acknowledgment remained an essential element in Williams's practice, but as an aesthetic governing the entire progress of a career it is quite narrow and limiting, since it does not allow for the passionate interrogations of history and memory which one finds throughout Yeats and Crane. In a sense, Williams's career is a demonstration of the values and limitations of the two modes, noticing and interrogation.

Following Whitman, for whom the mere recognition of the self among others was occasion for poetic speech and for whom the poem could be, if nothing more, a bearing witness to the stuff of the world, Williams broke down some of the traditional confines of occasionality. Unlike Yeats and Eliot, he did not require a thematic or meditative occasion. His practice was at once a mild-mannered assault on the vestiges of decorum as well as a redefinition of the poetic moment. Again following Whitman's practice, all varieties of experience and degrees of perception, all orders of vision and recognition, from the high to the low, from the symbolic to the literal, were admissible in the poem. Williams was a devouring presence, and if his manner is not as boisterous as Whitman's and Pound's, his impulse is the same: welcome the plenitude of the world, junk and jewels alike, take it all in, get it down, register it.

The danger of holding too rigorously to the notion of poetry as an act of enthusiastic noticing is that enthusiasm will finally be made to do the work of the selective imagination, that it will become little more than a feeble exertion of will upon the wonderfully resistant materials of the world. This limitation was still evident in the posthumous *Pictures from Brueghel*. There are two strains or impulses controlling the poems there: the devouring act of noticing, and the recuperative act of recollection. The former leads Williams to try to generate an occasion for poetic speech from his interest in some detail, to squeeze lyric description from what seems finally to be nothing more than the need to write, to practice poetry, to take notice:

> Summer!
> the painting is organized
> about a young
>
> reaper enjoying his
> noonday rest
> completely
>
> relaxed
> from his morning labors
> sprawled
>
> in fact sleeping
> unbuttoned
> on his back

The occasioning impulse of these lines (section VII, "The Corn Harvest," from the title poem) is not summer, nor strictly speaking the painting itself, but rather the poet's willfulness to describe or annotate what seems to him an interesting arrangement of evocative details. In aesthetic terms, beauty is reduced to that which is for whatever reason interesting, and inevitably the poem—for all its apparent attention toward the painting—becomes an exercise in solipsism disguised by affectionate descriptive language. In the "Haymaking" section of that same poem, the genuine enthusiasm of poetic talk turns, by virtue of Williams's need to take notice, to strained glee:

The living quality of
the man's mind
stands out

and its covert assertions
for art, art, art!
painting

that the Renaissance
tried to absorb
but

it remained a wheat field
over which the
wind played

In the longer poems at the end of *Pictures*, the literalist
strain is absorbed and enriched by another, more luxurious,
in which patterns of recollection converge on the moment of
telling, the past intricated in the argumentative present. In
poems like "To Daphne and Virginia," "The Orchestra," and
"The Sparrow," the act of noticing figures as one stage in a
sequence, one apprehending selection in a vexing series of selections, the latest recognition in a history of recognitions. Description comes to serve the larger needs of interpretation
and interrogation. The process of recuperating history, scru-
tinizing its patterns, and then claiming that very exploration
as a subject for poetry, is announced in the opening lines of
"The Descent":

The descent beckons
        as the ascent beckoned.
            Memory is a kind
of accomplishment,
        a sort of renewal
            even
an initiation, since the spaces it opens are new places
        inhabited by hordes
            heretofore unrealized,

of new kinds—
        since their movements
                are toward new objectives
(even though formerly they were abandoned).

Here Williams translates the essence of Dante's invocation to
the Muses: memory as work, recovery, unveiling, spatial pattern, and movement. Toward this work all energies are directed. One such energy is of course the instantaneous recording of perception, but in these poems Williams is more
concerned with the way the mind engages and arranges and
learns from its own mnemonic materials. As in Dante, the
shape of the moment is significant insofar as it contributes to
the larger and more exalting configuration, the shape of the
mind and life.

In "Asphodel, That Greeny Flower," the histories of the
vegetative world—the dissolutions and reflorescences of nature—mix with models of historical discovery (Columbus,
Darwin) and destruction (the atomic bomb, the Rosenbergs)
that act as metaphors of the inquiring mind, even while the
poem is an exploration into the patterns of failure and promise that Williams recollects as the shape of his own life. Lament and need converge on the desire for the duration of
memory and the vigilant selectivity of the recollecting mind:

A sweetest odor!
        Honeysuckle! And now
there comes the buzzing of a bee!
        and a whole flood
                of sister memories!
Only give me time,
        time to recall them
                before I shall speak out.

Williams is determined still to "talk on / against time," to write
out of resistance to time's passing, a resistance that also characterizes his interpretive review of the physical world, which

he sees as a field of procreation constantly generating subject matter for poetry and thus nourishing the imagination. If there are "a thousand topics / in an apple blossom," the natural world accordingly presents itself to us as both challenge and offering. Williams's announcement that "the whole world / became my garden" calls up for reconsideration his own poetic practice: to tend the world in all its particulars, which is an act of love, is to tend the garden of poetry. The gardener, cultivating his plot, cultivates his own consciousness of mortality.

In Book II, Williams confesses to his occasional failure, especially in his later years, to discern the distinctive patterns of individuation in nature. This dissolution of the mind's discriminating faculties is yet another force to be resisted, even while the breakdown process is being analyzed. When he says that "All appears / as if seen / wavering through water," he admits to what he knows to be an undesirable condition of mind. His method here, as elsewhere, is to establish a procedure of intellection, then dismiss it as futile or impoverished. (In "The Desert Music," for example: "To imitate, not to copy nature, not / to copy nature // NOT, prostrate, to copy nature / but a dance! to dance . . .") In the end, he still wants clarity of the seen world, so that the emotional and intellectual correspondences will likewise be clear and exact. "Asphodel" is clearly a meditative preparation for death, and Williams's method of preparing himself is to test to the end life's possibilities. These possibilities are authorized by history; they issue from historical contexts. The asphodel, a common field flower in the New Jersey meadows so familiar to Williams, also grows along the fields of the underworld.

To say, as Williams does, that "I was lost / failing the poem" is to claim the writing of poetry as a defining of one's mortality as it shapes itself in the context of the near world. (In "The Desert Music," the dance of poetry is "an agony of self-realization / bound into a whole / by that which surrounds us.") The imagination, as it receives and meditates on the resistant materials of the physical world, redeems the mind from the imminent confusion of undifferentiated matter and ideally prevents it from drawing pseudo-truths from apparent correspondences. The imaginative faculty, for example, allows Williams to perceive that the Bomb too is a flower, since its vicious cloud conforms generally to that figuration; but the discriminating imagination also insists that the Bomb's destructive capacity, its sheer waste and terror, must in the end elicit outrage, all the more so for its coincidental resemblance to the asphodel. Although he does not spell it out, Williams is calling into question the act of metaphor-making for its own sake for which too many poets are unjustifiably praised in our own time. His self-interrogation implies the necessity of imagination informed by moral conscience. It is entirely logical, then, that his questioning of plenitude and waste in the public world should lead him to reconsider what he himself has wasted or squandered in private life, his failures of love and attentiveness.

THE CODA of "Asphodel" is a celebration of light, of the clarity that emanates from and supersedes the consuming fires of process that generate it. The verse enacts a wedding ceremony in which the will toward love, informed by all the changes of the past, becomes a source of radiance. And love— toward the world in all its particulars and toward the beloved who embodies universal elements—is bound to imagination: "Love and the imagination / are of a piece." The mind's movement toward love is therefore movement toward the impossible perfecting of the imagination as it takes in, sorts, and interprets the matter of history. Williams says that the present is suffused with the odor of the asphodel, which "has no odor / save to the imagination." In the poem his imagination has already reviewed the "sexual orchid" of Helen, the garden of the sea, the hierarchies in nature sustained by strife and coexistence; and he has recollected other forms of flowering—marriage, friendships, career. The present is in effect suffused with imagination nurtured by memory.

The passion for elective recollection is in no way deflected by Williams's awareness of the images issuing from oceanic memory. His concentration—thematic concentration—is fixed on the greening process of time evidenced in the particulars of his life. His argument had already brought him, at the end of Book III, to some understanding of the ordered sequence of harm, forgiveness, and recompense:

> You have forgiven me
> > making me new again.
> > > So that here
> in the place
> > dedicated in the imagination
> > > to memory
> of the dead
> > I bring you
> > > a last flower.

The "place" is poetry, the "flower" this poem, delivered in elegiac thanksgiving. At the end of the Coda, it is the odor which only the imagination can detect—"an odor / as from our wedding"—that not only revives him but also begins to seep "into all crevices / of my world." In its reckoning with memory and imagination, with nature's plenitude as it reflects the honeycombing of private life, with the value of metaphor and correspondences ("Are facts not flowers / and flowers facts?"), "Asphodel" must have been the poem Williams wrote to thank the Muse.

WILLIAMS and the others I've mentioned demonstrated an extraordinary enthusiasm for the physical world. They quite freely dispensed that information (all the facts and flowers) in their work. They are securely in the ancient tradition of told experience, struggling, at times by sheer force of will and nerve, to find and release that word which might, in Pavese's words, "translate the world." Whatever privileged knowledge they unearthed in their explorations was something to be made public, announced in the provincial meeting hall of poetry, set before the reader in well-intentioned (if at times ill-directed) radiance. There is a mode of telling in recent American poetry, however, which marks a diminution of this tradition and which is practiced so widely as to demand attention. It is a poetry suffering from a kind of agoraphobia: instead of seizing the occasion of poetic speech as one for recollecting, interrogating, and telling the experience of history in its changes, it withdraws from any kind of disclosure or public enactment of discovery. The result is enforced, cultivated mystification. Instead of the public unveiling of private mysteries, this poetry dramatizes the enveiling, the enfolding, of public meaning. The instrument of mystification is metaphoric speech:

> *Mother Tongue*
>
> Sold by a butcher
> Wrapped in a newspaper
> It travels in a bag
> Of the stooped widow
> Next to some onions and potatoes
> Toward a dark house
> Where a cat will
> Leap off the stove
> Purring
> At its entrance

This poem by Charles Simic (not among his best but fairly representative) issues from an attenuated aesthetic: any figure of speech, uttered in properly hushed tones, may signal the sublime which, given the bemusement of the speaker, is likely to be a self-deprecatory sublime. But the sublime must not be made in any way accessible, the poem exists in order to withhold it, and language is therefore its travesty. The figure of the mother tongue is meant, I think, to amuse; the tone is

mock-morose. There is some suggestion of lost history, cultural estrangement, language lost and retrieved. But it is difficult to define the poem's subject or theme in any more definite manner. Clarification is willfully denied. The overlapping
pictures (butcher, newspaper, bag, widow, etc.—bizarre laminations of ordinary details) are modeled on the pictorial
method of Magritte. The linguistic mannerisms, such as the
dilated turn of phrase "in a bag / Of the stooped widow," are
stylistic equivalents of the iconography of surrealist painting.
Like the flamboyant allegories of Dali, the poem seems an allegorical method in search of a theme. If it is wrong to read
the poem in this humorless way, if the poem is meant to be
bleakly comic, why should this intention be confused or deflected by the shadow profundity of the title, or by the omi-
nous presence of the "dark house"?

The American brand of hermeticism presumes that the occasion for poetry may be nothing more than the conceiving of
an elusive, vaguely spooky metaphor, and that evocativeness
takes precedence over definiteness. This certainly has little to
do with Italian Hermeticism. Even one of the more elusive
poems of that school, Ungaretti's "Mattina"—"M'illumino /
d'immenso" (Morning: I'm filled with light that is a bound-
lessness)—yields a privileged moment and defines, in an instant, the sensation of radiant fullness of being. Nor should
the new hermeticism be confused with the studious articulations of Williams's literalism. In his famous "Poem," for example, we are given, however minimally, the clicking stop-
action activity of recollection as it holds in the mind's eye each
sequential frame of the cat's movement: "first the right /
forefoot // carefully / then the hind." And "The Red Wheel-
barrow" recovers for us momentarily a prosody of the phe-
nomenal world, its beats and measures and arrangements,
even while the poet engages his own wish to measure the
meaning of what he sees. The new hermeticism insists instead
that poetry is privileged concealment that can afford to for-
sake or ignore the disciplines of remembrance. It also as-

sumes that the world of things exists primarily as a pretext for fanciful metaphor. Clarity of image, or pictorial artifice, disattaches itself from clarity of context, from the nest of intellectual and sensational experience which is the proper breeding place of poetry. As a result, it estranges speech from its social origins and stands aloof from poetry's traditional work of quarreling with human and divine orders.

IT MAY BE that no degree of sincerity can elevate a poetry that is already diminished, even before it is told, by its disposition toward the memorial presence of the world. Sincerity needs to be authorized by something more than mere good craft or slant perspective. Usually it involves a complex of historical influences at work in the writing of a poem that push the poet toward discovery and articulation of that discovery. Solipsism, which often translates itself into unhinged pictorial ingenuity, will more likely turn one away from the raid on the inarticulate that Eliot encouraged. (Sincerity may also of course be a coy expression of polite manners, which are not especially helpful in conducting that raid.) Whitman, while insisting upon his own huge sincerity, at the same time turns voraciously toward the thick and busy actualizations of experience. Though he insists on his role as operatic solipsist in "Song of Myself," the poem is occupied above all with the changing arrangements of the physical world as they are gathered up, recollected, charged and shaped by psalmic outcry. Mandelstam suggested in his essay "About the Nature of the Word" one reason for Whitman's enthusiasm: "Having expended its philological reserves brought over from Europe, America began to act like someone now crazed, now thoughtful. Then all of a sudden, she initiated her own particular philology from which Whitman emerged; and he, like a new Adam, began giving things names, began behaving like Homer himself, offering a model for a primitive American poetry of nomenclature."

Mandelstam himself, for all the allusiveness of his verse,

was aware of the dangers of agoraphobia and its conceal-
ments. Poetry for him was an investigation into the memory
of time. In another essay, " Word and Culture," he says that
poetry is a "plough that turns up time in such a way that the
abysmal strata of Time, its black earth, appear on the surface."

Even when poets insist that they write only for themselves,
they usually mean that they write in order to excavate their
own consciousness of time as it is recorded in memory; in this
sense, they write for history. Lyric poetry occupies a middle
ground between private reckoning and public recognition.
The poem is an act of deliverance, and deliverance will therefore be crucial to the poet's intentions. If those intentions are
thwarted or corrupted, if the poet becomes somehow persuaded that poetry ought to be an arrogant denial, or willful
enclosure, or arbitrary exercise in nomenclature, then that
poet elects dissociation and chooses poverty.   [1981]

THE POETRY OF WILLIAM BRONK

During the 1970s the Elizabeth Press published in fine limited editions several books of poems by William Bronk, including his first, *My Father Photographed with Friends*, written in the 1940s, and *Light and Dark*, which had first appeared in 1956. In 1964, New Directions brought out *The World, The Worldless*, the only one of his volumes to appear under the imprint of a trade press and now out of print, though it is arguably one of the best books of that decade. None of these received the public attention given to other verse collections which we now no longer read with much attention. The Elizabeth Press books were not even given the passing acknowledgment accorded other small-press publications. The only major anthology containing Bronk's work is Hayden Carruth's *The Voice That Is Great within Us*. In our literary democracy it's considered rude or unseemly to speak of official culture and its control organs, but the fact remains that the benign, gentlemanly inattentiveness of reviewers, editors, and anthologists has been responsible for this neglect. There is of course another reason for Bronk's marginality: his poetry does not conform to the expectations of readers normally accustomed to descriptive rhetoric and the cult of personality, the two predominant modes of poetic expression during the past fifteen years or so. Bronk's poems are argumentative, analytical, contentious, and they are unattractive insofar as they do not profess statements meant to draw admiration or commiseration from the reader. His manner of abstract lyric statement also has a kind of exotic detachment, an impassioned dissolution of ragged personality in the presence of refined mental activity.

Life Supports: New and Collected Poems (1981) collects all of Bronk's earlier volumes in chronological order and includes thirty-four new poems (all of them compact twenty-liners). His strengths and eccentricities are apparent from the start:

sententious statement; argumentation modeled on the practice of the Elizabethans; cranky inquisitiveness; gnarled disputations with meaning; intimate conversation with ideas. Like Keats, Bronk is a poet of the disciplines of joy, lending his mind out to greet its object of contemplation. The influence of Stevens also runs strong and clear in the early work, especially in the way Bronk's poems dramatize the mind's attempt to distinguish the particulars of the world from their absorptive universal context and to discover moments of permanent actualization in a world of pure change. (There are also traces of Frost's melancholy indecisiveness, the unwillingness of the analytical faculty to commit itself to moral choice.) One of Bronk's early poems, "Her Singing," engages his chief influences. His singer's subject is change ("the flight of time, of our mortality") but her voice at the same time momentarily suspends all process, suspends the very subject of her song. Behind her stands Stevens's woman of Key West who sings beyond the genius of the sea, and behind both singers is that idea of music rising in "unheard melodies" from Keats's urn: "She said the moment shaped was more than these. / Her singing took the flight and held it still."

In his early work, then, Bronk was conducting his education in public. As he emerges from these historical pressures, his poems become more assertive and distinctive, his rhetoric more his own. The poems also become more clenched and elusive. Stevens's vertiginous oratory gives way to Bronk's own roughened, uncertain interrogations of experience. "Colloquy on a Bed," from his fourth book (*The Empty Hands*), begins by insisting that the order of "celestial motions" is not, cannot be, a rational order; it is too unaccommodating, too out of scale. This recognition provokes the statement: "This place, this universe, / in any rational sense is hopelessly / insane." Yet in its hopelessness it possesses meaning and can be valued. "Hopeless" (like Keats's "forlorn") is "the saving word," though it saves the poet only so that he may then repudiate his lover. The encounter finally teaches him that "pas-

sion does exist / as hopeless and meaningful as the universe
is." Here, in miniature, are the rhetorical movements which
Bronk puts to larger effect in his long poems: the dramatic
reversal of assertion and denial; the conflation of the cosmic
and the particular; the mind's need to familiarize and domes-
ticate monstrous scale; the contest between rational inquiry
and instinctual cry.

Bronk distinguishes between two forms of actualization,
two spheres of knowable reality: *the* world, the brute complex
of nature's matter presented to human consciousness, and *a*
world, an individuated structure, a localized pattern of meaning which consciousness constructs from the universal field. A
house or garden is a world that fixes in time and space a hab-
itable version of properties selected from the world:

> To live in a hogan under a hovering sky
> is to live in a universe hogan-shaped,
> or having hogans in it to give it shape,
> earth-covered hovels, holes having a wall
> to heave the back of the heart against.

Bronk has written numerous poems about North and South
American Indian cultures, and he is drawn to them because
in these societies the ligatures binding the great world of natural stuff to a world of local domestic patterns are so immediate, so apparently indissoluble, that they become a rule of
life. Even this paradigm of twin worlds, however, becomes
subject to criticism and modification; every proposition advanced is sooner or later questioned, because of the mind's
power of fabulation and dissent. In "The Failure to Devise a
Better World," Bronk says: "If failure is what you mean to call
it, it's the mind, / I suppose, that fails, but what a word. It fails
/ by succeeding. A sneaky triumph."

Few poets dare the kind of self-neutralizing diction—or
rhetoric of cancellation—that Bronk has made the center of
his art. He seems by temperament a connoisseur of impossibility:

> Why should we not in reason ask why
> it should go on so, always this and not
> more, why nothing otherwise than this?

These are the opening lines of "The Questions," a poem that seems to be about the impossibility of striking a fixed attitude toward time's passing. But here the argumentative impulse takes leave of its motivating concern, the habit of mind becomes dissociated from its subject matter. Whenever this occurs, Bronk's powerful rhetoric breaks down into sophistry, a crabbed delectation of denial. "The Questions" concludes: "Well, there are all sorts of positions to take. / One works as well as another, but none of them works." The surrender of disciplined thought to mere mental reflex may be an inherent limitation of Bronk's method. He is certainly aware of this, for in other poems he criticizes this reflexiveness.

Bronk's most recurrent theme, his "intensest concern," is the discovery of permanence in the near world, of what he calls "the real unchanged." But this aspiration is set against the felt need to escape the familiar terrain of habit and substance (the "stink and dirt" and "mean wrongs" of our lives) into a rarefied mentality purged of changing matter. He admits to the mere "seemings" of our world, in all their agonizing elusiveness, even while he praises them. And he questions the reasons for praise, yet offers praise nonetheless: "Landscape is metaphor / and only metaphor. But, oh, I have loved it so." In "On *Credo Ut Intelligam*" he attacks knowledge as one more provisional support system: "I plead the permanence / of ignorance, that we acknowledge it." But unknowing, too, may become a complacency or comfort, so he has to think his way out of a dilemma which his own ambition has designed. He suggests, therefore, that habitual ignorance is finally a nurturing illusion, a means of restoration. The *re*discovery of what we do not know becomes "The day's adventure, the same surprise." And the habit of belief "comforts our incoherence, offers to teach / some simple terms, the easy speech of the land."

Bronk's longer poems are a full, rich testing of Keatsian Negative Capability. That condition of suspended certainty, of the dissolution of personality in favor of intense attention to the object presented to the mind, becomes for him both subject matter and procedure. Like Dickinson, he speaks readily of vacancies rich with Edenic light, of deprivations which nourish, of absences bursting with spectral presences. In one of his most self-declarative poems, "The Real Surrounding: On Canaletto's Venice" (which ought to be included in future anthologies, along with "Skunk Cabbage," "The Outer Becoming Inner," "The Various Sizes of the World," "The Thinker Left Looking out the Window," "The Body of This Life," "June Comes, Janus Faced," and "What Form the World Has"), Bronk refuses dazzlement as motive for praise. He wants not Turner's vision ("all he saw / was concentration of light. There is something to say / besides glory all the time"), but Canaletto's, whose sensibility made him see the huge Venetian light as something lacking, a sign of magnificent emptiness which Canaletto "felt an urgency to paint . . . / as a positive presence, not as something gone." This is a clear statement of Bronk's intention to analyze and celebrate the processes of thought by which we try to spell the sense of the world. And it inevitably entails the often uncongenial mixture of self-effacement, pridefulness, intellectual aggressiveness and tenacious quarrelsomeness which distinguishes his poetry and gives it a severe beauty.   [1982]

A LIFE CONTINUOUS WITH
OUR OWN

In 1819, when Keats enclosed the first draft of his "Ode to Psyche" in the long letter of April 30 to his brother George, he explained that unlike his previous poems, which had been written quickly and hurriedly, the "Ode" had been composed with greater patience and deliberation, a new discipline which would encourage him "to write other thing[s] in even a more peaceable and healthy spirit." The poems he wrote in the next several weeks—"Ode on a Grecian Urn," "Ode to a Nightingale," and "Ode on Melancholy"—were presumably written according to the new prescription, leisurely, carefully measured, though now those weeks seem a fever spell in literary history. In light of those subsequent poems, with their high resolution of theme and fully experienced encounter between the inquiring spirit and its object, the "Ode to Psyche" is a rough and hesitant piece of work. Keats was scrupulously self-corrective. He sensed that the "Ode" was a preparation for other efforts and as such could be quickly put behind him. The version in the letter is signed off with typical, self-effacing swagger: "Here endethe ye Ode to Psyche."

Keats was unafraid to conduct his education in public, displaying in his published work the mimicry, indulgences, and defective artistry which poets of lesser power choose to disguise or conceal. He wrote and published *Endymion* in part because he felt a poet of ambition should at some time early in his career declare himself by writing a long poem. (Wallace Stevens and William Carlos Williams, both deeply indebted to Keats, later voiced the same opinion.) Writing *Endymion* schooled him in the broad, self-impelling narrative of Spenserian epic and prepared him for the later, scaled-down narratives of "The Eve of St. Agnes," "Lamia," and the "Hyperion" fragments. *Endymion* was a performance, a "trial of

149

invention." The dismissive flourish at the close of the "Ode to Psyche" (which I think is Keats's less dour equivalent of Milton's "twitch't his mantle blue") is a sign that he regarded that poem, too, as a trial or rehearsal.

Though conceptually shallow in parts and often tinny with the conventional pieties of odic address, the "Ode to Psyche" is the most interesting poem of self-instruction that Keats wrote. He explained its origins in the letter to George: "You must recollect that Psyche was not embodied as a goddess before the time of Apuleius the Platonist who lived after the Augustan age, and consequently the Goddess was never worshipped or sacrificed to with any of the ancient fervor—and perhaps never thought of in the old religion—I am more orthodox than to let a heathen Goddess be so neglected." The amused, self-conscious remark about his "orthodoxy" suggests that Keats regarded the poem as something serviceable and that he was, with some ostentation, *taking on* a subject. He is writing the poem to remedy an unhappy situation. He will make himself over into Psyche's priest and celebrant, singing her praise even while he keeps her secrets. The decision to ordain himself is brought on by a dream or vision: "Surely I dreamt to-day, or did I see / The winged Psyche with awaken'd eyes?" It's an arbitrary question and serves mainly to engage the matter of the meditation. The distinction between dreaming and that active reckoning with the processes of consciousness which is the visionary condition is here a rhetorical switch mechanism. It is not a formulation *arrived at* after a fully experienced investigation of thought, as it is at the end of "Ode to a Nightingale."

From the very beginning Keats is more concerned with flickering self-conscious mood than with the meaning of the announced object of his concentration, the goddess herself. He goes on to describe his discovery of Psyche and Eros in a forest, and his picture is a warm pastoral portrait which later, in "Ode on a Grecian Urn," will be completely denatured in the "Cold Pastoral" of the urn: "Their arms embraced, and their pinions too; / Their lips touch'd not, but had not bid adieu." Then, in the most peculiar moment in the entire poem, Keats curtly acknowledges the presence of Psyche's lover: "The winged boy I knew." This is the only mention of the divine lover in the poem, and the recognition is almost dismissively familiar in tone. It is also a little out of joint. Keats recognizes Eros (Love, or Sensation) before identifying Psyche (Soul, or Undefined Spirit), but then turns his attention from Eros for the rest of the poem until the final line, when Love is welcomed ("a casement ope at night, / To let the warm Love in"). Keats's greeting of Psyche—"But who wast thou, O happy, happy dove? / His Psyche true!"—is strained, as if the poet were momentarily tempted to say more about Eros (and perhaps change the direction and shape of the poem accordingly) but feels duty-bound by his original conception.

Already twenty-two lines into his poem, Keats is still presenting his subject and doing it in a way that suggests real difficulty in concentrating on it. He becomes almost trapped in the elegant maneuvers of delayed disclosure which had been so appropriate to "The Eve of St. Agnes" and which would be burnt away entirely in "To Autumn" and "Ode on Melancholy," poems of pure foreground. Keats had complained in letters about the difficulty he had in commencing a poem and his tendency to rely too much on rhetorical scene-setting. He felt that a long lyric poem, in which the poet's spirit moved outward to greet the object of its attention and in that greeting intensified the reality of the object, required first of all the situating of the object in relation to the poet; once the relation was established, the field between poet and object could be explored. But at the same time Keats wanted the sustained simultaneous rush of intellection *and* sensation, knowledge and sensuous thrill. This aspiration, I think, describes the central activity in the "Ode to Psyche," the wedding of Soul and Love consecrated by Mind. The process by which that union is achieved, however, is relayed in fits and starts, as if Keats were not yet convinced of its possibility and had therefore not yet thought through the dramatic structure of that possibility. He witnesses the union, or *a* union, early in the poem when he finds the lovers in the forest. But it is not yet ritualized, and at that point the ritualization of the union becomes one of his reasons for continuing the poem.

This delay and indecisiveness result from an even deeper divisiveness. Keats is never quite certain if he is addressing the story of Psyche and Eros or if he is writing an allegory of artistic self-declaration. The two intentions never quite resolve as one. In a sense, the poem finally has little to do with the myth, as Harold Bloom once pointed out. But Keats initially meant to oblige the myth and its central action, not merely the figure of Psyche in isolation. His concentration is split between the story and himself. While asserting that he will be Psyche's servant, he also wants the goddess and her story to serve him: "I see, and sing, by my own eyes inspir'd. / So let me be thy choir, and make a moan / Upon the midnight hours." But neither does this reciprocity become the central matter of the poem.

The Psyche story attracted Keats because it would justifiably occasion self-definition. At that point in his career he wanted a richer texture of story and relation along with a more detailed realization of what he had called the Chamber of Maiden-Thought, that room in life where we drink the light of differentiation, unlike the "infant or thoughtless Chamber" where all is undifferentiated eros. Once we pass into the Chamber of Maiden-Thought, he explained in a famous letter to his friend John Reynolds,

> we become intoxicated with the light and the atmosphere, we see nothing but pleasant wonders, and think of delaying there for ever in delight: However among the effects this breathing is father of is that tremendous one of sharpening one's vision into the heart and nature of Man—of convincing one's nerves that the world is full of Misery and Heartbreak, Pain, Sickness and oppression—whereby this Chamber of

Maiden-Thought becomes gradually darken'd and at the same time on all sides of it many doors are set open—but all dark—all leading to dark passages. . . . We feel the "burden of the mystery." (May 3, 1818)

He needed to absorb into poetic speech both the wayward moods of erotic sensation and the insistent clarity of Apollonian thought. The closing stanza in "Ode to Psyche" is the most powerfully argued, since here he finally vaporizes all the residual traces of the story as he had found it in Apuleius and turns his attention entirely to the formulation of his own ambition: the preparation of Mind to welcome the wedding of Love and Soul. The nature that surrounds the temple of intellection which Keats will build "in some untrodden region of my mind"—a sanctuary dressed "with the wreath'd trellis of a working brain"—is a nature whose proliferation will be assisted by the faculty of imagination or Fancy, and as such it will be a place of fructifying possibility. The shrine will be dressed "With buds, and bells, and stars without a name, / With all the gardener Fancy e'er could feign, / Who breeding flowers, will never breed the same." Although the poem itself has been rather improvisatory, the ambition it finally defines is that of orderly, methodical preparation of mind. The poem is best understood as a proofing of possibilities and a purifying of self for the later poems. It advances in search of a definitive subject (discovered only in the last stanza) because Keats had not fully internalized the content and occasion of his initial subject.

If a long lyric poem is a formalized casting of thought characteristic of—issuing *from the character of*—the poet, lyric speech must be grounded in intense meditative preparedness, the *inwarding* by which the poet internalizes the object of his concentration (an urn, a panther, an asphodel), tests it against his character, and answers the occasion. The answer is simultaneously an articulation of occasion. This process cannot be measured in time. Rilke studied his "thing" subjects for long periods before writing poems about them. Keats wrote "Ode to a Nightingale" in about two hours, evidently provoked on the spot into writing the poem. Whatever the actual physical circumstances, without this internalization and schooling of self the poet will write a poetry of improvisation where the formalization of artistic truth depends too much on the titillations of momentary feeling. Or he may write a poetry of charged instances, of flushed phantasmal presences. Such poetry has real value, but it should not be confused with Coleridge's ideal of bringing the entire Soul of mankind into activity, or with Keats's own ambition expressed in the closing stanza of "Ode to Psyche": the form-making impulse of Mind, suffused with possibility generated by Imagination, is the fullest and most accurate preparation for the transforming integration of Soul and Love.

The two books I want to look at here, the first in a series of new poetry volumes published by Elpenor Books, display some of the difficulties and questions which Keats tried to work through in "Ode to Psyche." William Hunt's *Oceans and Corridors of Orpheus* contains a sequence of poems derivative of the Orpheus and Persephone myths, and a prose Afterword intended to ground the poems. The Afterword is more provocative than explanatory. In it Mr. Hunt suggests that our individual lives are versions or variants of the Orpheus story, and that his own sequence of poems is a lament on the dawning of sexual fullness. The opening poem, "Of Serpents," deals obsessively with this anxiety. Mr. Hunt calls this fullness "puberty," but he means the term more generally to signify an adult's encounter with the world as he finds it, not as he might wish it to be. It is not only a world of work but also comprises the network of "those seemingly long-buried connections of soul-life—passionate alignments with others." He admits that the poems are a commentary on that time of review and initiation when he took stock of his life and used his mood of "complex sorrow much as an organ of sense might be used."

Mr. Hunt's regard for myth is complex, and he has clearly been influenced by Cesare Pavese's *Hard Labor* and *Dialogues with Leucò*. My general impression, however, is that he has not been assertive enough with regard to his chosen stories and has not personalized them as completely as he might have done in order to reveal precisely his own tale of becoming. The mythic presences in the poems undergo transformations: Eurydice becomes Persephone, Persephone becomes the woman in Mr. Hunt's life who occasioned the poems; the figure of Orpheus is shadowed over by that of Christ and of the poet. In order to avoid equivocation, however, this kind of multiple seeing needs to be defined unequivocally in the art of the poems. Here I find a problem, since the story that emerges from the Orphic material is not very clear, does not define itself as a *lived* pattern. In his Afterword Mr. Hunt says that gods are beings "who cannot embody themselves in the physical," that they exist in our thoughts, their existence signaled and confirmed by ideas, and that the process of thinking is itself a sign of myth. This argument is very like the one advanced some years ago by Jane Harrison, who said that only our ideas of the gods can be said to exist, and that ancient divinities were mental creations born of local circumstance, of regional needs and aspirations.

If ideas, as Mr. Hunt says, are "indicators" of divine orders, they are necessarily signs of that order, clear traceable emblems. It does not automatically follow, however, that the gods are images or embodiments of thoughts. To say that consciousness, in its image-making activity, affirms the existence of the gods, and that the gods in turn exist primarily as sanctions of consciousness, is to assert each as a sign of the other. The conception is circular and in artistic terms self-neutralizing. Meditation on the gods too easily becomes a hall of mirrors—wherever we look we see ourselves. For this reason a poet cannot afford to ignore that (sometimes embittering) quality which is the inexplicable otherness of the divine, even as it interpenetrates at will the human order.

The poems in Mr. Hunt's book treat the relation between Orpheus—singer, light-bringer, enchanter, privileged visitor—and Persephone, one of the queens of darkness, daughter of the Corn Mother. In the poems she is "the image of our being wide-awake," though her wakefulness is a vernal phase only. For the rest of the year she is *of* Hades. The occasionally opaque thinking in the Afterword perhaps lies behind what seems to me a troubling divisiveness in the poems. The sequence—ten poems—places the poet and an unnamed companion as witnesses to mythic occasions and transformations, the chief of which is the encounter between Orpheus and Persephone. Because for the most part the poet simply bears witness (or, in a few poems, thinks thoughts attributed to Orpheus and Persephone / Eurydice) the activities of consciousness which the mythic figures enact are set apart from the poet, who is thus maneuvered into the position of commentator. He is consequently divorced from the dramatic cause, the occasion-in-thought, that impels the poems.

In "What We Have Known Knows Us," a poem about reciprocity of consciousness, Mr. Hunt spells out the mutual projection and creation by which the gods come into existence as human thoughts. The poem opens with a full statement of shock and dismay at the discovery of self-consciousness:

> What is this gift that turns in upon
> itself, this consciousness of self?
> It bears the eyes of Eurydice
> withdrawn on the stairs,
> whose I we experience as our own.

When this self-consciousness is offered to the gods, who presumably authored it, it is refused. Existence is thus measured as a constant falling away from the divine; this is the consequence of self-consciousness. The lines beginning with "It bears the eyes of Eurydice," however, seem to me a too dispassionate explanation of the thought formed in the opening two lines, and perhaps also a withdrawal from its conse-

quences. The turn toward Eurydice is a gloss on the lived experience expressed in the opening. The continuity of consciousness and mythic trace is abruptly disjointed, and the
tone becomes slightly didactic. Something similar happens in
"Breathing in Death: Stillness in Life":

> He was everywhere he had ever been.
> Perhaps Eurydice would shudder
> in stupor of a death she was not
> rid of, or not having yet endured its thrust
> as an event of the future, when the rain
> of light would appear, to touch his wrists
> from within this corridor of red clay—

That opening statement is stunning. It expresses complete
sympathy of poet and subject, disclosing an essential quality
of Orphic consciousness. But Mr. Hunt then looks away from
this and steps back to offer a somewhat vague hypothesis
about the meeting between Orpheus and Eurydice in the Underworld. The myth is no longer a lived medium but rather
an implement or serviceable "version." This poem, like a few
others, seems to me only half-formed; it does not achieve that
total absorption of singer and subject which is the Orphic
model.

One poem which does seem fully formed is "How I Died,"
in which each line speaks naturally of the way in which our
consciousness of mortality allows us to inhabit our dying and
thus live fully, with little remorse, in the condition of pure
becoming: "Orpheus found the world was entering into him /
as if his limbs were caverns in which hung / the disk of the
sun." Every poem in the collection contains lines of equal
power: "He had fallen / out of the progressions of time"; "the
dead have become one / and we are among them, / differing
only / in the memory of our perished beauty." These lines
have the excitement of thought that William James spoke of
in his lectures on mysticism in *The Varieties of Religious Experience*, where he refers to lyric poems as "irrational door-

ways . . . through which the mystery of fact, the wildness and the pang of life, stole into our hearts and thrilled them." James goes on to say, however, that lyric poetry (and music) are vital and meaningful "only in proportion as they fetch these vague vistas of a life continuous with our own." In the finest lyric poetry this continuity is itself enacted in the art of the poem, where what James elsewhere calls "auroral openness" is sustained, a condition not quite sustained in Mr. Hunt's book.

Kenneth Fields's *The Odysseus Manuscripts* also treats myth and legend, but I think that before writing the poems Mr. Fields more fully internalized the form of ancient story. His poems, most of them drawn from Homeric material, are deliberate; that is, they are products of deliberation. They do not so much represent thought in process, or meditation, but rather the condition arrived at after such meditation has taken place. Perhaps because our literary culture has become so accustomed to poetry that catches life on the quick at any cost, Mr. Fields's poems may strike some readers as being unusually even-tempered, even when they speak of horror. The odd blend of fear and equanimity is unsettling, and something rare in our poetry.

The first poem in *The Odysseus Manuscripts*, "Athene: The Owl," is proof of the inward turn Mr. Fields urged on himself in an earlier poem, "Imperative" (in *Sunbelly*, 1974): "Leave off / Following the old sun for a little while. / Within, there is another; to the source / A quiet brother, humming as you hum." Athene is the straight way of wisdom, the complex of deliberation, justness, and value that both oversees and issues from the hundred ways of Odysseus. She is "The quiet voice within, / not the loud word above." (In another poem she is characterized as "the daughter, not the mother" of Odysseus's choices.) Athene is the norm of wisdom against which other more extreme kinds of knowledge may be evaluated, just as Odysseus is the human center around which the stories of other personages are constellated. Achilles, for example, now among the shades (in "Achilles in the Underworld") is a figure of memory outside the margins of time. He spins off, for Odysseus's benefit, fragments from his great life—his wrath, his "opulent withdrawal," the death of Patroklos:

> These are mere fragments, only parts of speech,
> Each moment fading in the fading reach
> Of past and future: through the breathless air
> Slowly these shades appear, then disappear;
> And we conclude our stories to no one.

His is prideful mourning for a life defined by warrior custom. Now in Hades' house, cast from the world of action and sensation, from the competitive field of *arete*, the great chieftain is so stricken as to say that the life of a peasant would be superior to the ghostly noncontinuity of the Underworld. Anything would be better than his doomed condition, anything that transpires in time: "We are what we are in time, not in these grim / Explosive symbols: bright, like you, then dim." The Achilles poem has a companion piece, "And Elpenor," in which the drowned sailor tells Odysseus that he and the other lost sailors depend on the tribute of memory. Achilles, in his poem, did not ask to be remembered. Elpenor, however, worries about fame: "I think my name here is . . . forgetfulness. / See that I'm not forgotten, Captain." His voice singularizes the general complaint of the lost crew (whose speech opens and closes the poem). Their final words to Odysseus, however, come as a threat:

> Beware,
> Honor us in your memory, and tell
> Our stories, set our oars along the shore
> And make your living mind our cenotaph.

These poems are followed by another thematic pair having to do with temptation. "Come: The Sirens" is the finest poem in the book. Its premise is that whatever nourishes most fully also consumes, that the most extravagant promise of gifts threatens to absorb and obliterate the acceptor. Calling to

Odysseus, the perfect voices ask him to see the sun's reflection in the water as the most fabulous shield in antiquity, "Achilles' little world," desirable because it exists without labor and does not change. Their song is an incantation of Allness and is thus a devouring promise. All history is rolled up in their song: "Everything that happened at Troy, everything / That has or will ever happen, everything / We know, and will tell you. We know everything, / So let us tell you." If he surrenders, Odysseus can free himself of all custom, the habit of mere becoming, the containments and definitions of reason, will, desire. The fullness of being they promise, however, is annihilation, the dissolution of intellection and hence the renunciation of Athene. They will give him "The Alpha and Omega of the world: / The perfect story." In the desire for knowledge, Odysseus would have to dissolve himself as knower. The Sirens' "perfect story" is oblivion. In the companion poem, "Just Afterward," Odysseus recalls his trial and makes it clear that he would have given himself over to the powers. He also realizes, though, that he would have lost the sensuous delight he takes in the world of process which he quietly celebrates in the poem's first line: "The bones in the flowery grass / are beautiful." Of all the heroes of antiquity, Odysseus was the one most privileged with a wide range and variety of experience, so that his opportunities for choice—for exercising the different faculties—were plentiful and various. His capacity for choice, and the consequences of choice, figure in some way in nearly every poem.

Between the two Siren poems occurs a short lyric, "The Ear of Being," intended to evoke Odysseus's ecstatic (and gluttonous) response to the Sirens' song. The poem never really passes beyond mere description of Odysseus's surroundings in that charged moment of passage, except perhaps for the final line: "I am the Center of a Single Ear." There are other lyrics in the collection, some only two lines long, which strike me (like "The Ear of Being") as preliminary studies for larger poems. They arrive as brief notes tenuously linking one poem

to another. The thematic pressure created by the longer
poems, however, is so strong (and the narrative continuity
generally so seamless) that the shorter lyrics are disruptive. I
would even suggest that Mr. Fields may be aware of these limitations. His long poem "Adrift" gives some evidence of this.
There the sprung surprise, the abrupt unveiling proper to
epigrammatic poetry, is adjusted slightly to serve a larger purpose. Odysseus considers what he left behind in Ithaka and
what he might expect to find on his return. His attempt to
think this through is shaken and disrupted by intrusive pictures, the accumulated unstrung images of his journey:

> And when my son, a baby, called my name
> *my own   or a gods fabulous bestiary?*
> And when I was a young man. Only my hair,
> *seaweed   or hemp?*
> Surprising me momentarily into time

The poem seemed to me at first a mere virtuoso piece, with
its odd turbulent manner. But by the end of the poem intention and manner fuse to dramatize Odysseus's attempt not
only to prepare for his homecoming (he's filled with vexed
nostalgia) but also to prevent the tearing apart of history and
nature. "Adrift" ends as a prayer or invocation that his homecoming be a return to nature and mortal history, to normalized relations, out of the trackless wandering of his journey,
the metamorphoses, giants, and monsters of voyage. Ap-
proaching home, he welcomes the cycles of change that in-
here in nature's patterns:

> I can ripen toward the gods, in their native time,
> *here is no time   no place*
> Can love the consequence of living there,
> And woven back into nature
> *where I can die*
> Can take delight in her
>   beautiful, aging face.

The anticipation culminates later in "Stringing the Lyre" when Odysseus, claiming his bow, is restored: "The old man runs his mind along the bow, / Familiar after nineteen years." The form-making mind, not the sensational eye, is crucial to his restoration.   [1982]

A SOMETHING OF SELF:
BYRON'S LETTERS

In the two concluding volumes of *Byron's Letters and Journals,*
A Heart for Every Fate (1822–1823) and *For Freedom's Battle*
(1823–1824), we have the final definition of the man Goethe
called the First Gentleman of Europe, and the gentlemanly
qualities of discretion, business sense, decorous compassion,
wit, and self-possession are all on display. The letters take up
shortly after Shelley's drowning near Viareggio and follow
Byron through the acrimonious break with his publisher
Murray, the composition of the later cantos of *Don Juan,* the
contributions to Leigh Hunt's new journal *The Liberal,* and the
endless tedious preparations for the last journey to Greece as
chief envoy for the English Committee in supporting the
Greeks in their war of independence against the Turks.

Many of the letters Byron wrote between October 1822 and
his death at Missolonghi in April 1824 were addressed to his
banker and business agent Douglas Kinnaird, and the subject
is money in all its transfigurations—taxes, patrimonies, royal-
ties, letters of credit, investments, and the like. The object of
these busy financial maneuverings was the Greek expedition,
and Byron was brilliantly single-minded in generating cash
badly needed to shore up the unstable situation in Greece. He
was no stranger to political intrigue; a few years earlier, during his stay in Ravenna, he had been closely involved with the
Carbonari. (Excerpts from the Ravenna Journal are included
in the *Selected Letters and Journals* [1982], a judicious and useful sampling that Leslie A. Marchand, Byron's most astute
biographer and the editor of the letters, has drawn from the
now completed series of eleven individual volumes.) But the
late letters make clear that Byron was quite consciously trying
to make himself over into a more intensely practical personality. The Greek rebellion offered him a ready-made context

163

in which he might redefine himself, be *of use*, perform an act of self-overcoming. The tone of these letters is no less mercurial than that of the earlier letters, but there is much less of the flamboyant theatricality and flair for self-dramatization which had made him the somewhat hideous darling of British and European society and which caused so many readers to see Childe Harold and Don Juan as figures for Byron himself. The voracious sensualist whose fiery accounts of wild Venetian nights were a measure of his self-absorption begins to take a more critically objective view of himself.

As Byron's commitment to the Greek cause grew more intense, his erotic adventures cooled and were replaced by a deepening favor for friendship. His "love perils" are now pretty much over. In a letter of October 10, 1822, he writes with gentle flirtation to Lady Hardy that "a man and a woman make for better friendship than can exist between two of the same sex—but *then* with the condition—that they never have made—or are to make love with each other. Lovers may (be)—and indeed generally are—enemies—but they never can be friends—because there must always be a space for jealousy—and a something of self in all their speculations." Because of his high origins Byron had greater cause than most to worry about his use in life, and we can see that worriment take shape as he notches his life into five-year stages. He certainly could not fall back upon his activity as a poet to justify his life (he would have mocked the very idea), and no amount of high-spirited joking about his love of money and leisure can disguise his deeper anxieties about energies wasted in cultivated idleness. In a journal he kept during 1813–1814 he wrote: "At five-and-twenty, when the better part of life is over, one should be *something*;—and what am I? nothing but five-and-twenty." Perhaps the last thing we expect from Byron is envy, but it is strongly present whenever he speaks of Burns who, had he been born a patrician, "should have had more polish—less force—just as much verse, but no immortality." Five years later he is still worrying the need for self-restoration. Because of his unusually privileged indulgence in sense and appetite, Byron found it more difficult than any other Romantic artist to unify the intellectual and practical life once those youthful passions had been exhausted. On July 18, 1823, he writes to Kinnaird from Genoa: "I always looked to about thirty as the barrier of any real or fierce delight in the passions—and determined to work them out in the younger ore and better veins of the Mine—and I flatter my-self (perhaps) that I have well done so—and now the *dross* is coming—and I loves lucre—for one must love something."

In 1813 Byron wrote to Annabella Milbanke—his marriage to her in 1815 would last only one year—that the great thing in life was sensation, "to feel that we exist—even though in pain—it is this 'craving void' which drives us . . . to intemper-ate but keenly felt pursuits of every description whose prin-cipal attraction is the agitation inseparable from their accom-plishment." That same year he declared in another letter that poetry is the product of sensation and therefore does not rank very high on the scale of intelligence. Eight years later he was still insisting that poetry is almost exclusively "the expression of *excited passion*." He would not allow for the pro-cess of contemplative deliberation in the making of poetry, that methodical testing of all the faculties which made for the "organic sensibility" so celebrated and valued by Wordsworth and Coleridge. Like Byron, the young Keats (in 1817) was in-tent upon a life of sensation rather than of thought, but within a short time Keats arrived at the more mature, com-prehensive view of poetry articulated by Coleridge, that com-position calls the entire Soul of man into activity. Keats and Byron make an odd pair in any historical view. The stable-keeper's son and the patrician, the tragic lyricist and the comic poet of human failings, Shakespeare's challenger and Pope's admirer. Some of Byron's most searing remarks are aimed at the poorly educated Keats, at his "*p-ss a bed* poetry," his "*Onanism* of Poetry," his "viciously soliciting his own ideas

into a state which is neither poetry nor any thing else but a
Bedlam vision produced by raw pork and opium."

Keats's earlier attack on Pope hardly explains Byron's vitu-
peration; more is going on here than a literary disagreement
on the value of one predecessor. However much Byron fashioned himself a rebellious literary bad boy, he found something in Keats's poetry that either outraged his inbred sense
of good manners or piqued his envy for a kind of noisy, savage, rude genius. He admired this quality in Burns, who
wrote a more sociable poetry than Keats and whose ambitions
were not nearly so grandiose. Byron's letters, like those of
Keats, are peppered with quotations from other writers; but
whereas Keats's attention to literary ancestors was largely the
angry affection of a student for vibrant, threatening teachers,
one who internalized and alchemized his reading in order to
school his own art, Byron's manner of quoting other poets is
often rather supercilious, the mark of a well-lettered gentleman. Keats was hungry, Byron was merely acquisitive, at least
until his decision to go to Greece. At that point there are more
and more references in his letters to *Henry IV, Part I*, the story
of the young cunning profligate whose public history becomes
an emblem of moral self-conquest, of heroic self-definition.
Some of Byron's most moving and tortured verses were written in his journals at the time of the Greek expedition. In a
fragmentary lyric of 1823 he writes: "The Dead have been
awakened—shall I sleep?" And the opening stanza of the last
verse entry in Missolonghi (which Mr. Marchand sets as an
epigraph to the final volume of letters and journals) puts
plainly Byron's need to ennoble and revitalize his power to
love by discovering a new and worthy object for his love:

> 'Tis time this heart should be unmoved,
>   Since others it hath ceased to move:
> Yet though I cannot be beloved,
>   Still let me love!

Byron's insistent notion of poetry as the product of volcanic
excitability (he says he was "half mad" when writing the third

canto of *Childe Harold*) was tempered by his more practical attitude toward actual composition. While his letters were often designed to shake or undercut his reader's expectations, they express sincerely enough his notion of writing as a habit, a normalized pastime, and his image of himself as a slightly world-weary practitioner. His remarks sometimes have the sound of self-instruction, or admonition, as if cautioning himself against the very engulfment he elsewhere so eloquently describes, and like many poets he defines his own position by reacting against those held by others. His salvoes against Wordsworth, the "Arch-Apostle of mystery and mysticism," usually serve this purpose. Writing June 1, 1818, to his good friend, the Irish poet Thomas Moore, Byron remarks on a comment made by Leigh Hunt: "Did you read his skimble-skamble about [Wordsworth] being at the head of his *profession*, in the *eyes* of *those* who followed it? I thought that Poetry was an *art*, or an *attribute*, and not a profession." By 1823, when all his energies were being directed toward the practical demands of the Greek expedition, he was insisting all the more on writing as quotidian custom: "I continue to compose for the same reason that I ride, or read, or bathe, or travel— it is a habit." Though he confesses that it is also hard work, "a task and a painful one."

Wary of what he felt to be Wordsworth's intellectual self-indulgence, Byron was equally suspicious of the allegorical strain in Romantic thought which regarded human circumstances as an emblem of spiritual activity, and he did not share his friend Shelley's patient, deliberate curiosity about the nature and functions of consciousness. He reckoned himself one "who thinks much, rapidly—perhaps deeply—but rarely with pleasure." That quickness and restlessness, however, finally account for much of the charm and forcefulness in his letters, which are dashed off, *hurled* at their recipients, full of ellipses, offhanded observations, odd curves of attention, and that aggressive common sense which in so many British writers lacking Byron's great fire and generosity becomes torpid, boring, trivial. The letters are testimony to Byron's admiration for

Pope and the celebrated values of neo-Augustan rhetoric—
strong sense, sententiousness, caustic satire—at the necessary
expense of sustained analytical or speculative attention. Byron ignites his opinions like matches: a bright flaring, a
tweaked extinction. On the Greek situation: "When the limbs
of the Greeks are a little less stiff from the shackles of four
centuries—they will not march so much 'as if they had gyves
on their legs'." On political personages: "A bad minister's
memory is as much an object of investigation—as his conduct
while alive—for his measures do not die with him like a private individual's notions, he is matter of *history*." On patriot-
ism: "Though I love my Country—I do not love my Country-
men—at least such as they now *are*." On social values: "In
England the only homage which they pay to Virtue—is hypocrisy."

Although Byron clearly enjoyed the good fellowship and
imminent danger which the Greek situation offered, he became increasingly disillusioned and cynical about the motives
of those who professed ideological causes, literary men and
Greek partisans alike. The Suliotes, the most volatile of the
Greek factions and the one to which Byron was instinctively
drawn (they made up his swaggering, colorful bodyguard),
exploited his generosity at every opportunity. He complains
in his last letters that the Greeks want of him only "money,
money, money," which is not entirely surprising since Byron
himself reckoned his income to exceed that of the president
of the United States. The later cantos of *Don Juan* turned
rather bitter, their portrayal of human corruption less gay
and endearing, so much so that his publisher pleaded with
him to "let us have your good humor again and put Juan in
the tone of Beppo." That return, however, was obviously
closed to Byron once and for all. The journey to Greece, his
public commitment to a nationalistic cause, was his final act of
self-exile from which he might have emerged, like Prince Hal,
a more finely articulated moral being and certainly a different
kind of artist.   [1983]

ON TRANSLATION: A REPLY
TO HANS MAGNUS ENZENSBERGER

In 1983, *Northwest Review* published a "Translation Sympo-
sium," for which a number of translators were asked to reply to a statement from *The Consciousness Industry* by Hans
Magnus Enzensberger, published by the Seabury Press in
1974. What follows are Mr. Enzensberger's remarks (in italics)
and my response to them.

*In the few decades that have passed since the stormy year of 1910,
modern poetry has established its dominance throughout the world. Its
poets have established a rapport among themselves that has lifted the
national barriers of poetry as never before and given the concept of
world literature a lustre inconceivable in other ages. . . .*

*This supranational trait finds exemplary expression in the careers
of a number of writers. In 1880 a certain Guillaume-Albert-Vladi-
mir-Apollinaire Kostrovitsky was born in Rome; the register of births
contains an entry under the name Guillaume-Albert Dulcigni. The
child's mother, born in Helsinki, came of a Polish-Russian family; the
father was a Sicilian named Francesco Constantino Camillo Flugi
d'Aspermont. Throughout his life Guillaume Apollinaire, as he later
called himself, wrote in French, like the Lithuanian Oscar Wenceslas
de Lubicz Milosz, the Chilean Vicente Huidobro (who also wrote in
Spanish), the black poet Aimé Césaire from Basse-Pointe, Martinique,
and the Alsatian Jean Arp, who signs his German poetry Hans Arp.
The Peruvian Vallejo died in Paris, the Turk Hikmet lives in Moscow
as a Russian citizen, and the American Pound lived in Italy. Super-
vielle, who was born in Uruguay, was a citizen of both hemispheres.
The Chilean Neruda wrote his poems in Djakarta, Mexico, Madrid,
Paris, Buenos Aires, and Moscow. The Greek Kavafis was born in
Constantinople, educated in England, and spent his life in Egypt.
The list can be continued almost indefinitely. A person setting out to
claim poets such as these for any one country would find himself in no*

small dilemma. Today it is less possible than ever to demand of poetry
a passport. . . .

Only in the twentieth century has "world" become the prefix to every
productive and destructive possibility: world war, world economy,
world literature—in earnest this time, in deadly earnest, and as a
condition of survival . . .

This conversation, this exchange of voices and echoes, is becoming
more and more obvious, and one has only to place side by side meta-
phors, cadences, techniques, and themes from a dozen languages to
become aware of this. In other words, the process of modern poetry is
leading to the formation of a world language of poetry.

In the old imperial railroad stations of American cities the rituals of departure are determined by systematically arranged
architectural zones. In Philadelphia, one descends from the
huge marbled light of the terminal into low-ceilinged cloisters
where the passenger trains arrive and depart alongside grim
narrow platforms. In Chicago, one passes from the echo
chamber of the old Union Station terminal to a bare, square-
pillared waiting area, then out onto cluttered poorly lighted
platforms where from no point can one see the entire length
of any train. Here, as elsewhere, only ticketed passengers are
allowed trackside. The actual departure of trains is pretty
much shut away from view. Passengers say good-bye to
friends and relatives in the genial light of a terminal where no
humming diesel intrudes. The platforms serve as efficient de-
compression chambers, landing stages, set apart from the
emotional complexity of greetings; they are, in a sense, privileged spaces, unpublic. In Italy, departures are not segre-
gated in this way. The terminals are public spaces where the
activities of both the transient and the settled mix and spill
one into another. Passengers, personnel, vendors, cabdrivers,
tour guides, and waiting friends and relatives swarm and min-
gle around arrivals and departures, a kind of public theater
at trackside, an accessible and commonly shared experience.
An Italian friend once said to me that rail terminals have had

a traditional specific attraction for poets and intellectuals and that you can *feel* those affections not only in their work but also, somehow, in the places themselves.

This is not to say that Italian stations are in any way better or more humane than our own, but they are surely different, their feeling-tone and function determined by different social and political forces. The human surround is crucially different, and so the tone of human encounters is also different. There is both a melancholy and a festiveness that many Americans visiting Italy find delightfully strange, and these feeling-tones are in part the result of historical circumstances which Americans find likewise strange. Italian trains have carried occupation armies, have been blown up by nationalistic terrorists, have sheltered refugees (and political exiles and peasant bandits), have become a grotesque historical joke because they were once made to run on time, and they cross frontiers. Vittorio Sereni's poem "Winter in Luino"—Luino is Sereni's birthplace, a town on Lake Maggiore—ends on these lines:

> I will leave when the wind
> slams against your shores;
> the waterfront people know it's hopeless
> to try to protect the transparent days.
> At night searchlights chafe the land,
> the town rimmed by sleepless fires
> wandering through the countryside,
> a muffled uproar of distant
> trains nearing the frontier.

If the full understanding of poetry requires integral completion of feeling, I am not sure that any American, myself included, can ever fully understand this poem, mainly because the quality of feeling released by its language has been shaped by political and social currents unfamiliar to us. Or is a train merely a train, a sign everywhere equivalent? Can any Western European fully understand what Whitman says about railroads, the mechanized plow that carved up our own early frontier? Could an Italian catch the feeling-tone of one of our own cultural facts, that in the nineteenth century many travelers paid for the sport of shooting at random into buffalo herds from the windows of passing trains?

Because I am not as enthusiastic about internationalism as Mr. Enzensberger clearly is, I cannot share his enthusiasm about a world language, a transcendent poetic idiom everywhere equivalent. His examples of poets who cross or transcend national borders are too exclusively chosen. What of William Carlos Williams, Rocco Scotellaro, Wallace Stevens, and Eugenio Montale? Each led a comparatively settled life, each set apart in his own time from literary schools and movements, each resolutely independent from what Mr. Enzensberger calls a world language of poetry. (Nor did they regard themselves as "professional poets"; Montale in particular liked to speak of poetry as *dilettantismo*.) Local custom, idiom as determined in part by regional dialect, cranky temperament, all the heterogeneous strains that make up a country's literary traditions—these are not reducible, should not be reduced, to any homogeneous world language or international style. The private life of poetry should not be curtailed or constricted by the apparent exigencies of public transmission.

I do not think that an international style serves the essential enterprise of translation, so much of which is aimed at redeeming and conserving as best as possible what is most provincial, idiomatic, and eccentric in foreign poetries. To conserve, in other words, the individualizing nuances of thought and feeling which make good poetry in a sense unworldly and noninternational—the textures and evocations of Montale's Ligurian shorelines, the Lucanian paganism of Sinisgalli, the Piedmontese hill mysteries of Pavese, the spectral trains of Sereni, Gatto, and Penna. And there is a practical reason for resisting all calls to a world language. Recent communications technology has brought about an increasingly standardized presentation of data and events. Its reductive milling process strips experience of nuance, suggestivity, feeling, and histori-cal resonance. Poetry resists such standardization, resists being reduced to a communications product, a foreign trade item or export good. Pound may have behaved like a cultural impresario but his translations are alert to the irreducible strangeness of the original, such that his methods still strike us sometimes as mere crankiness. Several years ago, Montale (who translated Emily Dickinson, Thomas Hardy, and several other poets) told me that he felt a translator's job was to find equivalents in his home language for the otherwise intractable materials in the original, even though true equivalents were often difficult or impossible to find. If a translator fails, better to fail at ideal conservation than to allow poetry's localized energies to dissipate into stylistic amiability.

I once asked a Brazilian friend of mine to help me read some poems by Carlos Drummond de Andrade. We had on hand some translations done by two American poets, none of which satisfied him. He explained that Drummond de An-drade's poems often bear—in tone, diction, form, attitude—values associated with his upper-middle-class background and in particular with the mining country he hails from. "It's a kind of *iron* poetry," he explained. "Hard and dry, but gritty, laconic, not at all tropical. It's peculiar and singular, certainly not representative of Brazilian poetry but only of one of the provinces of Brazilian poetry." Translation, when it fails, ought to fail through obscurity or overmuscled awkwardness, not through reductiveness. Drummond de Andrade is just one more foreign poet who is in danger of becoming a North American citizen, one who writes a poetry virtually indistin-guishable from that dehydrated, homeless international mode practiced by some of our own poets.

If a world language is espoused in this country, it will sooner or later seep into the university curriculum where it comes to be taught as a "contemporary convention." The pro-cess has already begun. A few years ago Richard Pevear, writ-ing in *The Hudson Review*, saw the situation taking shape:

young people in writers' workshops who read widely in translations done in a world language or international style are themselves influenced by that style (or nonstyle); they claim it as their own and Americanize it. They become influenced not by poetry but by a translation *product*. Thus a rootless, denatured style comes to be accepted as an American style. Back of this stands the desire to become internationalists. Lacking a naturalized style, they seek a poetic identity by other means, usually by choosing odd subject matter. This has led not only to the cult of idiosyncratic subject matter in our poetry but also to forced or strained regionalism, nativism as a last resort. I don't think young writers should be encouraged to become literary brokers in the marketplace of communications technology, and translators should not contribute, unknowingly or otherwise, to that encouragement.   [1983]

SOUTHERN

Somewhere in his *Autobiographies* Yeats refers to Keats as one of the "great lesser writers." The heavily embroidered textures of Keats's poetry, especially in the later odes and sonnets, were an expression of his powerful hunger for the lush, diverse appearances of things; and this hunger, this specialized aspiration, was rooted in his personal history. Deprivation produces a proportionate desire to value, perhaps too much, the voluptuous mass and colorings of the visible world. Yeats's famous image of him in "Ego Dominus Tuus" as a schoolboy with his "face and nose pressed to a sweet-shop window" is followed by this judgment:

> For certainly he sank into his grave
> His senses and his heart unsatisfied,
> And made—being poor, ailing and ignorant,
> Shut out from all the luxury of the world,
> The coarse-bred son of a livery-stable keeper—
> Luxuriant song.

His genius lay in his passionate restoration of the thick beauties of physical reality, a compensation for his youthful deprivation, and Yeats valued him for precisely this sensuous music. He was among the lesser poets because his metaphysical inquisitiveness was not equal to his desire to evoke the forceful immanence of the visible world. Unlike Spenser, the young Keats did not quite possess the patient rhetorical conviction of allegorical romance that might have allowed him to dramatize the more finely demarcated zones of metaphysical reality. *Endymion*, for all its small, local passions, lacks moral persuasiveness and thoughtful nuance; it is, in its way, too literary, too much a mere exertion of ambition. The "Ode to a Nightingale" and "The Fall of Hyperion" are great poems, major poems, because of their patient and fully impassioned calibrations of states of being, more than simply states of feeling.

175

A major lyric poet is one who not only explores in a sustained way, but who also tries to determine and *place*, the graduated registers of actual and metaphysical reality, and who is willing to assert the precise relations between the worlds of the living and of the dead, the relations between the here-and-now and the *aldilà*.

In modern Italian poetry the most insistent definer of relations is Eugenio Montale, and the publication in 1981 of Rebecca West's good critical study of the poetry, *Eugenio Montale: Poet on the Edge*, has begun to make clear to American readers the extraordinary range of registers that Montale commanded. We tend to think of him as the premier Hermetic poet, and yet his famous "*tu*" poems are grounded in social relations, relations which in poems like "*La primavera hitleriana*," "*Il sogno del prigioniero*," and the later lyrics in *Diario del '71 e del '72* and *Quaderno di quattro anni*, become explicitly political in content. Because of Montale's achievement, the fine lesser poets of the subsequent generation are too soon eclipsed by his long shadow, especially when the machinery of publication in America can "process" only translations of a few select poets. The quality and volume of translation defines for us the dimensions of foreign poetries. For Italian work, the cultural lag is usually about fifteen years, sometimes much longer, as in the case of Guido Gozzano, a very important poet active early in the century (and a deep influence on poets of Montale's generation) whose work only recently was presented here in Michael Palma's excellent translation, *The Man I Used to Be*. The translators most responsible for introducing us to distinguished Italian poets who might otherwise pass ignored are Ruth Feldman and Brian Swann. Their several books have gone a long way toward filling out and rectifying the sometimes misleading anthologies by Carlo Golino (*Contemporary Italian Poetry*, 1962) and Robert Lind (*Twentieth-Century Italian Poetry*, 1974), which for a long while were the most accessible points of reference for readers interested in modern Italian poetry. Those anthologies, like Lawrence

Smith's recent volume *The New Italian Poetry: 1945 to the Present*, are useful introductions to the variety of Italian poetry but they also erect critical categories—Crepuscularism, Hermeticism, Experimentalism, Classicism, and the like—which inevitably distort individual achievements. (Montale himself was quick to ridicule "isms" of any sort.) Feldman and Swann have not been guided in their choices by such arbitrary categories. Their selections are for the most part carefully edited, and the translations are idiomatic, accurate, and properly adjusted to the tone of the originals. If there is any bias in their choice of poets to translate, it is toward poets of the south, the *mezzogiorno*, as much an economic designation as a geographic one.

As commentary on the mysterious values and character of the Mezzogiorno, Carlo Levi's *Christ Stopped at Eboli* (1945) has become, in Italy and elsewhere, almost legendary. Exiled for antifascist activity from Turin to Gagliano, a small village in the southern province of Lucania, the cultured northerner discovered a region where Christ never passed, where rites and customs seemed to antedate the colonializations of antiquity and where Roman Catholicism survived as a fragile and not always identifiable flower of pagan roots. The peasants of the Mezzogiorno are traditionally poor tenant farmers exploited by absentee landlords. The terrain is rocky and mountainous, or arid and dusty, with scattered patches of arable land. Centuries of deforestation have turned once woodlands into barren scrapland. Organized efforts to rescue the Mezzogiorno from its traditional poverty, usually through massive industrialization and land reform projects, have failed miserably, while the government in Rome since World War II has continued to collapse and reconstitute itself, each new coalition government offering a plan for "renewal" of the southern regions. Years of neglect and widely publicized failure have made the people of Lucania and other areas hard, independent, cunning, xenophobic, and suspicious of all promises. Levi, a doctor and artist from the north, found himself suddenly a stranger in his own country. One episode in *Eboli* could stand as a sign for the enterprise of poets hailing from the south. The summer heat in Lucania was so suffocating that Levi was finally forced to find refuge from the sun in the local graveyard, where freshly dug graves provided a shaded nesting spot for noontide contemplation. Each day he would climb down into the cool pit, stretch out, read, nap, die a little, then resurrect himself and return to the life of the village.

Resurrection and return are the two strong themes of southern poetry. Several notable poets of the Mezzogiorno (Bartolo Cattafi and Leonardo Sinisgalli are the best known) left to pursue professional careers in Rome or the industrial centers farther north, and the pull of nostalgia is strongly felt in their poetry. Even poets like Bodini and Scotellaro who did not emigrate to the centers were bound to feel a degree of cultural estrangement from their sources, their pagan origins. The nostalgia that draws them back often takes the form of a withdrawal into the earth where Levi found repose, a willed surrender to absorption, obliteration, with a shadowy promise of resurrection.

The will to return, and to define oneself in terms of the desire to return, is Vittorio Bodini's most compelling subject. The desire is manifested as an urge to bind himself to the objects of his attention and, in a familiar Romantic way, to lose himself in that conjoining, surrendering reason and will to the landscape, to orange and lemon trees, tobacco patches, blood moons, goats. The yearning, always crepuscular in tone, is most strongly felt at sundown, "the worst hour / in which to die alone." "Finibusterrae," one of the poems in *The Hands of the South* (a selection edited and translated by Feldman and Swann, published in 1980) offers Bodini's most concentrated vision of a place where day's end fuses with land's end, where the landscape swarms with fugitive images of closings, retreats, "women collapsing in flight / in doorways." Twilight is the small terminal combustion of a country too notorious for its long history of defeats, internal strife, and unstable governments: "Italy, / you end meanly in a small riot / of waters at the foot of a lighthouse."

Bodini (1914–1970) was born in Bari and his poems are often set in the Salentine Peninsula, the heel of the boot, with its famous Bourbon legacies and its tufa houses in villages thick with the details of poverty and waste, images which fill Bodini with affectionate outrage:

> Here there were academies
> and most learned monks:
> O glorious cities
> of filth and abandon!
> In the mornings manless women
> suckle their babies on doorsteps
> or comb their hair endlessly.
>> ("In the Salentine Peninsula")

Sensitive to the dispossession he sees (and the displacement he feels) in southern locales, Bodini writes two different kinds of poems in order to clarify his own equivocal feelings. In a poem like "Moon of the Bourbons" he is the tough-minded modern pastoralist trying to see into the interfusedness of things and enter into that unity of all matter in which simple human loneliness might dissolve. He values such oneness over Christian individualism, and his vision is consequently earth-bound. There are none of the volatile signs of transcendence that one finds in Montale. Bodini is spokesman for the down-warding of things, for immanent blendings and absorptions:

> I live now in the things my eyes can see:
> I become olive tree and wheel of a slow cart,
> hedge of prickly pear, bitter soil
> where the tobacco grows.

He writes other poems, however, which answer and beat down these prideful assertions:

> The ivy tells me: you'll never
> be ivy. And the wind:

you won't be wind. And the sea:
you won't be sea.
        ("Simple Song of Being Oneself")

To define himself as what he is not, as that which is painfully
not anything else, is Bodini's least happy activity. He does not
want to be told by things, "try to be yourself / without us. /
Spare us your love." The argument is one he himself makes,
of course, and yet he also knows that solipsism is no useful
alternative: "I try to stay alone. I find / death, fear." If love of
things—of those olives, oranges, goats—is finally self-serving,
the lover is bound to be punished accordingly for his selfish
piety. The landscape takes its own revenge: "Green boredom
kills / idolatrous hearts."

Modern Italian poetry is a history of different breeds of an-
tieloquence, formal departures from the hendecasyllabic line
(more or less the historical equivalent of our blank verse line),
renunciations of vapid gorgeousness, skeptical attacks on solipsism and poetical self-regard, and deliberately roughed-up
styles drawing on regional dialects. Bodini was a distinguished
professor of Spanish literature, a translator of Cervantes,
Lorca, Alberti, and others. Lorca's influence has left heavy
scorings on the surfaces of his poems, particularly the Lorca
(Bly's leaping Lorca) who opens the poem to alien objects that
suddenly present mysterious correspondences between odd
disjunctive pieces of reality. One of Lorca's small but evocative
poems, "The Moon Rising," is a good example:

When the moon rises
the bells go quiet
and small paths
loom thick and closed.

When the moon rises
the sea covers the earth
and the heart becomes
an island in the infinite.

> Nobody eats oranges
> under the full moon.
> You have to eat
> fruit that's green, chilled.

> When the moon rises
> with its hundred identical faces,
> silver coins
> sob in your pockets.

The oddly considered events—coins sobbing, earth inun-
dated, moon faces multiplied—are really intimate valuations
of moonrise, mental events shaping and loading each stanza
with its own measure of feeling. The dartings of apparent unreason find their reason in the formal balance of elements in
the song; the instinctual figures released by Lorca's remarkable associative powers are situated, localized, in the completed
figure of the poem.

Bodini, too, intensifies feeling by such leaps, arcs which give
shape to apparitions and numina indigenous to his native
ground:

> The trees were nourished by the eyes
> of mournful birds. All light
> had disappeared from the sky
> when among tree trunks I saw fleeing ghosts
> burst forth, their breasts pierced
> by visible arrows, which they tried
> to tear out as they ran.
>   ("The Trees Were Nourished by the Eyes")

His poems become less passionate, and more mannered,
when their surrealist quirks arbitrarily disfigure reality. (This
willful disfiguration is the legacy of Spanish surrealism so apparent in our own poetry.) The wild veerings of attention
among alien objects, the violent surprise of correspondences,
are so heavily *laid on* that the verse turns wooden and a paralyzing estrangement sets in between concept and emotion. If
the splitting or shattering of familiar light becomes the norm

in a poet's practice, surprise is likely to be extinguished or
made dully habitual:

> All the clocks in your house
> are restless flowers,
> or pulse with temples of lemons
> in fruit dishes, in the rooms' dark.
>   ("Olvido")

Surrealism can abruptly reveal the fossil fires of the psyche, a
diabolism crazily released into intelligible forms. In its deca-
dent application, as mere technique, it produces just another
kind of local color, gaudy exoticism for its own sake, coy and
titillating perhaps in its disfigurements, but in the end a feckless sort of literary dandyism.

Both manifestations are present, and at loggerheads, in
"Tobacco Leaves." In one section of this poem Bodini is so
busy with distortions that his passionate statement sounds
contrived and studied:

> The lunar shell hardly
> raises false mountains that look murdered
> and a dull shining on the rails,
> your name, full of teeth, begins to cry
> in the shadow, and bites in the throat
> the palm tree and the church of the Rosary.

Later in the same poem, however, once he has found his
theme of loss and restitution, once his method has been naturalized and situated in a recognizable mental locale, he
writes the most powerful lines in the book:

> When I went back to my Southern village
> where everything, every instant of the past,
> resembles those terrible dead men's wrists
> that spring each time from the clods
> and, unappeased, eternally tire the spades,
> I understood then why I had to lose you:
> my face was made here, far from you,
> and yours—in other countries I can't picture.

These lines have a peculiarly southern sense. In *Eboli*, the village grave digger who discovers Levi one afternoon in his hideaway, tells him, "The village is built of the bones of the dead." To the old man, a wolf tamer before he became a grave digger and hence a man who had mysterious power over animals ("though he could not wield it over women"), all the emblems of life and death, the bleached bones poking from old graves, are a daily presence in the quite ordinary configuration of reality: "The bones, the dead, animals, and spirits were all familiar things, bound up as indeed they were to everyone in these parts with simple everyday life."

In the Preface to the 1963 edition of *Eboli* Levi speaks of Rocco Scotellaro as one "who is dear to me above all men," and I think most readers of *The Dawn Is Always New* (1980), another superb collaborative effort by Feldman and Swann, are likely to feel similar affection for the personality that emerges from the poems, though this affection is certainly not necessary to an appreciation of the work. Scotellaro was born in 1923 in Tricarico, a small town in Lucania. Unlike many artists and intellectuals of the south, he did not emigrate to the metropolitan centers but remained in his hometown and in the spring of 1946 was elected its first Socialist mayor (and the youngest mayor in Italy). All his poems, written between 1940 and his death in 1953, were published posthumously.

Scotellaro's critical reputation in Italy is still not so secure or distinguished as those of some of his less interesting contemporaries. His poetry has not appeared in many of the standard anthologies of postwar verse. According to Geno Pampaloni in his 1974 *Il sindaco poeta di Tricarico*, Pasolini found the poems mere entertainments too closely modeled on Levi's radical politics and derivative of the work of Scotellaro's fellow Lucanian Leonardo Sinisgalli. Other critics view him as a "case," a cultural oddity, the peasant poet engaged in small-town politics who never broke loose from provincial culture. These prevalent attitudes led Franco Fortini, in his Introduction to *La poesia di Scotellaro*, in 1974, to refuse to promulgate "the myth of the peasant poet" and "the legend of the little poet-mayor."

That "little" calls up all the patronizing attitudes that mandarin literary culture assumes toward a figure like Scotellaro. These attitudes have in turn endorsed false or hurried assumptions: that Scotellaro grew up in rank poverty (his father, a shoemaker, earned a modest living, the family was not dirt poor); that he was so steeped in the rituals and habits of provincial culture, *lived* that culture, that he could not fully mature as an artist (thus equating provincial art with arrested development, metropolitan art with maturation); that his learning was makeshift and eccentric and therefore inadequate to a mature literary artist (he had a classical convent and *liceo* education, studied the Greek and Roman authors, and struggled like other modern Italian poets with the great predecessor Leopardi, another "provincial"). When he completed his university education, at an age when most young writers would flee the provinces for the cultural buzz of big cities, Scotellaro returned to Tricarico and threw himself into all the administrative problems involved in running a municipal government. In his very good Introduction to Feldman and Swann's translation, Dante Della Terza describes the stress inherent in Scotellaro's position. He had to mediate between the landowners, who now found themselves divested of direct political control and who perceived in Scotellaro an "educated" man they could manipulate, and the peasants themselves who saw in him an ally, a country son who readily shared their company and invited their counsel in running his administration. This tension was increased by the internal needs felt by the poet. As Della Terza describes it: "We have on the one side the epos of the deprived, on the other the devastating autobiographical utterance of a Southern intellectual from a peasant family, torn between his allegiance to a reality in need of modification, and the ancestral needs of the family clan."

For many southerners the "capital" is Naples—Della Terza

calls Lucania "no more than Naples' extended back yard"—
and Scotellaro, who spent three years there near the end of
his life, inevitably felt ill at ease in a town which, then as now,
was sick with fatigue, decay, political corruption, and poverty.
Naples had also been the launching point for southern emigrants departing for the legendary New World shores. In
"First Farewell to Naples" Scotellaro catches that mood of estrangement and bartered hopes felt by so many emigrants
(his own father had made a brief voyage to America). He is
not taking off for the New World, however, but preparing to
return to Tricarico. He is no less a "foreigner," with his bag
of mountain possessions, passing through an alien place that
could never become home to him. His feelings about returning to Lucania are mixed. If the province is the open space of
his soul, the free air beyond the bleak confines of the big city,
within that free space is another kind of enclosure, another
cell:

> I'm going back to my dark hole of a village
> where we're jealous of one another;
> I'll pass a sleepless night waiting
> for the little houses whitened by dawn.
> And yet it is a cage suspended
> in the free sky, my house.

The keeper of the cage is the matriarch, and Scotellaro's
affection for her is complex and strained. His freckled face
bears the marks she imprinted before his birth. (In my own
family we still warn a pregnant woman not to rest her face on
her hands lest the pressure mark the unborn child's face.)
And she controls her son by withholding affection: "I see you
always straining / to rob me of a little affection. / You who
never accustomed me to caresses." He instinctually responds
by withholding his own love for the seamstress mother who
raised him "under the Singer's violent wheel." Only when his
double unexpectedly arrives—his father's bastard son, also
named Rocco—does the natural son begin to care for her. His

love is born of jealousy and self-protection, and I think it is
fair to say that this helps to define him as a son of the South
("where we're all jealous of one another").

In the small cage of the household, the father is a striking,
animated presence, and Scotellaro's affection for him is more
forthright and unequivocal. The father, selling his "expertly-
made shoes / at dust-choked fairs," is impetuous, cunning, ar-
dently opposed to governmental authority, a man who dies
suddenly without ever making peace with the world. He also
has some mysterious violence in his past which confers on him
a menacing nobility:

> Once he spilled
> a bastard's guts.
> It happened on a night better forgotten
> and when people asked him about it
> he screwed his eyes up angrily.

The knife he used is probably the same he now keeps hidden
up his sleeve "for the tax-collector's belly." The village cob-
bler, in other words, is at least half bandit, and in his small-
town way he is a barely domesticated version of the southern
outlaw. Banditry in the Mezzogiorno has by tradition been associated with the politics of poverty, and for the young activist
Rocco, who would later spend some months in prison falsely
accused of embezzlement by his political enemies, such a father could be a useful and fortifying model.

Scotellaro's fearlessness is edged with the bitterness of a native son who sees the land made barren—"the fleshless land
of parcelled-out patches"—and peasants humiliated for generations by mean tenant farming. (It is the bitterness and anger we hear in Danilo Dolci's 1966 *Conversazioni contadine*.)
One of his most disturbing poems, "Capostorno," takes its title
from a brain disease that strikes horses, cows, sheep, and
dogs, causing intense intracranial pressure that brings on fits
of dizziness and disorientation. Any other poet might have
played this subject for its nightmarish possibilities—Hardy

might have turned it into one of his rural parables—but for
Scotellaro it becomes an occasion for addressing actual economic circumstances, the cruel reality of which is sharpened
by an almost hallucinatory vision of poverty and hard-scrab-
ble farming which endure even under a provisional land reform program which doles out small plots of land (*quote*) to
peasants (*quotisti*):

> They've set the mountainsides on fire
> with oil-torches;
> they convoy the mule-train
> among the mirrors of stones and fens.
> They are the famished owners [*quotisti*]
> on their night march.

Only at the end of the poem does the title fully emerge. Sheep
feeding on malarial estuary grass feel their brains about to
burst:

> Seized by the staggers
> they chase their tails,
> banging their heads against stones and tree-trunks,
> the way peasants lose the horizon
> in the dark of night.

A poet of Scotellaro's practical moral intelligence and clear
hard vision of actual human suffering needs no surreal disfig-
urations to heighten speech. The small world of modern *con-
tadini* that he writes about is already so characterized by real
moral distortions and real physical deformations that his chief
objective in many poems is to bind his anger and fondness to
visionary anecdote—visionary in a way similar to Yeats's "Par-
nell's Funeral," grounded in recognizable historical-political
situations.

The date in the title "Black Puddle: April 18" refers to the
first postwar general election in 1948, when Scotellaro's Socialist party was defeated by the Christian Democrats, whose
victory was in large part bought by American dollars which

not only paid for thousands of votes but which also helped
win broad support from the clergy, the "black" element. The
triumph of the Christian Democrats meant that the movement for land reform which claimed so much of Scotellaro's
time and energy would probably be discreetly ignored or crip-
pled in endless parliamentary deliberations. The time when
the bosses and landowners, the *padroni,* dispensed food to
peasants and day laborers would have been a brief holiday:
"That day we were all brothers, / we had bonfires and band /
as on holidays." Soon enough the peasants would be left to
their traditional isolation and impoverishment. Scotellaro's
outburst in the closing lines of this remarkable poem has a fire
which I do not think any liberal patrician poet, however *im-
pegnato,* could achieve. The "we" in the following lines is no
rhetorical self-regard:

> And if death drowns us
> no one will be with us,
> in sickness and bad luck
> no one will be with us.
> They've barred the heavy doors to us;
> the ravines are flung wide open.
> Again today and for two thousand years
> we'll wear the same clothes.
> We're still the mob,
> the mob of beggars,
> the ones who rip off the bosses' masks
> with our teeth.

ITALY'S REGARD for the New World has been made up of
nearly equal measures of infatuation, despair, and cynicism.
Like so many reformist intellectuals, Scotellaro was troubled
by the tides of emigration begun in the late nineteenth century that had practically emptied southern villages of men-
folk. In 1898 Italians constituted the largest immigrant group
to America, and by 1927 there were already nine million Italians living abroad, three-and-a-half million in the United

States and millions more in Brazil and Argentina. Denis Mack
Smith, in *Italy: A Modern History*, tells this story: When the Italian prime minister visited the small southern town of Moli-
terno early in the century, the mayor welcomed him "on behalf of the eight thousand people in this commune, three
thousand of whom are in America and the other five thousand waiting to follow them." After the twenty years of Fas-
cism, the American liberators brought with them a renewed
image of the American character. America was not just a place
of wealth and military might, it was also a rich cultural re-
source. Cesare Pavese and Elio Vittorini were among a number of Italian writers who translated, and transmuted into
their own fiction, the work of Fitzgerald, Faulkner, Heming-
way, Whitman, Lewis, London, and others. An Italian friend
of mine once described the almost magical hold that John
Ford's westerns had on the imagination of leftist intellectuals
after the war. Those rough and ready mule drivers, frontier
gamblers, and scouts—men of conscientious action—were
imaginative models for independence, self-reliance, self-de-
termination. As it had been at the turn of the century, America still was not so much a locale as a state of mind, still *"bella,
lontana,"* beautiful and far away. One attribute defines the
other: beautiful in large part *because* far away from the familiar grinding limitations on promise which Italians, southerners especially, had accepted as cultural and economic deter-
minants.

The dream of America began to fade quickly enough in the
postwar years, and Scotellaro was sensitive to the shift in relations. In a poem written in 1951, "There Was America," he
compares the land his father had visited briefly many years
before as a twenty-year-old with the present frayed remnants
of that vision. His father was among the hundreds of thousands who returned to Italy after testing their chances in
America. The American promise was not so all-absorbing and
compelling as the statistics I quoted earlier would have us be-

lieve. That older America, his father's America, "managed to
break his heart." In a sense he was lucky to return:

> My friend died shot down in that land;
> they put wax on his face,
> a wax face just like his.
> They came back from so far away
> with a house and a vineyard
> for a bed of straw.

There's a deep ambivalence in Scotellaro's attitude toward the
New World. The last thing he wanted was an Americanized
Italy. As a Socialist it was a matter of faith that an Italian
political-economic situation required an Italian solution and
that cultural crossbreeding was liable to interfere with reform.
But he was also so much the conscience of his people that he
knew how the minds of several generations of landless peasants and destitute tradespeople turned instinctually toward
the American dream. The closing lines of "There Was America" repeat a refrain from the opening:

> *America qua, America là,*
> *dov'è più l'America*
> *del padre mio?*

> America here, America there,
> where is it now,
> my father's America?

The lines are childlike, almost a nursery jingle, but the playful
innocent nostalgia is darkened considerably by the realization
in the poem that there really should *not* be any more escaping
to a place, any place, where the faces of the dead are waxed
in a debased simulacrum of nationality, and that any notion
of redemption outside local circumstance, outside the historically determined situation of the Mezzogiorno, is bound to be
a barren, useless, and finally humiliating aspiration.

   The most orotund and declamatory of Scotellaro's poems,
and one which demonstrates (if proof be needed) his consid-

erable rhetorical skills, picks up the theme of emigration. "Psalm to the House and the Emigrants" is a rhapsodic cry of uncertainty and despair for the sons of the south whose fathers are constantly leaving home to find work elsewhere. The poem was written in 1952, so it is no longer only a remembrance about the lure of America but a statement of the new emigrations north to the industrial centers of Milan and Turin during the Boom years (a story told in Luchino Visconti's *Rocco and His Brothers*), and a fore-vision of the new displacement of southerners to Switzerland and Germany which Ann Cornelisen so movingly describes and analyzes in her book *Strangers and Pilgrims*. In the poem, Scotellaro gives voice to the puzzled anger of the sons who are left behind:

> Bowed to the earth, at the small worn house-door,
> we are the sons. The door is soaked with other sweat,
> and the land, our portion, stinks and smells.
> Let them kill me, let them arrest me. I'll die of hunger,
>   stifled,
> because under the door's edge wind and dust burn the
>   throat;
> no other woman will love me, war will break out,
> the house will collapse, mama will die and I'll lose my
>   friends.

The doorway, the threshold where this historical drama is played, is a figure for crossings, departures, estrangements, and it is also quite literally a frame for life in southern villages. Sinisgalli's Lucanian poems present the same kind of "framings"; Gramsci writes in one of his letters from prison about Sardinian women who spend the better part of their lives sitting in doorways; Paul Strand's famous photograph "The Family" is a classically composed image of this way of life. In Scotellaro's poem the doorway framing the generations of departing fathers and isolated sons is finally a black-bordered requiem announcement:

You are leaving too, fathers of the land, leaving
the door-edge blacker than black smoke.
What gleam of hope for the children you've sired
when they go to bed in the evening?

One of Scotellaro's clearest memories (which like so many
others is an explicitly historical-political one) is of the ninety-
year-old *garibaldino* in his town. His portrait of the man who
fought among Garibaldi's *Mille* is composed of two contradic-
tory overlapping figures: he is "an old ox soaking up the sun"
and a "*statua di neve*," a snow man. The helpless old warrior,
carried outside on a kitchen chair and spoon-fed by his niece,
was a kind of plaything for the child Rocco who played hide-
and-seek ducking under the old man's big wool cloak. For
what he embodies as history lived, event still warm with consequence, the *garibaldino* is "warmer than an ox in the stable."
But for his silence, the magnificent aloofness which would
soon melt away without having revealed anything of what he
knows to the boy, the aging monument is "colder than a snow-
man." Scotellaro's presentation is fairly plain, almost ingenuous, but the form-giving intelligence behind the poem that
enjambs these two ways of "receiving" history is anything but
the good-natured innocence suggested by the title "peasant
poet."

I have done some injustice to Scotellaro's genius by concentrating so exclusively on the poems of public, "social" content.
He wrote many brief evocative lyrics as well. One of these,
"Sea of Mist," left among a large group of poems in Levi's
possession after Scotellaro's death, is a strange vision of an
inland sea, symbol of voyaging (and so really not too far removed from the themes of the political poems), streaked with
the poet's grim taciturn humor. The sea is only mist, an apparition, but this natural transfiguration allows for a rare moment of things interfused:

It's the morning mist
and the highest mountains with their villages—

what slim peninsulas!
Its edges shatter
against the villa's pines.
The olive trees breathe.
It's true: the sea
illuminates the land.
Backbones of mountains
touched by the light winter sun.
You can see the shining pool
that becomes our stream.

Scotellaro's political and artistic ambitions come together in "Manifestos," one of his few poems about poetry. The jubilant tone verges on panicked abandon, the need to spread the word, to toss from his window his letters to the world, hurling his "paper manifestos / from the high attic-window in the desert / of roof-tiles." It is a liberation, but a dispersal too, and a feckless one, since his messages mainly serve the "deadly pillaging" of the trashman. The peasants who might read and learn from the manifestos are still bound by their historical situation; they "eat dust / but fear for their eyes." The poet's papers ("good only for trampling") will jam and pile up just outside those familiar doorways of peasants' houses. Scotellaro's last thought is one of equivocal promise: "But if there's wind—what a whirling!" If agitated, his words will spin into wild flurried activity—activity dizzied, purposeless, impotent, undirected, unreceived. That final possibility, that appearance of busy activity, is uttered with such blind enthusiasm that its hysteria points up all the more the rocky irony of consequence. The whirling of papers in the wind, new trash outside locked houses, mocks the profound intentions of a poet like Scotellaro, who knows that even while he writes in the current of tribal history, giving voice to genuine historical need, he is yet writing against history, against the future.

[1984]

FOUR NOTIONS
ABOUT J. V. CUNNINGHAM

1. "Fierce Impersonal"

One agenda of English and American poetry was spelled out early in the century. Eliot insisted that poetry was an escape from personality. Yeats wrote: "All that is personal soon rots; it must be packed in ice or salt." Frost contrived cunning impersonations as a strategy against personalism. Crane wanted visionary speech. There were several reasons for this: to purge from poetry Yeats's "bundle of accident and incoherence" that sits down to breakfast; to make poetry a purer expression of value uninhibited by the accidents of personality; to revise the legacy of psychologizing passed down by the Romantics; to infuse, after the achievements of Swinburne, Browning, and Tennyson, a more quickened, ironic, Nietzschean fire into poetry. J. V. Cunningham's statement of like ambition, his valuing of the crystalline forms of verse scrubbed of mere personality, comes in the last stanza of "L'Esprit de Géometrie et L'Esprit de Finesse":

> I know such men
> Of wild perceptions.
> Conceptions
> Cold as the serpent and as wise
> Have held my eyes:
> Their fierce impersonal forms have moved my pen.

Cunningham liked to say that his poems were few and short. (The 1971 Swallow edition of *The Collected Poems and Epigrams* runs to 142 pages.) Most of them are driven not by wild surmises of feeling or by the devastating (and distorting) assertions of will, or by the "violence of reason." His is the middle ground between the two impassioned biases, between the extreme claims of reason and sensation. He did not have

anything like Yeats's phantasmagoria, those ancient forms
and figures which the poet could drive toward renewed symbolic meanings. Nor did he have the equivalent of Stevens's
mental landscapes, dioramas where the pressure reality exerts
on imagination could be dramatized as scenes in a pageant.
Cunningham, desirous of excluding personalism from his
work, had lesser means, stricter and more deterministic ambitions, and smaller stanzas.

And yet he would often write about the way the will seeks
to make over the object of attention into an image of itself.
The will, driven to conceive then conduct itself to its own pro-
jected images, its loves and delights, will lead us into a solipsism at once the worst and most natural imprisonment of
thought and feeling. The terms of that bondage, and possible
escapes, help define Cunningham's poems. In "The Beacon"
he tells of the distant landmarks that contrive the cool objects
of meditation in his work, the cold impersonal forms that
make him write: "I praise / Far lamps at night, / Cold landmarks for reflection's gaze." He glossed the lines himself:
"Men give their hearts away but cannot pass judgement on
this act so long as they construct the object of love according
to their desires, for the will takes pleasure in begetting its own
image. I on the contrary choose an object other and distant, a
cold landmark toward which contemplation looks. The object
remains apart, but let us hope that in time it may be possessed."

2. "Exclusions of a Rhyme"

It's difficult to sound generous when describing Cunningham's poetic gifts. A plain style. A puritan discipline for worrying the consequences of pleasure. A Roman Catholic terror
of (and attraction for) the Absolute. Brevity. An austere
speech whose power lies in impassioned denials. Definition by
exclusion. Brevity. A belief that practice proceeds from definition, so that no definition, no outline of figure, gets redrawn
or revised in the process of composition.

His quest for the expression of pure impersonal forms persuaded Cunningham to give up much else. The minute particulars of lived experience, the specific sensations by which poets articulate our place in the order of nature, the details of memory's chronicles, these are often absent from his poems, cooked away by the desire for abstract summative declaration, for gnomic or aphoristic assertion, rhetoric (that is, persuasion) normally taking precedence over description and evocation. And in many of the earlier poems, like "Obsequies for a Poetess," "Lector Aere Perennior," and "Fancy," one hears very little of actual speech, the spectral cadences of the spoken language, the suggestive quotidian idiomatic turns that bear forth the changefulness of language. This particular kind of clearance or purification of language sets him apart from even a poet like the Crane of *White Buildings*.

The stanza for Cunningham is a little furnace where all the grit and frivolous impurities of language get burnt off. The stanza is a discipline, or habit, of denial; its brevity dramatizes all the exclusions that preceded the casting of the lines into their fixed form. One pays a price for such discipline (which loosens up in a few of the late poems). Cunningham's familiarity with, and consequent suspicion of, the unpredictable movements and flashing obliterations of sensuous experience causes many of the poems to be emptied of the circumstances of sensation. The poems get abstract, are too unflinchingly arrived at. The famous "For My Contemporaries" is a model of one aspect of Cunningham's art: the poem has no interest in enacting the process or strain of self-reclamation, of redefinition. It simply presents its conclusions:

> But rage who will.
> Time that procured me
> Good sense and skill
> Of madness cured me.

To a poet like Cunningham, the exposure of a mind quarreling with its own dearest assertions would probably seem in-

decorous, and faintly shameful. In choosing to write a particular sort of poetry (does the work of any other contemporary
so clearly bear the stamp, the impress, of the determining
choice?), a poetry so forcefully shaped by what it chooses to
exclude, Cunningham knowingly surrendered much: a Horatian delight in rangy, high-spirited talk; a dramatic mixing
of tonal registers and idioms that one finds in Catullus; Ovid's
densities of physical experience. These were among the authors he knew best, along with the Elizabethans, and so his
choice was informed as well as deliberate. But one of the
strangenesses of his poems is that they unembarrassedly wear
all the marks of their own energetic decisiveness, the scorings
of harsh, clear definitiveness. And so they remind us that a
conventionalized skepticism, a nurturing of our capacity for
ignorance, has become perhaps too unchallenged an assumption in much of our poetry. That we have become, in other
words, too mindlessly proud and accepting of "being in un-
certainties, Mysteries, doubts, without any irritable reaching
after fact and reason." Cunningham's work scrubs that.

3. "Of Madness Cured"

It's certainly an odd sort of realization Cunningham presents
in some of his poems:

> Let us not live with Lear,
> Nor ever at extremes
> Of ecstasy and fear,
> Joy in what only seems,
> Rage in the madman's hut
> Or on the thunderous hill,
> Crying *To kill, to kill!*
> Nor in a blind desire
> To sire we know not what
> Ravish the eternal Will.

The exhortation formulates the perilous extremes we are
urgèd to abjure. The poem is so neatly put, and so spare, that

its rhetoric persuades us that the poet has indeed known the
enticements of extremes and has resolved to deny them. The
substance of the exhortation has been determined before the
poem begins; its lines are an engraving of the formula. Cunningham does not "work through" things. One of his most
constantly enacted refusals was that of Wordsworth's plasticity
of form. In "Ripeness Is All" the stately certainties of holding
to the mean, to normative measures, are impeccably delivered
in those trimeters. Yet back of this poem, and of even more
steely ones like "A Moral Poem," there is a second voice, an
unhappy prickling drone inside the apparently tight-shut
stanzas. That second voice (the first metrical disturbance in
the lines above come with the quickened stress on "Joy" and
"Rage") repeats another phrase of Lear's spoken much earlier
in the play: "O, let me not be mad, not mad, sweet Heaven!"
Quiet terror rears up in other poems as well. The beautifully
composed description of the wheat crop in "August Hail" is
disturbed by the one question in the poem: "Who shall revenge unreason?"

4. "Handpump in the Sink"

One waits in vain for unguarded moments or reckless disclo-
sures in Cunningham's poetry. The arbitrary, wilder notes
have all been sung before the poem gets made. In some of the
later poems, however, we do get moments of trouble, de-
rangements, the "falling ember that unhinged Pascal." Cunningham was the least prodigal of speech among his contemporaries. Even compared to Louise Bogan, with whom he had
so much in common, Cunningham's remains the more austere and astringent practice. The most troubling exclusion
from his work is that of the particularized world of circumstance. The stress of the object world against our imaginings
is a contest, an unhappiness, that Cunningham must have ap-
preciated, but in so many of his poems he had no interest in
the drama of contact between the mind and the minute particulars of the physical world. I have not read his essays on

Stevens, but I cannot think he agreed with Stevens's conten-
tion in "The Noble Rider and the Sound of Words" that "the
subject matter of poetry is not that 'collection of solid, static
objects extended in space' but the life that is lived in the scene
that it composes: and so reality is not that external scene but
the life that is lived in it." I say Cunningham would have had
a hard time accepting this because in his poems often the human scene comprised of circumstance is bled of its particulars, its realizations. But this is not the whole of his art.

One appeal of Cunningham's work is its calm, deliberate
form so candidly presented, so unapologetically self-possessed
even in the presence of terrors. If he does not show the religious excitements of Hopkins, Herbert, or Yeats, he was nonetheless a religious poet in his analysis of the resolute contemplative self-possession won only *after* suffering excitements.
"Timor Dei," "To my Daimon," "Choice," "This Tower of
Sun," and "Montana Pastoral" are distinguished by the tension of enthusiasm held in check, wrestled down momentarily
in form. The announcement of discovery at the end of "Montana Pastoral" is like a powerful beast momentarily staked to
the ground:

> So to this hour. Through the warm dusk I drove
> To blizzards sifting on the hissing stove,
>
> And found no images of pastoral will,
> But fear, thirst, hunger, and this huddled chill.

The later poems—"The Aged Lover Discourses in the Flat
Style," "To My Wife," "Monday Morning," and the master-
works "Montana Fifty Years Ago" and "To What Strangers,
What Welcome"—are his finest achievements not because
they serve up "physical details" ("the front door locked and
nailed, / A handpump in the sink"), which consequently make
the poems more "real" or dramatic. It's because without dis-
engaging those rational powers which make the other poems
so severe in their determination, Cunningham also calls into

the struggle of the poem the figures of circumstance, the stuff of speech, the quickening of sensation and desire.

One of Cunningham's most forceful traits was his capacity for profound ironic concern. In "To What Strangers, What Welcome," that mind, still possessed of its ironic concern, yet construes "in disordered fantasy" the rasping passion of loss. Even while the mind of the poet knows itself to be a fabricator and arranger of images, knows that its will seeks love objects made after its own shape, that mind enacts the stages of suffering from the initial journey (or migration) to love, through loss, to the return in constant memory of that love, and that loss.   [1984]

ON JAMES WRIGHT AND THOM GUNN

In 1962 James Wright wrote an essay with the unlikely title "The Delicacy of Walt Whitman." Seeded in that essay are notions that eventually blossomed in Mr. Wright's own achievements as a poet. He says, for example, that as a stylist Whitman "did not begin as a solitary barbarian (in Ortega's sense of the word). He is many things that are perhaps discomforting and even awkward, but he is not a smug fool—he is not an imitation Dead End Kid pretending that no poet or man of any kind ever existed before he was born upon the earth. Whitman realizes that the past has existed." He is also speaking for himself. There are elements of the American Primitive in Mr. Wright's poems, in their colloquial diction, intensely regional subject matter, sometimes unsavory anecdotalism and attraction for the grotesque. But he realized that the past existed. Like Whitman he was candid, cunning, receptive, and refused to be embarrassed by his enthusiasms. Back of those enthusiasms stand years of diligent study, a discipline quite evident in the essays and reviews he wrote during the late fifties and throughout the sixties. These, along with excerpts from his early Ph.D. dissertation on Dickens and interviews from the seventies, are available in the *Collected Prose* (1983), edited after his death by Annie Wright. In the writings, especially the earlier work, he was clearly trying to define a position for himself as a poet, an articulated space for his activity, even when his remarks seem innocently descriptive. When he speaks of things he values as a reader of poetry, we know he is holding to these same qualities in his own work. Generally, he is more precise (and provocative) in the writings than in the interviews. He writes with terrific freedom and aggressiveness, without sacrificing delicacy or nuance; and he does not seem to care what others might think of his remarks. In the later interviews, this changes. His tone softens, he is less assertive of his judgments, he seems to want to be liked.

With this change in manner—the *poetry* didn't become any less independent as he got older—there creeps into the interviews a notion which is only faintly prefigured in the essays and which has become a literary commonplace related perhaps to the ironclad humility celebrated by so many poets of my generation. With Mr. Wright, whose mind was so precise and keen to historical changes, the question is more troubling. (I also realize that none of us is innocent of generalization, especially when we want to drive hard an idea that matters to us.) It first appears in a note on his translation of Hermann Hesse's poetry in 1970, just when he had pretty much ceased to write prose: "This is what I think Hesse's poetry is about. He is homesick. But what is home? I do not know the answer, but I cherish Hesse because he at least knew how to ask the question." This is a little too passive and unquestioning a judgment. Poetry does, or ought to do, more than ask questions clearly. The question of home, of habitation, of finding one's power place, like the questions "What is belief?" or "Where is the Divine?," are already largely formulated by our place in the world as circumstance has helped determine it, by our singular presence as mindful, rational, self-controllable, essentially disordered creatures painfully aware of otherness. I don't believe it is the office of poetry to resolve and conclude such questions—this would result in a poetry of moral sentences and righteous orthodox definitions—but I do feel that the role of poetry is at least to answer to, respond to, the pressure of, such questions as arise from our mindful suffering in nature, without denying or ignoring the mysteries of this condition. To view poetry as reply or answer (not wistful questioning or resolution) is also, practically speaking, a guard against solipsism. Nostalgia was one of Mr. Wright's subjects. We are such a nation of once homeless (and still homeless) populations that this is bound to remain a central subject in American verse, but it need not be a vainly or idly evocative one. Mr. Wright, in some of his poems, settled for the inarticulate sentiments of homesickness. But he wrote other poems, especially those in his posthumous volume *This Journey*, in particular the poem "Apollo," which are a tremendous answering to the question of spiritual homecoming.

A unified ambition stood behind Mr. Wright's career, and I think it is summed up in his Horatianism. On several occasions throughout his life he affirmed what he called Horatian unity and wholeness as an ideal in his work. In his 1978 interview published under the title "Poetry Must Think," he puts it this way: "I believe in the 'whole' of a poem and the subordination of style to some wholeness of structure and some wholeness of vision about the nature of things." Not far removed from this is his reassertion of Dr. Johnson's belief in the superiority of "just representations of general nature" over the eccentric singular case. But the most important thing James Wright ever said about his own ambitions was said by him about Thomas Hardy, in a review written in 1961 but published for the first time in the *Collected Prose*: "A great poet possesses what I might call the religious imagination. He can see local and private details within a vision of the entire creation; and the facts of his personal experience include some kind of order, some tragic pain and the courage it evokes, and some kind of glory."

FOR A POET as reserved and private as Thom Gunn, the essay can be doubly important as a means of self-declaration and definition, especially since he chose to reprint in his collection of essays *The Occasions of Poetry* (1982) only those pieces which represent his position on poets who matter to him. His subjects are, among others, Hardy, Greville, Jonson, and William Carlos Williams, and his essays on these poets are never chatty or rambling, though they do have a charm that consists not in the slurred banter of personality but in scholarly attentiveness and rigorous curiosity. Mr. Gunn's ideas come clear quickly. He is concerned above all with clarity and efficiency of diction in poetry because diction is the instrumentation of moral value. The book gets its title from a remark in his essay on Jonson, that all poetry is necessarily occasional, "whether the occasion is an external event ... or an occasion of the imagination, or whether it is in some sort of combination of the two. (After all, the external may lead to the internal occasions.)" In a sense, Mr. Gunn has been for a long time now our most seventeenth-century poet, carrying over into his verse some carefully modified notions of decorum, measure, wholeness, and occasionality which had their most eloquent apologist and practitioner in Jonson. He sees these conventions still alive and generative even in some unlikely modern instances. He can admit to William Carlos Williams's aspiration, stated so candidly in the early poem "Tract" to bring *everything* into poetry: "Nothing shall be ignored. All shall be included." But he also sees into Williams's art and reveals its historical grounding, which Williams himself admits to on numerous occasions in his essays. Of "The Farmer," from *Spring and All*, Mr. Gunn says: "The poet organizes, plants, and meditates on what he has planted, 'in deep thought.' In spite of a hint at the organization of art, a hint that is undeveloped, the poet could as well be from the seventeenth century as from the twentieth." His most crucial statement on moral quality is also occasioned by a Williams poem, "By the road to the contagious hospital." He says that the felt particularity of observation in a classically ordered pattern leads naturally to a general feeling on the reader's part: "A perfect accuracy of description, by means of which the world is both mastered and lived in, becomes thus a moral perception."

Reading these essays, which include a few brief, even-tempered, and sometimes very funny autobiographical pieces, you are easily persuaded that Gunn has thought long and hard about what he needs and wants to say. The formulations he applies to others characterize his own art, revealing the assumptions on which his own practice is based, so he measures his statements carefully. Of Jonson's classicism he writes: "it is interesting that most of those who have succeeded best in writing so, i.e. within restraints both technical and passional, have been people most tempted toward personal anarchy. For them, there is some purpose in the close limits, and there is something to restrain." One of Mr. Gunn's most frequent subjects in his poetry is the shape and contingency of excess, of the need to find a form to contain personal anarchy. He has written many poems about social, cultural, and sexual anarchy; his preferred form has been rhymed meters. "Flooded Meadows," the poem in which he speaks most forcefully about "the unity of unabsorbed excess" in all of nature, is a sonnet. A later poem, "The Bed" (from *Jack Straw's Castle*), is short enough to present here:

> The pulsing stops where time has been,
>   The garden is snow-bound,
> The branches weighed down and the paths filled in,
>   Drifts quilt the ground.
>
> We lie soft-caught, still now it's done,
>   Loose-twined across the bed
> Like wrestling statues; but it still goes on
>   Inside my head.

The fullest treatment of this theme is the remarkable poem "Sweet Things" from his new collection *The Passages of Joy*. Mr. Gunn, needless to say, does not disdain artifice. It is one significant means of truth-telling: "What we must remember is that artifice is not necessarily the antithesis of sincerity."

[1984]

THE CINQUE-SPOTTED SHADOW:
COLERIDGE'S *BIOGRAPHIA LITERARIA*

Writing to Robert Southey in 1794, Coleridge said that he increasingly felt the need to ground his poetry in philosophical principles, "a *body of thought*,—hence my Poetry is crowded and sweats beneath a heavy burthen of Ideas and Imagery!" That burden is one of the distinguishing characteristics of the remarkable poems he wrote in 1797 and 1798. "Frost at Midnight," with its pantheism, its pursuit of the One diffused in the Many, certainly bears the philosophical burden that Coleridge both desired and worried over. There are a few lines in that poem which are for me among the most mysterious in their effects, where the poem seems momentarily free of the self-imposed obligation to philosophize. When that weight is lifted, it is as if Coleridge's nerves take over. He sets himself at the almost untenable center of a tight weave of forces. Sitting in his cottage, he is alert to the suspense of things outside—the frost, encroaching but "unhelped by any wind," the night silence pierced by an owlet's cry—and tense also with the arrangement of the near world his own mind is construing. His family has gone to bed, though his child Hartley sleeps by his side. The air, agitated by its own quiet, "vexes meditation with its strange / And extreme silentness." From the center of the tightening network of outer and inner life come these lines:

> Sea, hill, and wood,
> This populous village! Sea, and hill, and wood,
> With all the numberless goings-on of life,
> Inaudible as dreams.

The three sorts of landscape are marked off into discrete units which click through Coleridge's mind so that the world of external nature can be defined and contained. No sooner

does he fix this arrangement than he unmakes it, melts and
revises its neat organization into the more impassioned and
amorphous, less willed and categorical, procession of sea *and*
hill *and* wood pouring one into another till they become the
continuous ground for the countless hidden goings-on of life.
That first naming shows Coleridge's mind in its active discrimination and individuation of things outside itself; the second shows his powers of synthesis, the fusion obtained by passive submission to many-ness, to the indistinguishable. But
from final dissolution in silence and dreams, from the narcotic sea of undifferentiated impressions, Coleridge is called
back by one small thing of the world, the "thin blue flame"
that lies motionless on his fire. And his attention is renewed
by the fire-thing that *does* move, the "stranger" fluttering at
the grate:

> Methinks, its motion in this hush of nature
> Gives it dim sympathies with me who live,
> Making it a companionable form,
> Whose puny flaps and freaks the idling Spirit
> By its own moods interprets, everywhere
> Echo or mirror seeking of itself,
> And makes a toy of Thought.

In his encounter with the small thing seen and his instinct
to read the particulars of sensuous life by the mind's moods,
Coleridge gets caught up not only in viewing his own mental
operations but also in explaining them. In his few great
poems he worries these matters with an intensity that only
Keats and Shelley approach. Even in the lines I quoted earlier, apparently numb, scene-setting details bear the full force
of what his contemporaries felt was the most commanding,
restless, promising, ambitious mind of his generation. The
better part of Coleridge's life was spent mediating, or devising
explanations that would help him to mediate, the encounter
between self-consciousness and the natural world, and in

trying to construct a philosophical system that would satisfy, as he said many times, both his heart and his head.

The systematized presentation never took place. Its fragments lie scattered across hundreds of pages of articles, lectures, letters, notebooks, marginalia, and table talk. The self-censored skittishness of his career, his legendary inability to complete his "projects," his intense moral self-awareness that only increased his inertia, his habit of re-saying something he thought important—all these traits stream through those strangely repetitive lines above. In Coleridge's temperament there is a lurching, almost foolhardy aggressiveness blent into tentative, wobbling self-assurance. Sometimes his mind strikes out with the superior but damaging strength the infirm force their few actions to carry. "Frost at Midnight," "Kubla Khan," "Christabel," "The Nightingale," and "The Rime of the Ancient Mariner" came at a time when Coleridge, not yet thirty, was still able to concentrate all his considerable philosophic and artistic gifts on verse composition. But those few years proved to be just a momentary stay against other impulses, aspirations, and bad luck. The self-containedness and discipline which would have helped him to go on writing poems with the peculiar mode of attention (totally self-absorbed, totally *other*) that a poet needs to sustain his work, dissolved into years of confused ambitions, domestic upheaval, literary makework (though there was the heroic effort to concentrate his attention with *The Friend*), restless travel, and endless talk. When he emerged from those hard years, he came out talking. The result was the *Biographia Literaria*.

Coleridge was forty-three when he began dictating that book, and although he was famous, his career already seemed an almost incoherent series of misfired or wild-shot intentions. He was always getting ready to do something, or writing something while he was gearing up to write something else, something bigger, more systematic. The *Biographia Literaria* is an impossible book, inspired, irresolute, mercurial, untrustworthy, packed with other men's ideas, but driven at every

stage by Coleridge's singular (and, for some readers, endearing) self-postponing self-devouring obsessiveness. In a sense,
the best description of it came from Keats, in a letter where
he is in fact talking about his meeting Coleridge:

> I walked with [Coleridge] at his alderman-after-dinner pace
> for near two miles I suppose. In those two Miles he broached
> a thousand things—let me see if I can give you a list—Night-
> ingales, Poetry—on Poetical Sensation—Metaphysics—Dif-
> ferent genera and species of Dreams—Nightmare—a dream
> accompanied by a sense of touch—single and double touch—
> A dream related—First and second consciousness—the dif-
> ference explained between Will and Volition—so many
> metaphysicians from a want of smoking the second con-
> sciousness—Monsters—the Kraken—Mermaids—Southey be-
> lieves in them—Southey's belief too much diluted—a Ghost
> story—Good morning—I heard his voice as it came towards
> me—I heard it as he moved away—I had heard it all the in-
> terval.

Keats wrote that in April of 1819, four years after Coleridge commenced the *Biographia*. Madame de Staël, who had
met Coleridge in 1813, described him as a monologuist, not a
conversationalist. He charmed listeners and drew their love,
but he had little sense of social propriety; his talk was that of
a man more possessed by than possessive of his anxious need
to fill silence. The *Biographia* is a register of that sort of compulsive speech. Into its pages Coleridge talked literary history
and opinion, metaphysical speculation, practical criticism,
personal grudges, advice to writers, and much else, all of it
justified by the subtitle "Biographical Sketches of my Literary
Life and Opinions." It is one of the many dissonances or "dis-
harmonies" of the book that while Coleridge claims to be writing it in order to set down "fixed canons of criticism, previ-
ously established and deduced from the nature of man" so
that literary judgment could be saved from "the arbitrary dictation and petulant sneer of book reviewers," those canons are

never established in detail, and the philosophy on the nature of man is postponed.

Coleridge's mixed intentions help us to understand the odd form of the *Biographia*. It was to be a crucial stage in clarifying his philosophy, in part by reviewing its development. Like Shelley and Blake, he struggled after some reasonable alternative to the mechanistic and materialist systems of the eighteenth century. As a young man he was so claimed by Hartley's theories of association that he named his son after the philosopher. But Hartley, Priestley, and Locke drove the ghost from the machine, and Coleridge's essentially religious temperament craved a system that would be host to the spirit. For a long time he was persuaded by Spinoza's pantheism, but even this could not satisfy him, since inside any system that claimed a polyvalent divinity, the divine presence diffused in material particulars, there lurked the atheist's formulation: If God is everywhere, he is nowhere. In the years before the *Biographia*, Coleridge had been dismantling many of the assumptions on which his philosophical faith had rested, and he was moving toward the restless but sustained conviction of transcendent Christianity and a three-personed God which would rescue him from pantheism.

But as the ground where this work of review and clarification would be done he chose the discontinuous, cluttered, elliptical, familiar semiwilderness of "a book of literary opinions." Even if we read it as autobiography, as a chronicle of the poet's intellectual growth, tracing his career from its early schoolboy years up to his work as a young journalist and poet, finally converging on the brilliance and failure of his friendship with Wordsworth, the narrative is strapped to the torture rack of prose least suited to such disclosure: authority-laden, irresolute, piecemeal enticements toward the massive presentation to come, the *Logosophia*, his *magnum opus* on metaphysics and religion. And yet the *Biographia*'s prose is the kind he wrote best: marginalia, notebook furies, self-annotations.

Coleridge's intellectual desire always outran his temperamental equipment to keep pace with it. From his early years he wanted to be a poet and thinker, but his nerves—and his huge appetite for books—made it hard for him to sit still and write, and the physical habit of composition became even more difficult as he got older. When he was only twenty-four, he wrote to his friend John Thelwall: "I am, and ever have been, a great reader—and have read almost every-thing—a library cormorant—I compose very little—and I absolutely detest composition" (Nov. 19, 1796). And yet the expectations he set for himself were agonizingly grand. His encounter and friendship with Wordsworth was a powerful goad, and out of that conversation came a redefinition of decorum in English poetry. But it also brought him too close to an almost monstrous example of diligence and industry. All of Wordsworth's patience and fluency must have devastated someone as prone to self-accusation as the young Coleridge. What interests me most in Coleridge's character is the way he made such extreme disquiet and impatience—his bad nerves—into a power. What is great and singular in his poetry is the felt struggle of nervous recognitions, instinctual flarings, and visions, driven by profound learning, all held menacingly momentarily in check by the willed suppleness of poetic form. "Frost at Midnight," "This Lime-Tree Bower My Prison," and "Dejection: An Ode," all seem to take for granted that clear thought about our relation to the world outside our minds takes place right at the edge of oblivion. The quiet and reserve in those poems, and especially the tensed reciprocities ("O Lady! we receive but what we give," "Great Universal Teacher! he shall mould / Thy spirit, and by giving make it ask") are stratagems for balancing on the abyss of formless incomprehensibility.

What is maddeningly predictable about Coleridge is that he also feels obliged to "think," to lay false tracks, to pretend to be something more than just a poet—not only a poet but also a critic who can clarify better than anyone his own poems, *and* supply the philosophical pedigree to explain the "positions" taken in the poems, *and* a well-reasoned defense of technique.

That supernatural phenomena seep into the normalized forms of nature and manipulate our desires, enticing us with apparently innocent promises of something *out there*, outside nature, and that this kind of formation takes place most normally, daily, unfailingly, in dreams—this persuasion accounts for the dark tone of "Christabel." It and "Kubla Khan" are poems by someone who travels half-worlds, who takes dangerous pleasure in studying the manner of voyage between consciousness and oblivion. But they are also written by a literary intelligence that feels obliged to introduce "Christabel" with this:

> I have only to add that the metre of Christabel is not, properly speaking, irregular, though it may seem so from its being founded on a new principle: namely, that of counting in each line the accents, not the syllables. Though the latter may vary from seven to twelve, yet in each line the accents will be found to be only four. Nevertheless, this occasional variation in number of syllables is not introduced wantonly, or for the mere ends of convenience, but in correspondence with some transition in the nature of the imagery of passion.

That metrical "principle" is the least interesting, indeed one of the most distracting, aspects of the poem. Yet Coleridge feels obliged to assure us that he knows what he is doing. He is a poet who is not content simply with having a set of principles or assumptions on which to base his poetry, he must *announce* that he has them. He wants to claim another source of specialized authority, that of discursive criticism, or of philosophy. The most disquieting sort of authority, however, is that borrowed from others but unacknowledged.

De Quincey said that Coleridge's mind "never gives back anything as it receives it. All things are modified and altered in passing through his thoughts." It was also De Quincey, familiar with Coleridge's intellectual habits, who posted early storm warnings about his borrowings. Difficult as it was for Coleridge to sustain one labor over a period of time, he was a fanatical encyclopedist, a note-taker on a grand scale, and a detailed annotator of his reading. This is not to say he did not know that in the *Biographia Literaria* he was repeating whole pieces from books of German philosophy that he owned, but rather that he believed that the larger design, the Great System he hoped to construct, rendered any niggling over source material the activity of small minds. In chapter 9, where he speaks of his debt to Schelling, he makes his famous claim, also a disclaimer: "I regard truth as a divine ventriloquist: I care not from whose mouth the sounds are supposed to proceed, if only the words are audible and intelligible."

Most writers borrow, or steal; and some sometimes remember, or are courteous (or pedantic) enough, to acknowledge their sources. Coleridge's intellectual reflex was to strike an apologetic tone as a strategy for shoring up his authority. He suggests that he is the helpless victim of his own voracious mind, which is too ample in its ambitions. It in no way discredits his genius to admit that he was a master of the machinery of self-exoneration, just as he also endured, in his daily physical existence, profound emotional and psychological torment. In the *Biographia*, he serves up a heavy, mixed dish, often from other men's ingredients and recipes, as his own; then he apologizes for using those recipes in part when he has in fact used them whole and entire. It is one of the many tense contradictions in Coleridge that while he could be almost tediously meticulous in worrying the details of a philosophical or literary argument (his argument with Hartley in chapter 7 and with Wordsworth in volume II are instances), he would also impatiently bull his way toward larger definitions, formulations of ideal harmonies, hierarchies of mind and affects. His famous assertions about Primary and Secondary Imagination, the esemplastic power, and the poet described in ideal perfection, are attempts at establishing general principles, even if the details have not been methodically worked through. Coleridge's eloquence, especially about poetry, sometimes has oracular power. The general statements possess a wisdom that seems both harmonious and hard earned, like the closing paragraph of chapter 14: "Finally, GOOD SENSE is the BODY of poetic genius, FANCY its DRAPERY, MOTION its LIFE, and IMAGINATION the SOUL that is every where, and in each; and forms all into one graceful and intelligent whole."

Should it matter that the detailed investigation standing back of such generalizations does not appear, or is promised at some later, never to arrive, date? It matters insofar as it reminds us that one of the reasons for reading Coleridge at all is to see into the nature of indecisiveness, self-divisiveness, and desire. We cannot dismiss out of hand his assertion in chapter 9 that "all the main and fundamental ideas [in *Biographia*] were born and matured in my mind before I had ever seen a single page of the German Philosopher," but the evidence compiled in Norman Fruman's *Coleridge: The Damaged Archangel* and Thomas McFarland's *Coleridge and the Pantheist Tradition* about Coleridge's debt to Schelling, Maass, Kant, Bruno and others, weighs too heavily against the truth of the assertion. I don't believe this was deliberate equivocation on Coleridge's part, but rather the contortions of a man whose intellectual yearning was always in excess of his temperamental equipment to realize, to transform into sustained prose discourse, those aspirations. In this sense, the *Biographia Literaria* is one of the most striking biographies of desire and its devastating claims.

The depth and gnarled complexity of that desire are fully presented in the new (1983) Bollingen edition edited by James Engell and W. Jackson Bate, which confronts the issue of Coleridge's plagiarisms and displays the evidence. Often two or three lines of text are strung across the top of a page, beneath which rise bricked columns of small print which annotate sources, point toward related ideas in Coleridge's other writings, and refer us to other commentators. Most of the footnote apparatus is made up of quotes from his notebooks (which he quarried in writing the *Biographia*) and excerpts from German writers. The look of the page is an emblem of

Coleridge's mind: the pressure of his omnivorous reading rising against the narrow margin that contains his own speech. That stress line where two forces press one against the other was the line Coleridge walked most of his life. In chapter 10 he says: "For a very long time indeed I could not reconcile personality with infinity; and my head was with Spinoza, though my whole heart remained with Paul and John." In chapter 13 he speaks of the philosophical problem, in him also an emotional need, to conceive two forces "which counteract each other by their essential nature; not only not in consequence of the accidental direction of each, but as prior to all direction, nay, as the primary forces from which the conditions of all possible directions are derivative and deducible: secondly, that these forces should be assumed to be both alike infinite, both alike indestructible."

The faculty that at once discriminates between and fuses the two eternally countervailing forces is the imagination, and it is one job of the poet to actualize these tense harmonies in language by fully exercising the secondary imagination, which "dissolves, diffuses, dissipates, in order to re-create; or where the process is rendered impossible, yet still at all events it struggles to idealize and unify." The editors' note on the "two forces" passage describes the very similar thinking of Fichte and Schelling on this matter and cites ten long locations in those authors where Coleridge may have found his inspiration (or which, as some critics say, he looted). More important than the question of attribution is the drama exposed in this scholarly presentation: Coleridge's deeply felt struggle with opposing powers in his own temperament, and his drivenness to harmonize them and justify the harmony philosophically, both are mysteriously implicated in the intrigue (to which he unmistakably contributed much) about the origins and growth of his ideas. Even when pursuing the great synthesis, the harmonious fusing, he felt most at home among dissonance and irresolute contestation. He desperately wanted to save himself intellectually, to rescue himself from materialist

and mechanistic philosophies. To perform the rescue operation, however, he invited all the moral equivocation of pla-
giarism.

In "Frost at Midnight" and "Dejection: An Ode" (which is a
cry of fear at having lost the imaginative power which, only
four years before, had helped him to write "Frost") the poet's
mind enacts alternating impulses, now active, outreaching,
and acquisitive, now passive and absorptive. In chapter 7 of
the *Biographia* Coleridge describes "the mind's self-experience
in the act of thinking":

> Most of my readers will have observed a small water-insect
> on the surface of rivulets, which throws a cinque-spotted
> shadow fringed with prismatic colours on the sunny bottom
> of the brook; and will have noticed, how the little animal *wins*
> its way up against the stream, by alternate pulses of active
> and passive motion, now resisting the current, and now
> yielding to it in order to gather strength and a momentary
> *fulcrum* for a further propulsion.

It is, first of all, a mark of Coleridge's judicious particularity
of mind that he should find concentrated in the pulse and
stillness of a water insect the proud stress of the mind exert-
ing itself against the press of external reality. The mediating
faculty between these two exertions is the imagination. In poetry, this mediation is exercised to "a superior degree" and is
necessarily "joined to a superior voluntary controul over it."
Voluntary control of any sort, over his affections, desires, ad-
dictions, work habits, scholarly acquisitiveness, and daily
truth-telling, was a quality Coleridge notoriously lacked. Except in the writing of his poems, where he has a surer control
over the powers engaged in composition than does Wordsworth. Coleridge could not sustain his control; Wordsworth,
orchestrating fewer and less intensely concentrated powers
over a longer stretch, knew how to measure out his strengths.

When he is talking in the *Biographia Literaria* about what it
feels like to compose poetry, to know that condition of con-

trol, ecstasy, and self-aware desire, Coleridge can chill us with
his accuracy. His discussion of the disciplined excitement of
meter, and the force it exerts against necessary "good sense,"
obviously comes right out of his own nervous experience as a
poet. But when he acts the part of Samuel Taylor Coleridge,
the esteemed man of letters whose every word of table talk
was valued as the best wisdom of his time, he becomes tedious.
In chapter 11 he urges authors to have a profession apart
from their writing; his vision of the author's daily return from
the workplace to the nest of family and "vocation" is contrived
and sickly sweet: "Then, when you retire into your study, in
the books on your shelves you revisit so many venerable
friends with whom you can converse. . . . Even your writing
desk with its blank paper and all its other implements will appear a chain of flowers, capable of linking your feelings as
well as thoughts to events and characters past or to come."
And if his remarks on meter in volume II are precise and useful, his strictures against Wordsworth's presumed defense of
the use of common speech in poetry are conservative, self-
protective rant. Wordsworth, his achievements and shortcomings, is the one subject in the *Biographia* that Coleridge finds
hard to let drop. One wishes he had been as unrelentingly
detailed in his discussion of the imagination as he was in cor-
recting the "principles" of a poet whose stream of work was
probably an unforgettable chastisement of Coleridge's early
quick decline as a poet.

For all his attempts to cover his own tracks, Coleridge's habits announce themselves everywhere in his writings. When
early in his career someone suggested he write an epic, he said
he would first have to spend ten years studying a wide range
of topics before he could even begin to write. He loved and
invited impossible contraries, resistances, irreconcilables. He
went round and round the problem of matter infused with
spirit, of the transformation of potential into the actual. He
remained a student—as he once had been the poet—of the
growth of mixed, contrary forces. That was the garden where

he worked best. It is where he wrote his few great poems. Whoever cultivates that condition, delighting in that tension, will also find that opposing forces, after too long and familiar an acquaintance, can neutralize each other and become a mere academic formula. The next stage is paralysis of the will to compose, or the lapse into self-imitation. In his later years Coleridge continued to conform to the description of himself in chapter 10 of the *Biographia*: "On my own account I may perhaps have had sufficient reason to lament my own deficiency in self-control, and the neglect of concentrating my powers to the realization of some permanent work." This was said while he was in the course of dictating what would become his most famous prose work. In the poems, which come more immediately off his nervous system, one of the most appetitive and, in its way, innocent minds of the early nineteenth century recites the alternating calm and turmoil of that condition. They do not have the symphonic movements and long, measured leisures of Wordsworth's important poems, but they have sharper edges, quicker and more intensely lived turns of phrase, and a painfully attentive tracking of the movements of desire.   [1985]

WILLIAM JAMES AND
HENRY JAMES

As a representative pair they are almost too available.
Their personalities and destinies express certain conflict-
ing traits in the American character so forcefully that they
nearly seem stage caricatures of pieces of the American psyche. William was the young aspiring artist "converted" to the
scientific discipline he spent much of his life interrogating and
whose intellectual life was changed utterly by a now-unread
French philosopher. William, long before Henry, was an internationalist who, apart from "tours" in his youth and lecture
engagements late in life, stayed home to make his stake in
America. Like William Carlos Williams, he chose his home
ground in the suburb of a big city. By all accounts, he was a
brilliant and earnest university teacher, guileless, excitable,
curious, physically and intellectually energetic, full of the ag-
gressively unprepossessing charm that Europeans perceive as
characteristically American. His was an advocate's energy
and, for all his erudition, he usually comes off as a passionately amateur explainer. The force of his personality gusts
through his letters, which are sometimes rude in their imme-
diacy. When he learns his sister Alice has a breast tumor, he
writes to her: "I know you've never cared for life, and to me,
now at the age of nearly fifty, life and death seem singularly
close together in all of us—and life a mere farce of frustration
in all, so far as the realization of the innermost ideals go to
which we are made respectively capable of feeling an affinity
and responding" (July 6, 1891).

While William, the peppery eldest son with a genius for affection, vacillated for years before deciding on a profession
and did not publish his first book until he was forty-eight, the
younger Henry became almost at once the prolific, industrious artist whose work, however, would seldom have the pe-

219

culiar sexual charge and vivacity of William's. If William stayed in Cambridge to become a renowned European American, conversant with the latest philosophical and scientific advances on the Continent, Henry left to become the most famous American European of his time. He was the analyst of affects, manners, and social economies, whose writings present a mind promiscuously *on view*, all externalized, insatiable in its ruminations. And yet for all the cascading articulations of feeling and experience that shimmer through thousands of pages of letters and reviews, he remained a creature of colossal reserve. The reserve was cultivated, I believe, not out of reverence for social custom but out of fear of the unshaped and the unshapely, of the chaos from which social history emerges as a controlled formulation of human energies. Henry was troubled by impurities that endangered established orders, by apparent manners which were not grounded in the experience of history. He was shocked but curious about raw things, the unformed and untransformed. William, who always felt more at home at his mountain retreat in New Hampshire than in Cambridge, was half in love with formlessness and wilderness; his curiosity fed on menacing possibilities, and much of his professional work was directed at violently changeful experiences, at dissolutions and conversions. He was, for all his professorial distinction, an original American hooter and hollerer. Readers of *The Varieties of Religious Experience* still shiver a little with embarrassment to learn that its author not only studied but also consulted mediums and mind-cure doctors. He described a visit to one of these "specialists" in a letter to Alice three years before he published *Principles of Psychology*: "I sit down beside her and presently drop asleep, whilst she disentangles the snarls out of my mind. She says she never saw a mind with so many, so agitated, so restless, etc. She said my *eyes*, mentally speaking, kept revolving like wheels in front of each other and in front of my face, and it was four or five sittings ere she could get them *fixed*" (February 5, 1887).

The brothers also represent two clearly articulated forces that wrestle in the American poetical character, and if the sketch I offered above suggests the plenitude of the James legacy, it should also suggest its unhappy, unresolved divisiveness. Any description of the legacy—short of the massive survey F. O. Matthiessen gave us in *The James Family*—runs the risk of codification, whereby personal and professional qualities are entered all into a mighty ledger, one column headed HJ, the other WJ. My purpose here is to sketch out a certain "character formation" which, though it did not originate with the James brothers (the elements are already there in Walt Whitman and Emily Dickinson), was most dramatically acted out in their work. That formation is, I believe, their legacy specifically to American poets. I have felt its tensions and its demands, and I see it in the poetry of my contemporaries and those who have come before.

The terms of the legacy were drawn up in a letter William wrote to Henry in 1887 (the same year he consulted that mind-cure doctor). Working to finish *Principles of Psychology*, he said he had "to forge every sentence in the teeth of irreducible and stubborn facts." Whitehead quotes this in *Science and the Modern World* to establish James's contribution to the "new color" of twentieth-century thought, namely the attempt to fuse "passionate interest in the detailed facts with equal devotion to abstract generalization." William's first aspirations were in art, but his drawings were fact-bound; what is missing is inventive, speculative, imaginative imitation *in answer to* the world of fact. Whatever his talent, it was not enhanced or challenged by the resistance of the given world. His ambition, which took him years to discover and attack, found its realization in psychology, where knowledge is born out of the constant mysterious encounter between irrevocable fact and the mind's attempt to generalize, to accommodate whole orders. In the essay "Reflex Action and Theism" he talks about the mind's inability to hold the general order or organization of synchronic facts, the "simply given order" of the sum of beings and events: "But can we think of such a sum? Can we realize for an instant what a cross-section of all existence at a definite point of time would be? While I talk and the flies buzz, a sea-gull catches a fish at the mouth of the Amazon, a tree falls in the Adirondack wilderness, a man sneezes in Germany, a horse dies in Tartary, and twins are born in France." We can conceive the category but we cannot fill it. Or we can dramatize the aspiration to fill it by accumulating and arranging selected facts. The project of holding in the mind serial cross sections of such matter, displayed in some kind of compelling order, was Pound's ambition in the *Cantos*; ordered thus, mental facts in the poem would illuminate the nature of goodness and evil. But the *Cantos* is also, as many have already noted, an anthology of transformations. If the trouble in that poem is the encounter with fact, the poem's conduct is transformational. William described the thinker's problem. Henry enacted the artist's procedure.

Henry's novels of the eighties, especially *The Bostonians* and *The Princess Casamassima*, met and absorbed the world of hard fact that William struggled with so obsessively, but that encounter was already beginning to dissolve in the more insistent transformational processes of consciousness that finally dominate in *What Maisie Knew*, written in 1897, where Henry's late style really takes hold. (James scholars point out that it was during the writing of that book that he began to dictate directly to the typewriter.) William became predictably impatient with the late style and announced his disapproval in a letter of May 4, 1907: "For gleams and innuendoes and felicitous verbal insinuations you are unapproachable, but the *core* of literature is solid. Give it to us *once* again! The bare perfume of things will not support existence, and the effect of solidity you reach is but perfume and simulacrum." William wanted an American Henry, and he had him really only in the early novels *Roderick Hudson* and *The American*. The elder brother, who never locked American idioms in quote marks, knew his own way was "to say a thing in one sentence as straight and explicit as it can be made, and then to drop it forever," whereas Henry's manner was to create the illusion of a solid object "by dint of breathing and sighing all round and round it." We can hear in all this the admirer of Tolstoy and Whitman, who cast his own lot with American vigor and directness, who believed that the world of expression is impelled by will and that willed intensity ought to be palpable in the velocity of style itself. William's excitability, and his slouching willfulness, shoot through the poetry of Pound, Frost, Roethke and Lowell. There is, however, a darker sign in his sensibility that also stamps these poets. With William's coltishness goes a profound, blotting morbidity; when this mixes with Jamesian playfulness the mood turns rueful and dangerous. It is the mood, I think, of "Home Burial" and "For the Union Dead." William at any rate was no artist; he was a scientist contending with fact. In most of his work he had no desire (except for crucial exceptions in *The Varieties of Religious Experience*), because no need, to transform.

Somewhere in his notebooks, Henry says that while sitting at all those endless dinner parties he repeated to himself, while conversation and gossip whisked politely across the table, *transform, transform*. The letters that sailed between the two brothers in the first decade of the century are emblematic of the soul split between the visceral excitement of raw American experience (Henry Adams was already gloomy about the Second Law of Thermodynamics, but William argued passionately that such a "law" does not affect the way we live in history) and a Europe where experience had for centuries been resolving and articulating itself in manners, and where the world of fact, as depicted in Henry's late work, dissolves into the watery flexions of consciousness and the elaborately orchestrated obliquities of "civilized" conversation. The split shows in the oddly crisscrossing opinions the brothers held of certain writers.

Whitman, for example, became one of William's specimens of the religion of healthy-mindedness. In *Varieties*, he is offered as "the supreme contemporary example of the inability to feel evil." This is not to say that Whitman's art was infantile or ingenuous, but that it was constantly expansive, acquisitive and inclusive, not "contractile," punitive or stringent. His optimism was driven by will, it was "defiant," flourishing where it met the sternest resistance. William knew, however, that Whitman's so-called pagan exuberance was a world apart from the tragic sense of the ancient Greeks, whose consciousness "was full to the brim of the sad mortality of this sunlit world." Henry too, in his last years, spoke of Whitman as a great poet; a charming anecdote by Edith Wharton describes the Master chanting Whitman's poems. But as a young novelist intent on discovering and cultivating his own language, and who would, like Pound and Eliot, make himself over into an odd-bird European, Henry wrote his most ill-famed review, a petulant attack on *Drum-Taps*. What annoyed Henry was the absence of ideas in Whitman's work; there are only, he felt, "imitations of ideas." But it was the abundant clamorous presence of the self in the poems that disturbed him most: "art requires, above all things, a suppression of one's self, a subordination of one's self to an idea." Henry's regard for Whitman changed (for sexual reasons, I think, after he read and warmly reviewed the Peter Doyle correspondence), but he never changed his mind about the necessary obliteration of self in art. As he matured, he became more patient and appreciative of the tension between experience and form. In 1907, in his wonderful introduction to *The Tempest*, he took up the same question. Shakespeare is distinguished by the frequent "momentous conjunction between his charged inspiration and his clarified experience, between his human curiosity and his aesthetic passion." Finally, however, it is aesthetic passion, the form-making faculty enacting experience in style, which exerts itself beyond curiosity, beyond the world of fact. That was the way his own imagination took. Other artists choose, as he put it, to knead another kind of dough, where the encounter with fact, the *demonstration* of curiosity, becomes the most salient quality.

For all his talk about method, William Carlos Williams was one of those after Whitman for whom the enactment of curiosity, the rub of intelligence against fact, is usually foremost. Frost, too, in poems like "Mending Wall" and "Birches," wrote a poetry in which the strain of aesthetic passion against apparently healthy-minded curiosity nearly tears the poems apart. They are poets who resist what James called "the independent, absolute value of Style." The balance tips the other way in Stevens, Crane and William Bronk, where the manner of formulating statements about mental experience purges the poem of its experiential beginnings, and where the fact-world is volatilized in Style. I don't mean to suggest that these are camps to which American poets can be handily assigned. I am trying instead to describe the twisted lines of descent in which we often find ourselves caught, and which may go some way toward explaining how it is that in our own time lyric poetry seeks sanctuary behind a thousand veils of pretty nuance even when the subject is hog-butchering or rock-climbing. The two pressures Henry described are still felt, still making trouble for the poet. For a stylist like himself, there is in Whitman so much crowing of fact that one finally distrusts the source, and no idea stands a chance. The poet closest to the vein Henry himself was probing, Emily Dickinson, was unknown to him. Whitman gave us mountainous "experience"; Dickinson, in the best of her poems, composes the shape of aspiration as it coils and clusters around an idea:

> Perception of an object costs
> Precise the Object's loss—
> Perception is itself a Gain
> Replying to its Price—
> The Object Absolute—is nought
> Perception sets it fair

And then upbraids a Perfectness
That situates so far—

The meeting of these two strains—of Fact and Style, curiosity and aesthetic passion—can be read in some of Stevens's poems, in "Anecdote of the Jar," "The Man on the Dump" and "The Latest Freed Man." It is the double Jamesian bind, of which Stevens was quite aware. In his "Prose statement on the poetry of war" he says: "The poetry of a work of the imagination constantly illustrates the fundamental and endless struggle with fact. It goes on everywhere, even in the periods that we call peace."

HENRY JAMES SENIOR was himself a prolific author of mostly theological works. The central problem for him was the existence of evil in a universe ruled by benevolent deity, and the central experience of his spiritual life was the "vastation" that struck him in 1844. He described it in his book *Society the Redeemed Form of Man*. Sitting alone at table after dinner, he was overcome by fear and trembling. The terror, which reduced him to a state "of almost helpless infancy," had no ostensible cause except for "some damned shape squatting invisible to me within the precincts of the room and raging from his fetid personality influences fatal to life." William had a like encounter with irrational evil, and he published an account of it in the chapter "The Sick Soul" in *Varieties*, attributing it however to an imaginary informant. While sitting in a darkened room, he was attacked by the memory of an epileptic he had seen in an asylum, a young man with black hair and greenish skin: "He sat there like a sort of sculptured Egyptian cat or Peruvian mummy, moving nothing but his black eyes and looking absolutely non-human. This image and my fear entered into a species of combination with each other. *That shape am I*, I felt, potentially. Nothing that I possess can defend me from that fate, if the hour for it should strike for me as it struck for him." The vision erupts, paralyzing reason and will by assert-

ing an image of their opposite, its clarity of visionary form
attacks the form we assume the self possesses. The fear and
the courting of such visions are at the center of our poetry.
Dickinson's poems recite the stages of desperate anticipation;
Tuckermann's sonnets woo the devastating "other." Lowell's
poems boil over with that turbulence. In "Skunk Hour" he
says his "mind's not right" because "I myself am hell. / No-
body's here." The eruptions of unreason are not so peculiar
to our poetry as our quickness to dare evil to show its face *so
that* we can test the assumptions we hold about the consistency
and robustness of the American character and see what it
takes to turn out the light. In "The Sick Soul" William de-
clares healthy-mindedness inadequate as a philosophical doc-
trine precisely because it refuses to reckon with "the evil facts"
of reality: "The normal process of life contains moments as
bad as any of those which insane melancholy is filled with,
moments in which radical evil gets its innings and takes its
solid turn. The lunatic's visions of horror are all drawn from
the material of daily fact. Our civilization is founded on the
shambles, and every individual existence goes out in a lonely
spasm of helpless agony." The menace, what William called
"the bat's wing of irrationality" that wheels over the normal
processes of life, is palpable in most of Lowell's poems, but
especially in "Home after Three Months Away," where the
sick mind, now "cured," feels "fizzled, stale, and small." The
fear, and the daring, can be heard in Roethke's poem "The
Bat": "Something must be amiss or out of place / When mice
with wings can have a human face." And that is a poem we
recite to our children.

I want to thicken the literary relations even more. The
brothers also shared an interest in Baudelaire and Hawthorne. In an article on *Les Fleurs du Mal* published in the *Nation* in 1876, Henry said that in his treatment of evil Baudelaire was "exactly what Hawthorne was not—Hawthorne, who
felt the thing at its source, deep in the human consciousness."
From the vastations in the James family we know that the fa-

ther and William had knowledge of "evil facts." William, moreover, believed that his brother's art, at least in its early phase, owed something to Hawthorne, "some real American mental quality." That quality, I think, is the knowledge of the reality of evil as it is expressed in the ordinary conduct of social relations. For William it was defined in solitary, spectral terms. *The Varieties of Religious Experience* is not about societies of belief but about confrontations between individual minds and the palpable reality of the unseen. In his chosen discipline, William investigated frontiers. For Henry, evil was inevitably social, issuing from desires activated by will, and its expression took the form of the corruption of the consciousness of others by manipulating it to serve selfish interests. (Pound, in his long essay on James, called it "personal intimate tyrannies working at close range.") Of Baudelaire, Henry said "evil for him begins outside and not inside," and that he knew evil "not by experience, not as something within himself, but by contemplation and curiosity, as something outside himself."

The relations between many of the characters in the novels beginning with *What Maisie Knew* are made up of small signs which enact, as he says in *The Wings of the Dove*, "the whole soft breath of consciousness meeting and promoting consciousness." Henry takes this as a given in all intimate human relations. (His brother wrote: "Something is always mere fact and *givenness*.") As early as *The Bostonians* he was already treating, though not so obsessively, the "moist moral impress" humans make on each other. When someone abuses this power of affecting the shaping of another's consciousness, by misrepresenting the truths according to which the will acts upon its choices, or by manipulating the desires of others in order to serve self-interests or to enhance one's material life, that person is committing evil. In *The Wings of the Dove*, when Densher goes to see Milly Theale in Venice, with full knowledge that he is making up to her in hope of inheriting her fortune, he encounters the maggiordomo Eugenio who, less disingenuously, is himself overcharging Millie for his services. In the gaze of the cynical, knowing Italian, Densher feels the whole force of his own playing with evil. The entire scene, in his consciousness, accuses him; it is one of the scenes in James's fiction where all his powers of transformation are engaged: "It was a Venice all of evil that had broken out for them alike, so that they were together in their anxiety, if they really could have met on it, a Venice of cold, lashing rain from a low black sky, of wicked wind raging through narrow passes, of general arrest and interruption, with the people engaged in all the water-life huddled, stranded and wageless, bored and cynical, under archways and bridges."

Many of my contemporaries are, like myself, the grandchildren of somewhere else, of southern or eastern Europe, of Mexico or Africa. If their poems are often stubbornly regional—the variety runs from C. K. Williams's tense redbrick cityscapes and Alan Shapiro's household estrangements from ancient religious culture, to Dave Smith's tidewater-region chronicles—it's because of the felt but usually unannounced need to ground one's work in a distinctly American place, to stake it down, however self-consciously, so that it won't be blown into homeless wandering by the other powerful impulse in our poetry, the need to migrate. There is also a species of recent poetry which is constantly in transit to somewhere else, to the works of others, to novels, paintings, poems, photographs, not because these other forms offer occasions for investigating the legacies of imaginative forms, nor to engage in meaningful dialogue with the dead. It results from our peculiar instinct to go *out*, to cross over, to appropriate, to resettle. (Such poetry is interesting only for its symptomatic cultural reflexes.) The same restlessness is felt in the three more substantial poets I mentioned above, all of whom have written about tribal removals and displacements. America's history is one of serial migrations anyway, and local populations are still liable to sudden alterations by the newly arrived who have followed the promise of jobs, property, better weather, *anything*. Even the poet most attached to certain American locales will, given the opportunity, travel or live for a time in Europe and be tempted by the subject matter of crumbling, glittering antiquities. In 1881, Henry James wrote in his notebooks: "[An American] *must* deal, more or less, even if only by implication, with Europe; whereas no European is obliged to deal in the least with America."

The brothers were second-generation Americans, descended from the royal-sounding William James of Albany— Albany, New York, by way of County Cavan, Ireland, and Baltimore, Maryland—who made his fortune in salt manufacturing. The restlessness of the recently-arrived continued in his son, Henry Senior, who took his brood on frequent European excursions. So William and Henry both spent considerable time in Europe as children and young men. William's eventual decision to remain in America, however, was a sustained act of will shivered by frequent doubts. Returning from a visit to Henry in England in 1893, he wrote his brother yet another letter about mixed impulses. He writes from "The Salters' Hill-Top" near his summer home in Chocorua, a region he loves dearly. But he sees it differently now. Compared to his recent memories of Switzerland, the American landscape is a "poverty-stricken land, and sad American sunlight over all—sad because so empty." His return makes him so melancholy that he is hardened in his resolution not to leave America again unless it is to go somewhere to end his days: "Such a divided soul is very bad." We must recall William's vacillating temperament. The philosopher of the power of will, whose pluralism seems the product of decisive, concentrated intelligence, had a hard time making up his mind about many things. When he was in Europe, he became twice as American; in America, he was quasi-European. The divided soul is in any event too familiar a condition for many American artists to be dismissed as one man's obsession. He says that all the orders of the Old World have been won by populations staying put for generations, and that Americans must now do the same. But he is fifty-one years old; it has taken him *that* long to decide. William is writing out of a particular fear and lonesomeness; from his beautiful hilltop he has been struck by the vision of "a terrible grimness, more ugliness than I ever realized in things, and a greater weakness in nature's beauty, such as it is. One must pitch one's whole sensibility first in a different key—then gradually the quantum of personal happiness of which one is susceptible fills the cup—but the moment of change of key is lonesome." That lonesomeness, the hilltop brooding on the waste, vacancy and thinness which are just the other side of American enthusiasm, runs through the poetry of James Wright, Gary Snyder, and A. R. Ammons.

Henry was more decisive. As if retracing his grandfather's route, after initial "test" excursions he went to England in 1881 (the year of the notebook entry) and did not return for over twenty years. One purpose of Ezra Pound's 1918 essay on James was to testify to his realization of an American European art. Pound was a wilder internationalist, and the sort of impresario and culture-mediator that James, whose impulse was always to dramatize and refine discriminations rather than preach them, could never have been. But in James, Pound saw an American performing a sort of necessary repatriation to the native Europe of the mind. It was a Europe which in Pound's case, as Europeans will insist, only an American could have imagined. But it was a powerful idea boomed by a powerful personality. For James, at any rate, the change of key was his way of situating himself in a culture which provided him material for the best of his novels and most of the stories. He could locate himself in a centuries-old culture where manners had been stabilized as the result and continuation of history, where behavior was an accurate codification and embodiment of experience. James's finest subjects, however, were the migrating personalities, the national character in transit, off-balance, suffering a change of key (even in *The Europeans*, where the usual pattern is reversed and Europeans are comically set loose in American society), the estrangements of worshipping a dead past, and the journey artists make to discover the fittest metaphors and most fertile habits. Lambert Strether, Milly Theale, and Isabel Archer are each at different stages of migrating to an idea of civilized order and delight different from what they have known in America. Strether, perhaps more than any character in James, remains shipwrecked in that lonesome moment William described.

In 1904, Henry returned to the States for a visit and collected his impressions in *The American Scene*. The question he himself could not resolve still troubles our artists: "Do certain impressions [in America] represent the absolute extinction of old sensibilities, or do they represent only new forms of them?" His most disturbingly eloquent pages are about the new aliens, the Italian and Jewish populations especially, who were swelling the population of New York City, bringing with them none of what James would ever recognize as "European manners." What he saw was "the *launched* foreign personality always in one's eyes." He barely controls his dismay and outrage, though he himself knew one form of that condition when he launched himself upon European society. The difference is in the degree of sensibility and development of manners (and of money). It is the fateful difference between steerage and stateroom. And yet, when Henry wrote in *The American Scene*, about the essential American condition of being alien, he was, I think, writing about a condition he experienced firsthand:

> Who and what is an alien, when it comes to that, in a country peopled from the first under the jealous eye of history?— peopled, that is, by migrations at once extremely recent, perfectly traceable, and urgently required. . . . Which is the American, by these scant measures?—which is *not* the alien, over a large part of the country at least, and where does one put a finger on the dividing line, or, for that matter, "spot" and identify any particular phase of the conversion, any one of its successive moments?

The erroneous assumption, or persuasion, back of James's analysis—impressions, I should say, since no questions are answered, though many troubling ones are put—was that there could be fixed and articulated and measured some homogeneous, unified, American mentality that was being violated by the aliens, that a "real" American now had to eat the bitter fruit of having "to share the sanctity of his American consciousness with the inconceivable alien." The "supreme relation, the relation to one's country" was now being carved into odd messy portions by the launched populations. That relation, by any European measure, had not been very long in the making here, and before it there existed Indian populations whose "relation to the country," to their land and their gods, was intruded upon by paleface aliens. The "supreme relation," in other words, existed only as inchoate American possibility modeled on European precedents. Henry imagined the existence of a European quality in a place whose "vacancies," as he called them, would not allow for the development of a concentrated homogeneous political sensibility over such a short period of time. More to the point, his native country was, as it still is, a palimpsest of alien cultures trying to lay claim to a commonly shared notion of civilization, commonly called "the good life," and to establish sound economies. Those economies, then and now, are unstable. The instability was evident to Henry practically everywhere he went in America. But not long after his return to England, Europe was at war, and Henry's letters are shocked but courageous testimony to the rending of the apparently stable social orders he valued and whose stability he had thought he understood.

THE EXERTIONS of American poetry have been those of experience over philosophy. If we have all learned something directly or indirectly from Coleridge about the unities of poetry, we have generally ignored his assertions about the sisterhood of poetry and philosophy. Eliot wrote a philosophical poetry in *Four Quartets*, and I suppose one could argue that

Pound's program in the *Cantos* was to establish a philosophy of culture. In a poet like William Carlos Williams, however, the attempts to "think in poetry" in the late *Desert Music* poems snag on the splinters of experience. There is no philosophy in Frost, Lowell, or Bishop. Stevens, on the other hand, believed that poetry can be defined as "an unofficial view of being," and that poetry and philosophy are such co-ordinate activities that one must take care in distinguishing them. In practice, Stevens took over from Henri Focillon's *The Life of Forms in Art* the idea that "the chief characteristic of the mind is to be constantly describing itself." In his poems the mind is often describing itself doing a specific sort of work, that of "the imagination pressing back against the pressures of reality." Stevens's poetry pursues the consequences of association, and a poem is accordingly an occasion for the mind's encounter with such consequences. Stevens was, in all this, very influenced by Coleridge, but the only poet since who follows Stevens in writing "poetry that thinks" (the phrase is Richard Pevear's, though I'm abusing it a little to fit my own purposes) is William Bronk. American poets generally do not share Coleridge's or Stevens's interest in philosophy. Most of us are, in Simone Weil's phrase, too much the children of the Age of Psychology. Whether we are aware of it or not, William James is really the closest thing to a representative philosopher—or antiphilosopher—that we have. Frost's "The Most of It" is a Jamesian poem: the reality of the self, its shape and its solitude, depends on the answer it gets from physical encounters with the world, where habitual regard and definition may be shattered by new fact:

> Instead of proving human when it neared
> And someone else additional to him,
> As a great buck it powerfully appeared,
> Pushing the crumpled water up ahead,
> And landed pouring like a waterfall,
> And stumbled through the rocks with horny tread,
> And forced the underbrush—and that was all.

William James's statement of purpose in the Gifford Lectures, which became *The Varieties of Religious Experience*, asserts what I believe to be the assumption behind much of our poetry and its procedures: "to defend 'experience' against 'philosophy' as being the real backbone of the world's religious life—I mean prayer, guidance, and all that sort of thing immediately and privately felt, as against high and noble general views of our destiny and the world's meaning." James always valued this kind of lyric subjectivism, the quick, sharp lash of the particular, over magisterial generalization. His career had its real beginnings in 1870 when he made this entry in his diary: "I think that yesterday was a crisis in my life. I finished the first part of [the French philosopher Charles] Renouvier's second 'Essais' and see no reason why his definition of Free Will—'the sustaining of a thought *because I choose to* when I might have other thoughts'—need be the definition of an illusion." His first act of free will, he joked, would be to believe in free will. The conviction sustained him throughout his life and preserved him from the "vastations" which I'm certain would have destroyed him. On the basis of free will—James's enthusiasm for Renouvier seems now a little embarrassing, but his enthusiasms often had a suffocating American hugginess—he built his philosophy of radical empiricism, of the experimental self finding its definition in a world of changeful experience. In the 1884 essay "The Dilemma of Determinism" he stated his belief in indeterminism, but one of his own design, in which "the free-will theory of popular sense based on the judgement of regret . . . represents the world as vulnerable, and liable to be injured by certain parts if they act wrong. And it represents their acting wrong as a matter of possibility or accident, neither inevitable nor yet to be infallibly warded off." His model for the universe was "pluralistic, restless," so that no summative, unified view could take it in. In our daily existence, this model as something lived with and *through* means that if free will fails, or is corrupted, the world must slow down to a sluggish, blandly unified, monochromatic field of vision such as Lowell arrives at in "Waking Early Sunday Morning":

> Pity the planet, all joy gone
> from this sweet volcanic cone;
> peace to our children when they fall
> in small war on the heels of small
> war—until the end of time
> to police the earth, a ghost
> orbiting forever lost
> in our monotonous sublime.

That entire poem, one more in the anthology of American Sunday poems, is about the painful, defeatist exertions of will in a world of reckless circumstance and meaningless ritual: "O to break loose."

It is instinct in poets to think there exists a unified view of things, that poetry can sooner or later, in William's phrase, "take in the whole scene." But it's also instinct among American poets to distrust ideal unities of any sort. Even if the field of vision seems one and coherent, we look for exceptions, monsters, or dismantle the whole view into sheared perspectives. Lyric poetry at any rate usually celebrates and enacts occasions, which are serial, discrete, empirical, extracted from the pluralist rush of mental and physical events. Giving form to those urgent selections is a stay against devastation. Lowell's career is in this respect representative, because so many of the poems beginning with *Life Studies* push mercilessly against the sort of grandiose, unified, but determinist and (in Henry Adams's term) entropic, view that concludes "Waking Early Sunday Morning." William James would have recognized at once these exertions, just as he would have recognized the conversion in Elizabeth Bishop's late poems, especially "In the Waiting Room." In *The Will to Believe*, James described the view of the radical empiricist: "For him the crudity of experience remains an eternal element [of the world]. There is no possible point of view from which the world can appear an absolutely single fact."

And yet there is that other profound instinct for unity, even in a country so dangerously and unpredictably diverse, for some coherent, summative view that would license poets to make general statements. I think that instinct, that real desire, is the pulsing afterimage of our knowledge of European culture, where the elements of civilization, and of poetic culture specifically, have been developing, struggling, cohering, dissolving, and redefining themselves for centuries, in countries with relatively stable populations and whose land masses would be just bright dabs on America's vastnesses. The American facts of history and nature will not submit to that afterimage dream, that second impression. So much was made harshly clear to Henry when he made his late visit: "In America we get our sanctity as we can, and we plead it, if we are wise, wherever the conditions suffer the faintest show of color for it to flush through." In Henry's Europe, the cultural formations were *there*, waiting for him. In America there were, and still are, fewer such viable formations at hand. We have had instead discoverables out there among the vacancies. For Henry, it was "the great adventure of a society reaching out into the apparent void."

For an American poet the void is always one more field of possibility. Instead of long-established cultural formations naturally evolved out of local historical circumstances, we have the swarming, indeterminate flux of American facts, themselves clapped together from fragmentary European or Asian or African facts. Reckoning with this is one task which naturally carries us back, sooner or later, to another country, or urges us to confront American Indian cultures. I am not saying that American poetry is essentially improvisation, or that all the historical resources of English verse should be closed to us; that sort of nationalism is just a grotesque kind of self-glorifying impoverishment. But the American poet who does not choose to become an internationalist like Pound or Eliot (or a vulgar Blue Guide version of them), and who therefore takes as given the extremely complex world of American facts, is bound to appreciate the sly humor in William James's remark about a friend who, possessing a mind in love with unity, criticized James's radical vision: "The thought of my universe makes him sick, like the sight of the horrible motion of a mass of maggots in their carrion bed." That vision, if uncongenial, is nonetheless at the source of our poetry. It is certainly the universe in which some of us have tried to do our work. An American artist is, I believe, historically determined to be half in love with what is unfinished, half-refined, and doomed to expect always to hear a shout in the desert. The motion of James's maggots in their carrion bed is a vile richness, a vital sign of rough continuance and replenishment.   [1985]

WORK

One of the demanding memories of my childhood is the mysterious textured space that seemed to surround the men on my block as they went back and forth to work. To us children, "being at work" meant not just an activity but a place, a temporary habitat outside our South Philadelphia neighborhood. Work was the surround that absorbed them every morning and restored them to us at day's end, a little transfigured by dust or grease, their hands smelling of borax, their breath sour with beer or whiskey. And around them was that aura. In the mornings it should have been crisp, remade by night's passing. But something careworn and irredeemable always wrapped itself about them. None ever seemed happy or expectant, as if the work, the need and the duty of it, was a mineral substance they wore like a coat. It impressed on me, before anything else, that work was never a lightness and gaiety, but something gravid, earthborn and earthbound. The departures were built on ritual morning preparations: the clatter of cups on saucers, the gurgle of coffee perking, the familiar (and threatening) cadence of feet down the stairs, the gulps and sluicing of water through old plumbing. If life's ordinary rhythms were repeated faithfully, they were charms that helped sustain a household. Observe the ritual and you were safe against most disruptions caused by your own laziness and stupidity. If bad fortune wanted you, it would have to come get you. But break the ritual, fail in some regular observance out of weariness or distraction, and a job would be jeopardized, and consequently a household, a family extending to grandparents and possibly a bachelor aunt or uncle. Fool with the rigors of habit and you became your own bad luck.

I had no sense of the daily humiliations many of them suffered in their jobs. Some had the hot, sharp intelligence intellectuals envy, but for one reason or another formal education

wasn't available to them and many had to make their way as
unskilled laborers. They seemed not so much beaten or embarrassed by their work, of whatever kind, as numbed to a
silence their children could hardly pierce. Nor were they heroic, though it is the tendency of those who learn about the
struggle of material existence from books either to falsely ennoble workers or, reactively, to "demythologize" them. Hannah Arendt says that since the nineteenth century we have
glorified labor as the source of all values. For us children, the
great thing was that our fathers worked with their hands,
built big things with big tools, drove loud trucks, put things
together on assembly lines, or mixed explosive chemicals in
oceanic proportions. They mended ship fittings in the Navy
Yard, tarred high roofs, laid brick for doctors' offices,
mounted pistons on locomotives, poured concrete for sky-
scrapers and walked out to the edge of girders forty stories
up, right there at the edge of nothing at all.

My memory is thickly colored by what I now know them to
have done. So that the chemicals man, in my mind's eye, always looks unnaturally scrubbed, his face blanched or
parched, and all around his stiff posture—stiffened in expec-
tation of some explosion or concussion—the air is tinted sul-
phurous yellow. And the man whose job was to us young boys
the most exciting, who broke pavement with one of those
jackhammer chisels, bore a chalky cowl around his head, as if
the job had cast a permanent proprietary veil. He had a sail-
or's rolling gait, always checking his balance after his jittery
day.

Only one had no aura, who was only what he was. Already
rather remote for living at the far end of the block, he walked
the entire length of the street morning and evening; the
promenade past all our houses seemed part of his job. His
distinction—and it may be this that rubbed out the aura—was
the shirt he always wore. A bright white shirt seen in fever, in
daylight, will make your head swim. His, day after day, had
that hallucinated candor. The shirt had no creases (I remem-

ber best spring and summer days, when everyone was in shirt-
sleeves), which meant he couldn't afford to send it to the laun-
dry, or chose not to. His collar was always open and starched.
I never knew for sure what his job was. Though he lived on
our street, his son never played in our games. The women
sometimes spoke in quickened breaths about "City Work,"
meaning city government. He was probably a civil servant
who could get by without a necktie but was expected to wear
that white badge. He had a movie star's baked good looks, in
a neighborhood filled with handsome southern Italians, and
he was trimmer than they, not quite as square and planted.
He was also the only adult ever to strike in anger a child not
his own, an event that nearly caused a riot and became legend
for years. The heraldic sign identifying the legend was the
white shirt.

As children assemble and organize all the mixed facts the
world blasts at them into classes of related things, into metaphoric families, I built up a class called "Working Men." My
neighbor in the famous shirt did not exist in that class. He was
slotted into a mongrel sort occupied by two other men. (It was
always and only men, in that sort of neighborhood in the
1950s; the first and only woman to hold a job also divorced
her husband and "broke" the block by selling her house to a
black family.) One was the angel idiot, a stricken holy creature
in his late twenties, whose hungry beauty seemed traced by a
Filippino Lippi. Because he was epileptic, he did not work
and was not expected to. He became the kind of friend and
protector to the neighborhood children that their fathers,
away from the house all day and many in the corner taproom
till late evening, could never be. His demon, the sudden
scrambling of the body's electricity that turned him into an
inexplicably self-punishing creature, pardoned him from the
world of work. But that torment was also his ethereal element,
the wild Ariel in him: when he lay convulsed on the ground,
he seemed least earthbound. His disease freed him. That

seemed to me at once the most horrific and desirable privilege.

The other exception to my class of workers was a smiling, snappily dressed young man from a large family, the only one of several sons who didn't work. Much later, his image became confused with the dramatic figure of Simone, the "fallen brother" in Visconti's *Rocco and His Brothers*, but by that time I had also found a sharper clarification of work and workers in the writings of Paul Nizan and the photographs of Lewis Hine. My neighbor, at any rate, did no work because he was a gangster. All the adults knew this and were shamed by it, though I think the shame was mixed with envious anger. The gangster genius had all the fruits of work and luck—beautiful suits, good shoes, his own auto, friends who dressed as well as he—without working. Like my tormented Ariel and the foreigner in the white shirt, the gangster exempt from work was unnatural, a gorgeous freak. Each in his own way was a monster whose aberration accentuated the norms of habit that ruled other lives. My workers with their auras were not monsters, but it took me a long time to begin to understand why I needed to preserve that space around them.

PAUL NIZAN was a son of the railroad. His father rose through the ranks during the great expansion of the French railway system at the end of the nineteenth century, advancing from the "low" position of engineer to the more prestigious levels of lower management. Nizan came of age between the big wars, and his intellectual companions were writers like Sartre and Camus. Like them, he became a political writer of all trades—novelist, essayist, polemicist. *Antoine Bloyé*, published in 1933, is the novel that established his small but controversial reputation. It expresses with angry clarity the structures of habit and how one destiny is determined, and ill fortuned, by the conjunction of habit and a certain kind of economy. The structures of habit are really overlayerings of desire, palimpsest chronicles of the unhappiness which in turn replenishes habit and gives it even stricter control over life. Habit, while it seems to publicize convenience and necessity, in fact hides and seals away from us the anarchy of desire; it wrestles anarchy into daily repetitions, actions without recognitions, ritualized offerings to necessity.

Nizan introduces the story of Antoine Bloyé, another son of the railroad, with an epigraph from *The German Ideology*: "If communism is to put an end both to the 'cares' of the bourgeois and the needs of the proletarian, it is self-evident that it cannot do this without putting an end to the cause of both, 'labor.'" Marx scholars note the contradiction between this remark and another that comes a few pages earlier: "Men begin to distinguish themselves from animals when they begin to produce their means of subsistence." Man is distinguished from animals because he labors, but the laboring process which is man's essential activity also binds him to larger natural cycles. Labor affects "the metabolism between man and nature." It is "an eternal necessity imposed by nature." In *The Human Condition*, Hannah Arendt describes the equivocation: "The fact remains that in all stages of his work [Marx] defines man as an *animal laborans* and then leads him into a society in which this greatest and most human power is no longer necessary." Presumably Marx intended the emancipation from labor to be the emancipation from necessity, and that is the most disarming utopian strain in his work. In the early *Economic and Philosophic Manuscripts*, he emphasized that labor is the expression of a human being's "sensuous nature" and in a communist society that nature could be expressed freely, not urged and constrained by necessity. In the course of his life, Antoine Bloyé advances beyond the menial labor his father performed and becomes a manager, a boss. In his passage he surrenders more of the opportunity to engage his sensuous nature in work, he becomes thus a stranger to his own nature, though no less enslaved to necessity.

As a teenager, studying at the School of Arts and Trades and working seasonally in the shipyards, Antoine is vital, expressive, answering the press of necessity without being reduced by his own answer. He is "endowed with strengths and with vast desires he will never be able to satisfy." He studies hard, works summers to pay tuition and gladly steeps himself in his work. Once he leaves school, however, he becomes a regular wage-earner. The difference between a worker and a wage-earner is that one ideally is defined by his activity, the other by the object or consequence of the activity. Antoine soon begins to live for the future in a present muffled by habit and expectations. He wants to win with his labor the prize of normalized relations in every sector of his life—wife, home, children, things. The necessity he feels now is defined not by natural "metabolisms" but by economic and social forces, which are the devitalized codifications of those metabolisms. Obedient to what he thinks are the "new" necessities, he suffers terrible reverses: he becomes a strikebreaker, betraying the class of workers which produced him; he loses his position finally because of poor "quality control" of war material; he backslides into a modest, miserable retirement punished by regret, reviewing unexpressed desires formalized into habits.

The ambiguity of our relation to habit—it sustains and reduces us, so do we celebrate or condemn it?—is caught in Nizan's description of Antoine's daily routine at the office:

> Each morning he went to his office; he hung up his umbrella or his overcoat. Winter came and then summer; first the season of derby hats, then the season of straw hats, of panamas. He sat down, lit a cigarette, and went and opened the door of the neighboring office as soon as he heard the sounds of a man, coughing, footsteps, a slight whistle, snatches of humming, the heavy sound of a body depositing its weight in an armchair. This meant the engineer had arrived.

The dull march of parallel phrases enacts what Nizan calls the "cotton wool" of habit in which workers wrap their lives. It protects, it softens the shock of the world, but it also packs us into a self-justifying indifference toward all that looms outside

the laminations of habit. It is the most available vaccine
against the contagion of political activism. Upon morning repetitions are laid the ritual organizations of the workday, in
turn covered over by the habitual return, the evening meal,
and the preparations for the next morning's round. The pattern is not limited to regular wage-earners. Rilke learned
from Rodin the lesson of ritual application to the task at hand.
For Nizan, the layerings of habit form an emblem of mental
habits, of insulation against change. It is the habit of thinking
about reality in a familiar way and living, unquestioningly, by
those steady lights. When Halley's Comet passes, Antoine's
neighbors try to joke about the perturbation in the familiar
sky, but they are obviously troubled by what they cannot control:

> They believed themselves wise, they believed themselves sta-
> ble, they believed themselves happy. They were capable of
> the greatest anger, the most reckless courage to defend the
> wisdom, the stability, the happiness of their small exacting
> lives against all change, all forces. They thought with deepest
> hatred of revolutions, of the workers who would make them.
> They were the kind of people who loved the gendarmes.
> And Antoine lived among them, he was one of them. Month
> after month, he sank deeper into this soothing languor of
> habits.

Habit is also a way of domesticating necessity so that we do
not feel so entirely subject to its demands. In Marx's communist society, once the need to labor is dissolved, so too will be
its fixed regularities. In *The German Ideology*, he says that in a
new society people will be able to "do this today and that tomorrow, who hunt in the morning, go fishing in the afternoon, raise cattle in the evening, are critics after dinner, as
they see fit, without ever becoming hunters, fishermen, shep-
herds or critics." But if we surrender the usually painless ca-
pitulations of habit, we also give up the illusion of controlling
our circumstances and being less tyrannized by necessity.

Nizan's sympathies are stretched thin in *Antoine Bloyé*. He looks for a Marxist formulation of class problems, but he demonstrates an artist's loyalty to the sufferings of an individual who is not so much the casualty of a social system as he is a powerful sensuous nature incapable of articulating his desires to himself. Although he does not know what happiness is, Antoine knows that he wants it. As a young man he hates the poverty he sees around him. He does not think to change it, nor to understand it; he wants only to escape it. He knows from his father's experience that in a capitalist economy one gets trapped in a job of everlasting repetitions. (Arendt's critique of Marx turns on her belief in labor as an almost celebrative participation in nature's processes, in its repetitions.) His father, a porter, tells Antoine what it is like to be "anchored to a certain lot in the world, a lot ordained for the rest of his life, a lot which he surveys as a tethered goat measures the circumference of its rope, a lot which, like every lot in life, was willed by chance, by riches, by the rulers." The Marxist element absent here is nature's rule of necessity. The sour irony of the story is that in order to escape the submissiveness described by his father, Antoine enters the middle class, where he is even more trapped than his father because more circumscribed by compound responsibilities and more implicated in an economic structure whose power he cannot share. He is even more ineffectual than his father. He may have his own garden behind his own house, but he is a tethered goat there.

Nizan shows us his characters in the workplace, their destinies tied to actions performed there. Henry James is the sort of novelist whose characters, with rare exceptions like Hyacinth Robinson, never work. In novels of manners the only work is performed by money busily reproducing itself behind the scenes so that its possessors might "live." Late in his career, however, as if to fit an explanatory filter on all his previous fiction, James described the work people in his fiction really commit themselves to. In *The Wings of the Dove*, Lord Mark is trying to win the favor of Maud Lowder and her niece Kate Croy, who live at Lancaster Gate: "He was working Lancaster Gate for all it was worth: just as it was, no doubt, working *him*, and just as the working and the worked were in London, as one might explain, the parties to every relation." James's view is that a system of "working," of exploiting or appropriating for social purposes, characterizes *all* relations, even those beyond the drawing rooms that are the workplaces of his fiction. Because it is a tacitly agreed-upon system, and one that does not threaten habitual relations with revolutionary change, it is self-preserving and self-adjusting: "The worker in one connection was the worked in another; it was as broad as it was long—with the wheels of the system, as might be seen, wonderfully oiled."

That industrial metaphor might well have come out of Nizan's political imagination, which bred characters whose lives are burnt out *because* the machinery of work is so attentively maintained. It is, in any event, clear in James's novel that the consequences of these unquestioned "working habits" are moral equivocation, paralyzed will, and tragic regret. The only character who does not enter directly into the working system is the dying American heiress Milly Theale. Though even she, late in the story, asks her traveling companion: "Work for me, all the same—work for me!" She keeps her distance from the machinery of social use, in part, because her vision of reciprocity is so pure and earnest. She may enlist an agent to work for her, but she remains the dove who requires no substance heavier than air to sustain her. Her wings lift her above the weighted manipulations of Kate, Mrs. Lowder, Densher, and all the others stationed around her mysterious fortune. Free of this world of work, she is ethereal, apart. Although this notion is peculiarly adjusted to James's art, work signifies, even in the drawing room, a gravity and flightlessness.

DIGGING and hacking the earth is a child's most powerful form of play. Even though my neighborhood was covered over with concrete and asphalt, we used to dig with sticks or knives in the puny cracks in the sidewalk, methodically refilling our ditch-work. Children may be charmed by stories of idle fairies performing good deeds, but they are compelled and deeply swayed by tales of dwarfs who go off each day to pick and hammer mines. The only man whose job we children envied, and which we mimicked in our play, was the jackhammer man. I have seen my daughter and her friends almost frighteningly caught up in the game of breaking a red brick with a hammer, crushing the shattered bits into powder, bagging it as if it were a precious mineral, then stirring it into water. With the brick-dust impasto they then drew pictures of houses. I'd never seen them respond so energetically, and so nobly, to any other game. While breaking the bricks—soon they went into mass production—they sang "I Been Working on the Railroad." As if the rhythms of bodies at work, the claiming and use of earth's stuff, breaking down its forms so that it might be transformed, were all carried out in obedience to a primordial cadence, the metabolic exertions described by Arendt, the expressions of which can still be read on the walls and ceilings of Altamira and Lascaux.

But that is play. Concentrated and passionate and repetitive, but also buoyant, unobliged, with no material relation to any society larger than that of children at play. Children working in real mines left no trace, but they had their chronicler in Lewis Hine, who dutifully recorded the contradictions of their work. When he decided in 1908 to quit his high-school teaching job and devote himself to photography, Hine went to work at once for the National Child Labor Committee to document the hideous working conditions in Indiana's glassworks, North Carolina's cotton mills, and West Virginia's coal fields.

The breaker boys were youngsters who sat twelve to fourteen hours a day bent over long chutes, separating slag from coal. They worked six days a week and were paid seventy-five cents a day. In Hine's picture, "Breaker Boys in Coal Chute," taken in the workplace, the children, all wrapped in coarse clothes, stare boldly at the camera. The few bits of exposed flesh, especially the gleaming knuckles and pale discs around the eyes, are impoverished instances of light in the gloom. That light, however, is called forth by Hine's interrogating flash; the sole electrical fixture, whose vertical line helps structure the image, is dead. The only natural light source is far left of center, behind the boys—a brief exhalation of sunshine stoppered in the breaker shed's window. In that strangely composed moment, when the boys turn momentarily from their job, they look mineralized, half-transformed into the material of their labor. The eyes that look so candidly at us seem as yet untouched, the remaining untransformed part, as if the buoyant illumination of mind shining there were the only energy preserving them from being utterly appropriated by work's gravity. Hine said of these children: "These processes involve work, hard work, deadening in its monotony, exhausting physically, irregular, the workers' only joy the closing house. We might even say of these children that they are condemned to work."

There is a code of forms running through Hine's images of workers. Twenty-five years later, when he goes up to take pictures of workers in high-steel raising the Empire State Building, we can read a continuation of the story he began years earlier in the mines. Hine called the men "Skyboys"; he saw in them the soul of early youth, of promise and passion, now at a different stage of industrial civilization. Earth's mined products are now made over into towering architectonic forms; their use has been taken up and transformed by the imagination. The darkling breaker boys, it would seem, have grown and gone out, *up*, into the air. The most compelling image in the Skyboy series is the one most catalogs call "Icarus." A worker is bracing a cable, his right arm extended tensely to do the job while his left clenches the cable for support. The long articulated forearm muscles imitate the visual rhythm of the cable. At his feet, the only stay against oblivion, is a huge loop that will be payed out as he makes his way higher. Lifted almost above the horizon, his head is literally in the clouds. But the figure that dominates the image, extending ineluctably beyond the clouds and city and river below, is that mineral black cable. It sustains the skyboy, it came before him, and its elements will outlast him. It is his medium for proving his identity as one who climbs too high. The image would be too blatantly ironic an arrangement were it not for the ambiguous blend of joy and strain on his face, as if the exhilaration of defying earth's pull and rising into the Ariel element also exhausts the will.

Hine was exceptional in that the sheer physical exertion and risk of his kind of photography imitated the toil of his worker-subjects. He lugged bulky equipment. He took chances, following his skyboys out along those girders. Because he was not a studio artist, he seems much more a worker than does a painter, sculptor, or writer. And among studio artists, it is the writer who does not act on or refigure matter; he does not produce material goods, at least not until the actual work is done, at which point another work process reifies his work into a book. Arendt says that poetry is "perhaps the most human and the least worldly of the arts, the one in which the end product remains closest to the thought that inspired it." In her analysis in *The Human Condition*, where she is mostly concerned with the process of objectification of work, the poet is always a maker, because his works are "thought things." Because of the thing-character of a poem, she says, the poet may be said to use "the same workmanship which, through the primordial instrument of human hands, builds the other durable things of the human artifice." This accounts for the object-laden quality of composition, and for the weighted, tactile sense a poet has of his or her work, that it is a thing-making labor. But it slights the thought-character of poetry, the intense immateriality of actual composition.

The absorption of composition is also closer to the dream state than is, for instance, the writing of history or philosophy, and certainly closer to the worldless attention of a child at serious play. The chief mental activity in composition is not directed toward thing-making; it is the contending of immaterialities, of utter non-things, of thought pressing against the emanations of imagination, which processes resolve into the "thought thing" of poetry. If the work of poetry is generally more patronized, and consequently presumed innocuous, in our own time, poets have protested all the more that they really do work, that a poem has a made or fabricated character and that composition takes place in real time measurable by the same units used to measure all other kinds of work.

I have heard Yeats's lines quoted too often in reverent knowing tones: " 'A line will take us hours maybe; / Yet if it does not seem a moment's thought, / Our stitching and unstitching has been naught.' " Poets and apologists close ranks around this statement as if it were definitive of a poet's work *and therefore* justifies the activity. Coming out of a nineties culture and the influence of William Morris, Yeats at the turn of the century still held residual notions of the decorative intricacy and morally compelling artisanry of verse composition, but when he wrote "Adam's Curse" he was trying to find escape from impressionistic solipsism by looking outside his own mind for a source of metaphors and stories. With that turn outward comes also the assertion of a poet's public identity, which is being served by the defensiveness of Yeats's position, that no matter how hard a poet works, harder than scullery maid or old pauper breaking stones, that poet will still be thought "an idler by the noisy set / Of bankers, schoolmasters, and clergymen / The martyrs call the world." Even if the poet describes his or her work in terms they of all people might understand—as tedious, time-consuming cottage industry, knit-craft—the poet cannot dislodge their assumptions. Yeats's argument is corrupted because it is forged to meet the expectations of those whose expectations the poem is meant to overturn. He is thus helpless to persuade, he can only assert, that poetry, like any fine thing since Adam's fall, "needs much laboring."

This is the bind that seizes modern poets when they try to describe the nature of their work. We would indeed like poems to be regarded as things, or as essential facts, because this would pull poetry farther into the thing-world and make it a more impinging piece of reality. This becomes all the more urgently felt in a civilization flooded with anonymous "products" and infinite replications. If poetry has a thing-character, it is now more difficult to assert its distinctiveness in a diluvial thing-world. Our instinct is to seek sanctuary in historical justifications by taking over traditional designations. But we assume too much too quickly when we innocently take over the Greek concept of *poiētēs* to explain that a poet makes things. That term does not refer so much to a poet's artisanry as to a poet's imaginative arrangements. Aristotle says that the author of a treatise on medicine or natural science written in verse is called a *poiētēs*. We come closer to what the Greek mind made of the work of poetry in Democritus's remark that Homer was great because he "framed a cosmos out of all kinds of words." The poet as maker was also a *tektōn*, a builder, framer, form-giver. When Sir Philip Sidney says that "Englishmen have met with the Greeks in calling (the poet) 'a maker,' " he was still using the term to mean harmonizer, integrator, unifier, and creator. Historians, philosophers, scientists, writing in prose, may be "makers" (and industrious, technically skillful versifiers may not be worthy of the title). Moreover, the poet's activity in these earlier conceptions was inseparable from the divine element in human intelligence. In *An Apology for Poetry* Sidney says we should "give right honor to the heavenly Maker of that maker, who, having made man to His own likeness, set him beyond and over all the works of that second nature: which in nothing he showeth so much as in Poetry, when with the force of a divine breath he bringeth things forth far surpassing her doings, with no small argument to the incredulous of that first accursed fall of Adam, since our erected wit maketh us know what perfection is, and yet our infected will keepeth us from reaching unto it."

Our assumptions may be inspired by ancient definitions, but they are articulated according to models of work that our own civilization offers. The most commonly accepted notion in our time is that the work of the poet is not to make a thing of beauty but to produce a beautifully functioning thing. No civilization has been so made of like products, and none has articulated its powers so massively by means of machines. Two great lyric poets, Eugenio Montale and William Carlos Williams, have called the poem "a little machine." The organic, associationist models of nineteenth-century literary criticism gave way to an industrial model; where criticism once borrowed its vocabulary from philosophy, theology, and the natural sciences, in our century it began to speak of "functioning components" and "lynchpins" in "well-tooled" poems. It is now second nature for many poets to speak of "dismantling" or "retooling" or "tuning up" their poems. The kind of work performed is by analogy mechanical, industrial. Our ordinary understanding of the poet's work, in other words, is much closer to *technē*, to the practice of a trade or the performing of a work operation. Poetry is neither diminished nor debased by the new model (though it is debased by the inauthenticity and professionalism the new model encourages) so long as it does not surrender its techtonic life, its complex and elusive thought-character, for this finally is what makes it the most human of the arts. The work of poetry is most human when it is like the work of philosophizing, less so when it is like knitcraft.

Poets are at any rate driven to such explanations and definitions by two immediate causes. Poetry can only be described finally in its own terms, but its terms are those of the imagination. In order to make comprehensible statements (which might justify the work of poetry as a task) we resort to analogue. The other arts have not borrowed so much from poetry's technical vocabulary as poetry has looted theirs. It is in fact the *search* for analogue, the irrational movements of attention and selection by which a poet discovers correspondences, which is more illustrative of a poet's actual work. But how tell or picture that movement without resorting to analogue? (It is *like* trying to describe the forms that stir and shift in a choreographer's thought as he shapes a new dance.) Secondly, the writing of poetry really is work: it is physically draining, though it is sometimes the exhaustion that follows exhilaration; it requires time, not only or primarily in the writing (which can happen fast) but in the discipline of preparation, of "framing"; and it may have some effect on another person's existence. The most accurate description of the sensuous labor of poetry was said of Nietzsche, that when he thought, he thought with his whole body.

To BELIEVE that poetry is a task in reply to living in a world of things, and that the poet's work is to receive the object world, may induce a sustaining fluency, at least for a while. It sustained Rilke through the composition of *New Poems* (1907–1908), but in the silent period that followed he looked back on that productive time, writing to Lou-Andreas Salomé in December 1911: "I expected nothing and no one and more and more the whole world streamed toward me merely as a task and I replied clearly and surely with work." On these conditions the work of poetry can respond powerfully and with great concentration to existence. But the conditions are narrow and dependent on the world's presentations, its object-occasions. In that extraordinary period Rilke's model had been Rodin; Rilke believed that a poet, like the sculptor, could each day take up the work of answering the given object, of acting on thing-material, of *laboring*. Those brief years gave way to silence, however, and Rilke had to revise his understanding of the work of poetry. It became pure inwardness, the dissolution of the world within the soul: the poet's new industry was as a bee of the invisible. If one remains too settled in the belief that poetry is a way of working the world's occasions, the poetry may repose in asking habitual (or friendly) questions of the world; or it may become all sheeted, adversarial resistance to it, so that poems become predictably argumentative replies to the pressure exerted by the world of things.

I know the adversarial position because it has sustained me in the writing of some poems. To understand its appeal, and to understand why the work of poetry as described by Yeats still jangles me, I have had to think back to my own initial formations. Because I come from a culture of working-class Southern European Catholics, I was bred to believe that work is, in conscience and in fact, the curse of the fall from grace, and that the curse determines and defines one's life. Adam fell, brought himself *down*, bound to earth; existence is the struggle to rise from the earth of work that compacts life in habit. Even if you were able to choose your work, you should not assume it would be pleasurable. If you found work you liked, you were lucky, but expect no more than this. And yet, obligatory and maledicted as work was, not to work was sinful, scandalous, and only the holy idiot or gangster was exempt from its pains. Work, in effect, was the necessary reply to being in a world characterized everywhere by exertions. The conviction that the work of poetry, though chosen (and by most measures unnecessary), is a dutiful adversarial engagement with the object world, and that the task of writing is a life-sustaining answer, however muted, to that world, had its roots for me in religious belief and a very localized culture. Work was the chief way of suffering redemption—a passion. But in these terms the work of writing is also a chastisement that can shrivel the imagination.

As a child I could read the gravities of work in the men I watched. But the reimagining or idealizing instinct let me see them as arrangements of energy, each with its aura, not to heroize them but to characterize their existence by reimagining their actual forms. Reviewing their working day, it was instinct in me to infuse their weightedness with some ethereal element. Lightened, lifted, they could be stopped and held in mind. The bricklayer on his scaffold is reshaping the sky. The ice man sails from the high black cab of his truck. My childish fancy was answering a real need, to rescue what I saw from the seductive life of habit, to see in work an ascendancy or upwarding. That instinct was really work's most important element. It was the hopeful Ariel voice asking: "Is there more toil?"

It took me perhaps too long to understand the obvious, that the economy of poetic work is not so exclusively dependent on the encounter with the world's presentations, though this is of course necessary in any representational art, but that there is a world elsewhere in every exertion. Caliban is enslaved, but Ariel does the important work. I have come to believe that the poet occupies the middle zone, mediating (but not making peace) between the two forces. The poet's workplace is what William James somewhere calls "that distributed and strungalong and flowing sort of reality which we finite beings swim in," but within this mineralized condition the poet moves toward some Edenic source of consciousness, and this movement is the work of the form-giving imagination.

As one gets older, poetry's share in the normal conditions of work—the habituations, obsessiveness, dutifulness—becomes more complex but also more regularized. The temptation then is to think of poetry as a job, or trade, or indeed as "work." We need common terms, of course, and work is the oldest and most efficient, and is especially apt in our industrial civilization. For me it has come to mean existence in the middle zone where the ordinary exertions of labor suck everything downward toward a leveling repetition of familiar forms, toward mannerism and the reassuring monotony of self-imitation. Contending with this is the Ariel instinct, the guiltless, unexplanatory transformations authorized by the imagination. Without the mineral counterweight, the Ariel instinct leads to alchemy, where the crude matter of existence is transformed in the poet's alembic into merely perfect world-less gold. It is the lure of gorgeous inanity. The middle zone, which exists only in the writing, is at least a provisional passage during which fact and inspiration may be unevenly, often unprettily, welded.   [1985]